This book belongs to

_____

_____

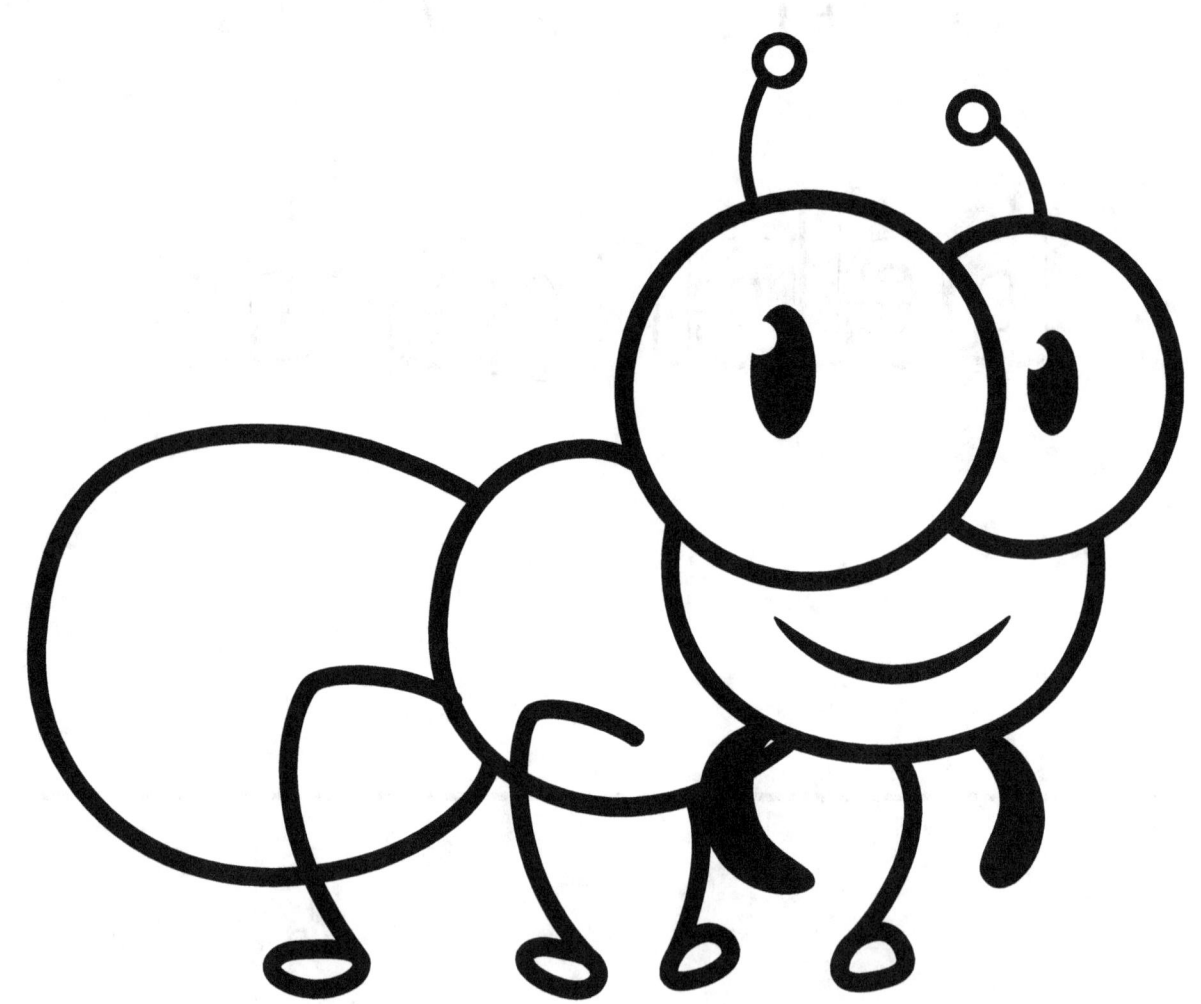

ant

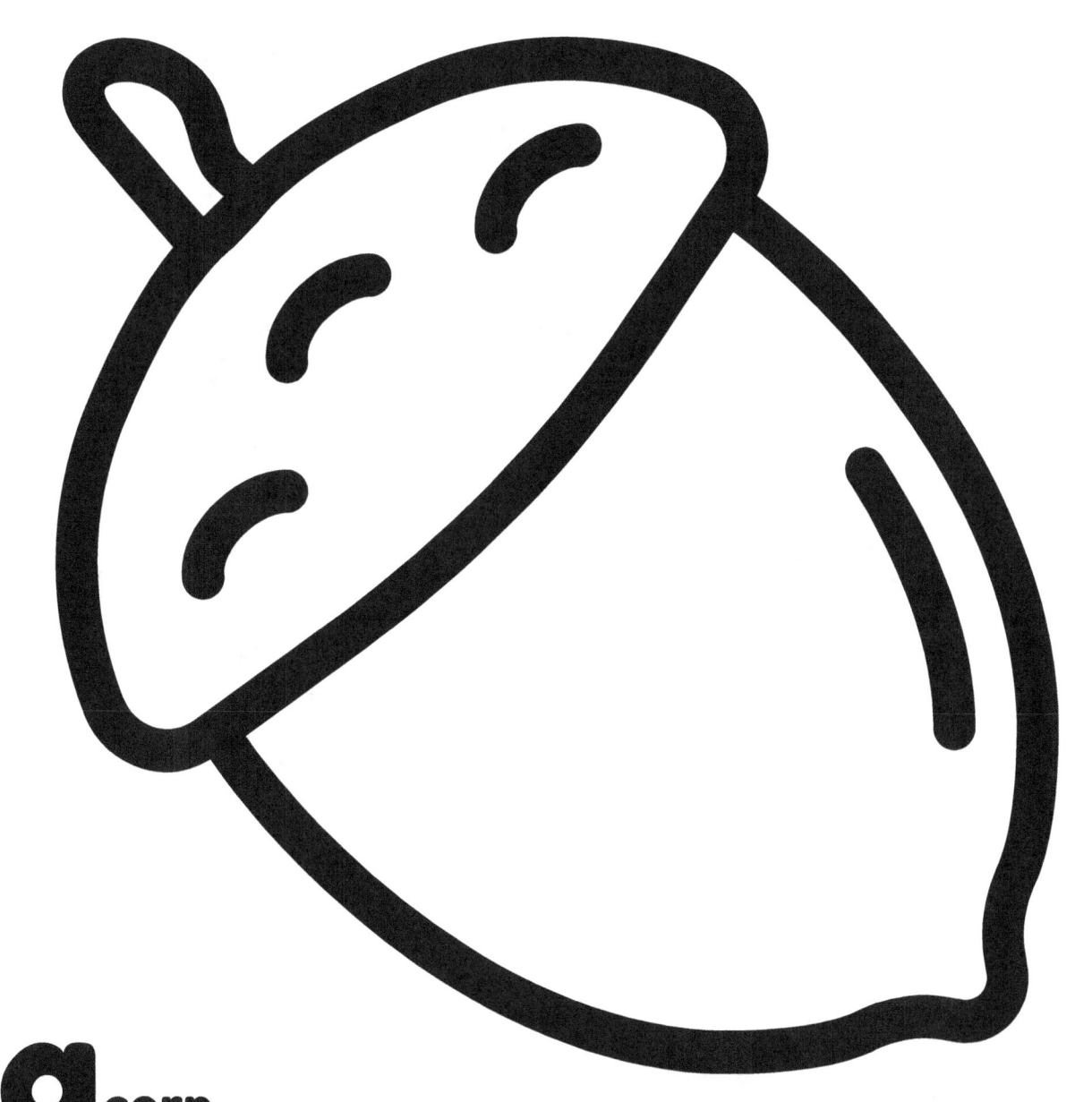

acorn

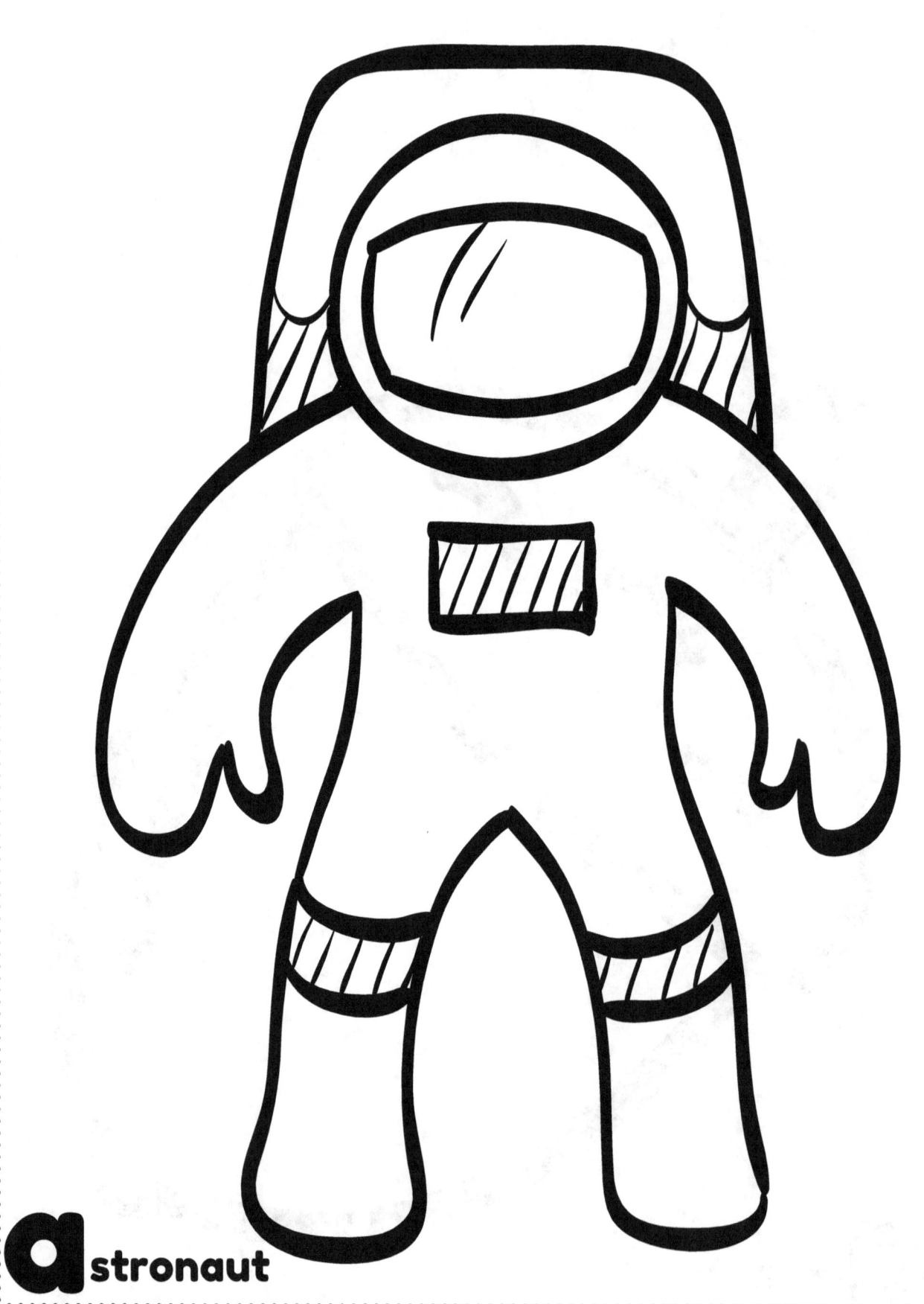

astronaut

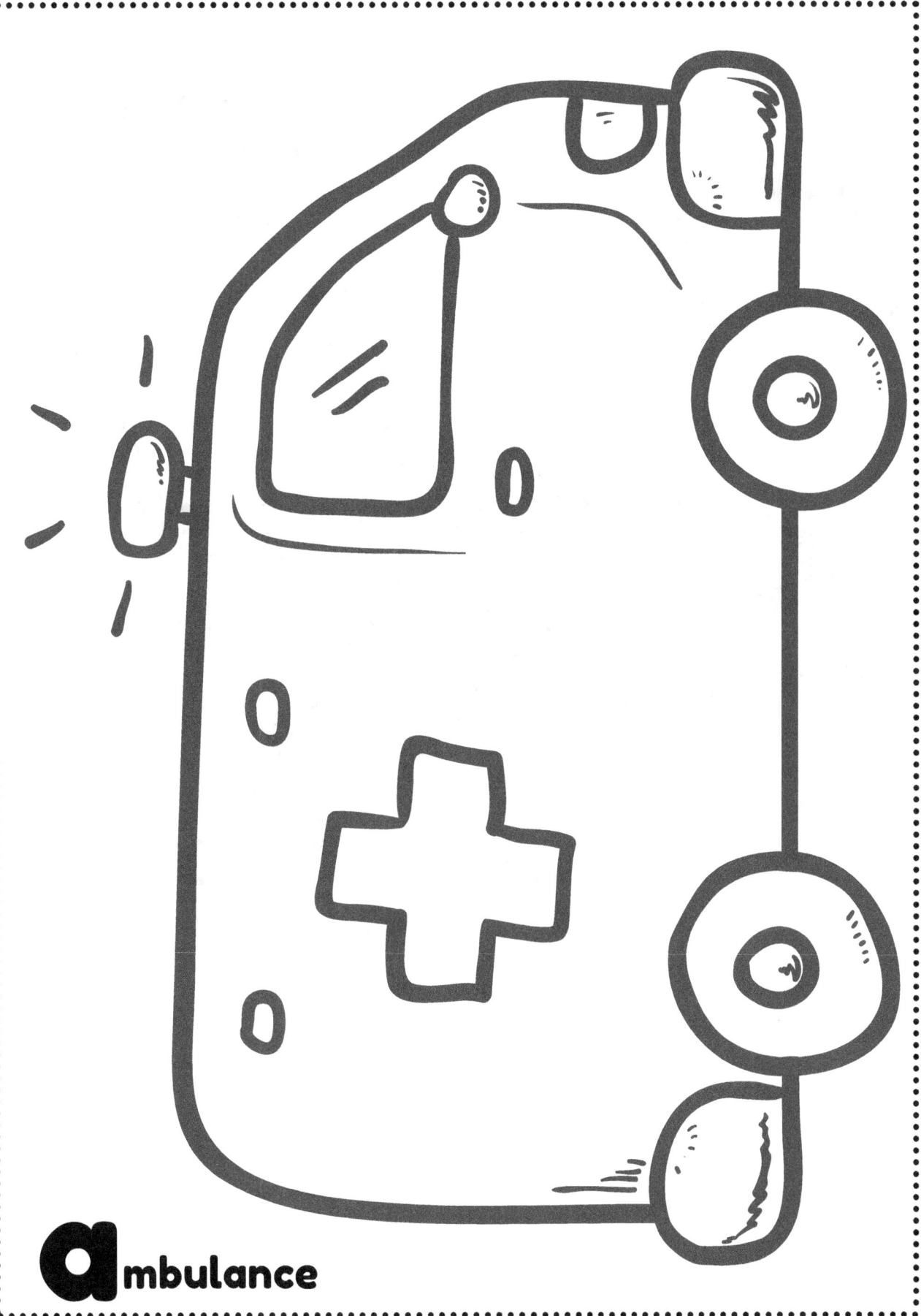

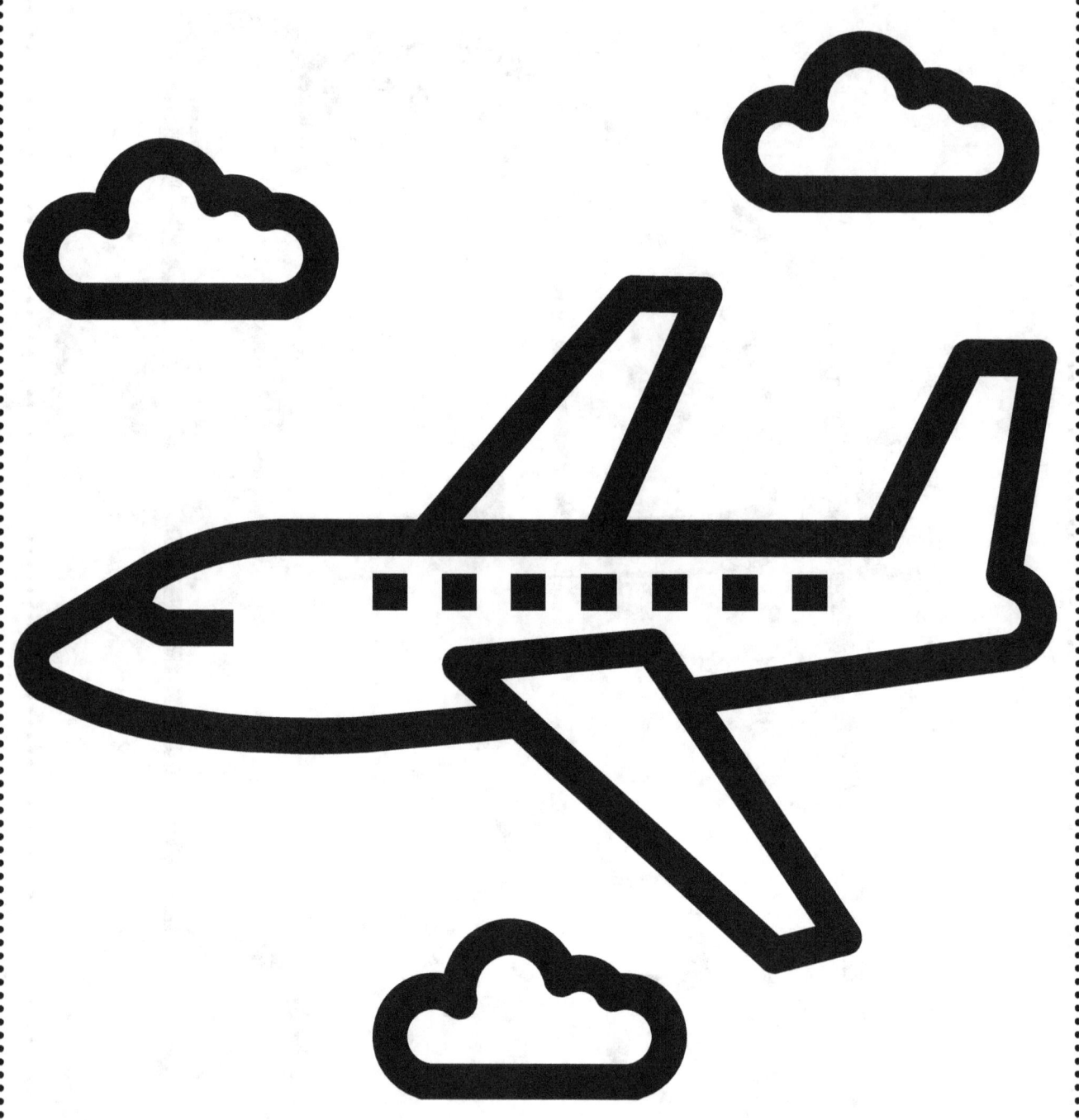

airplane

Name:

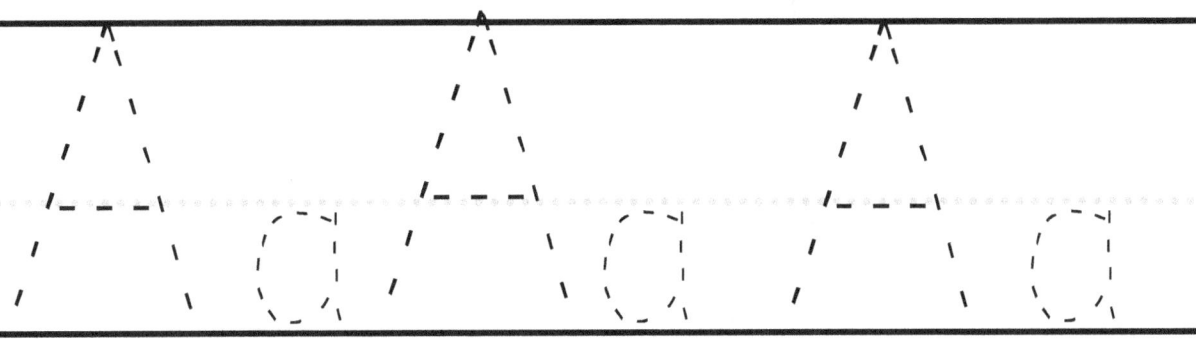

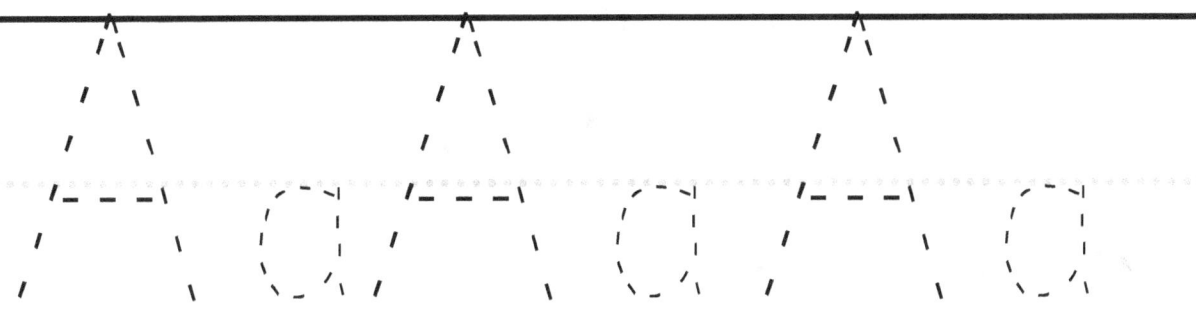

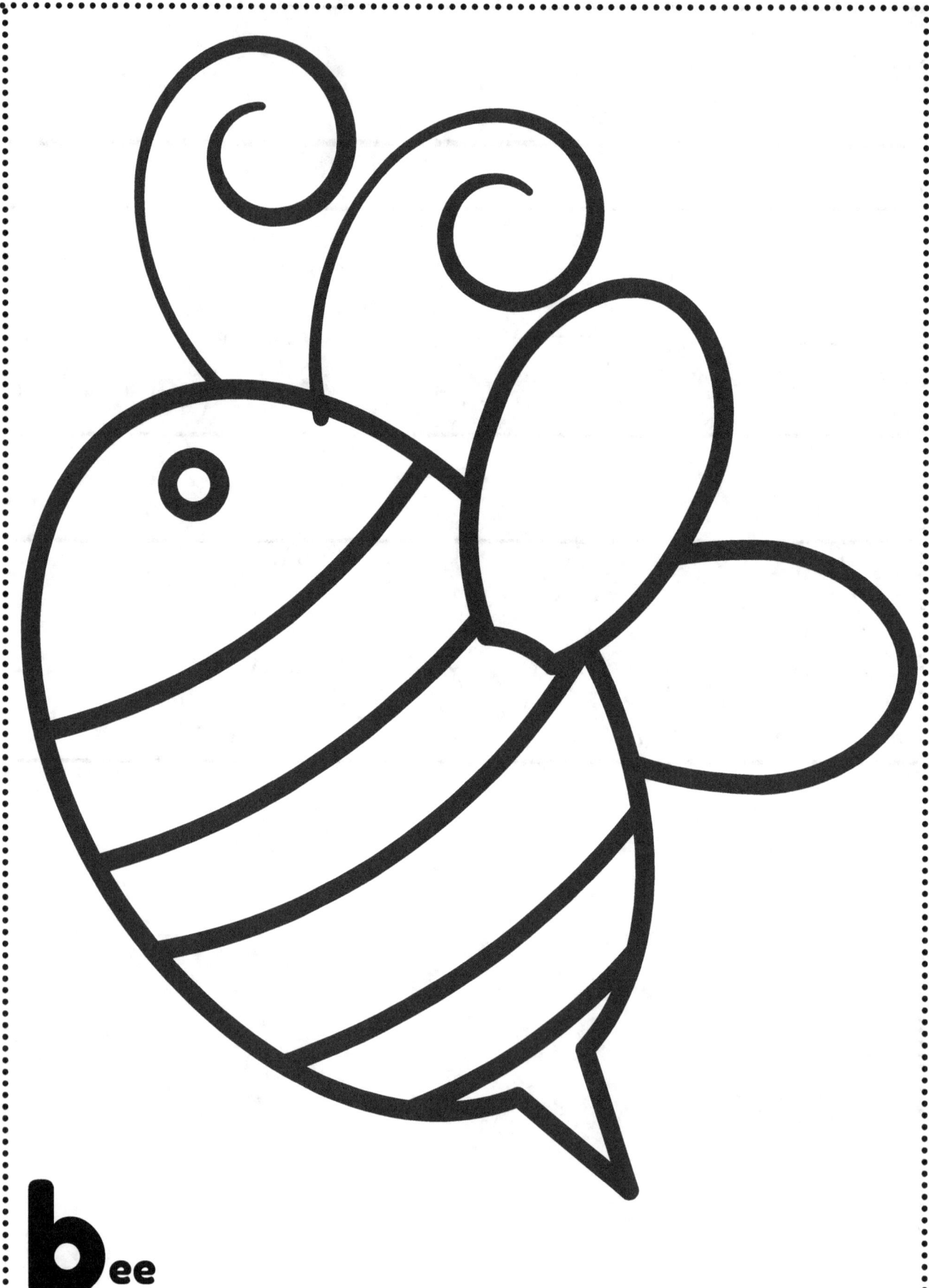

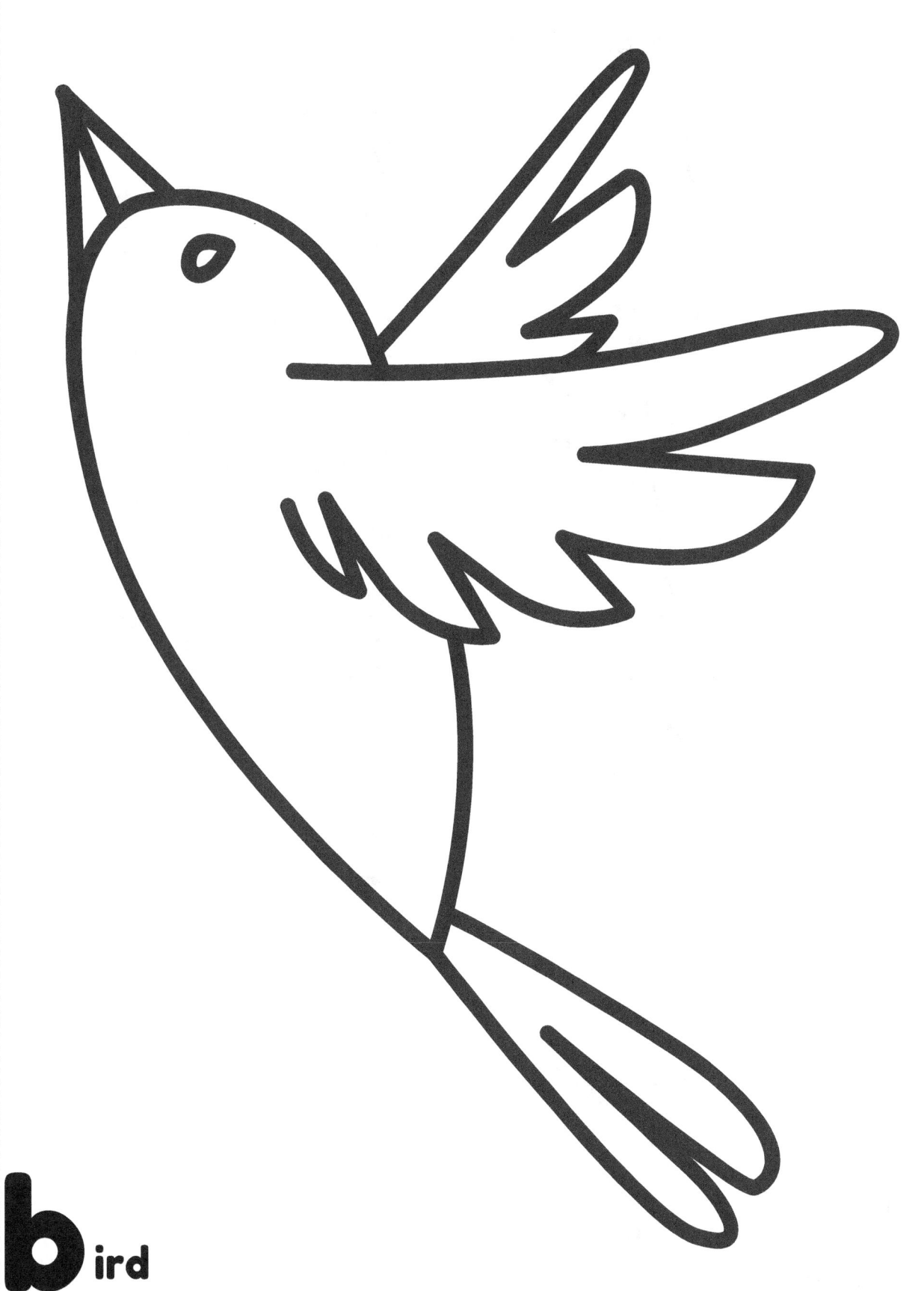
bird

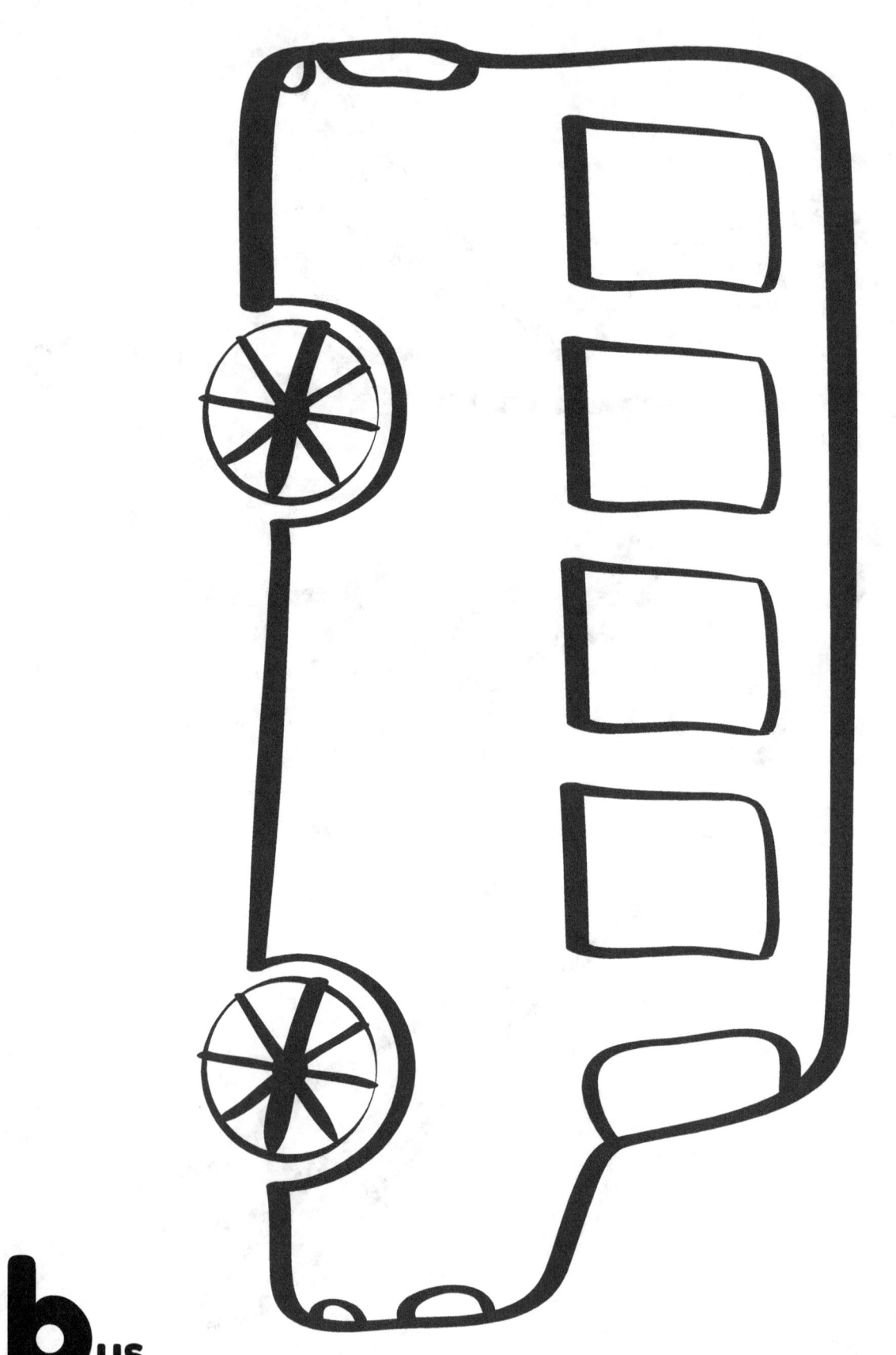

b us

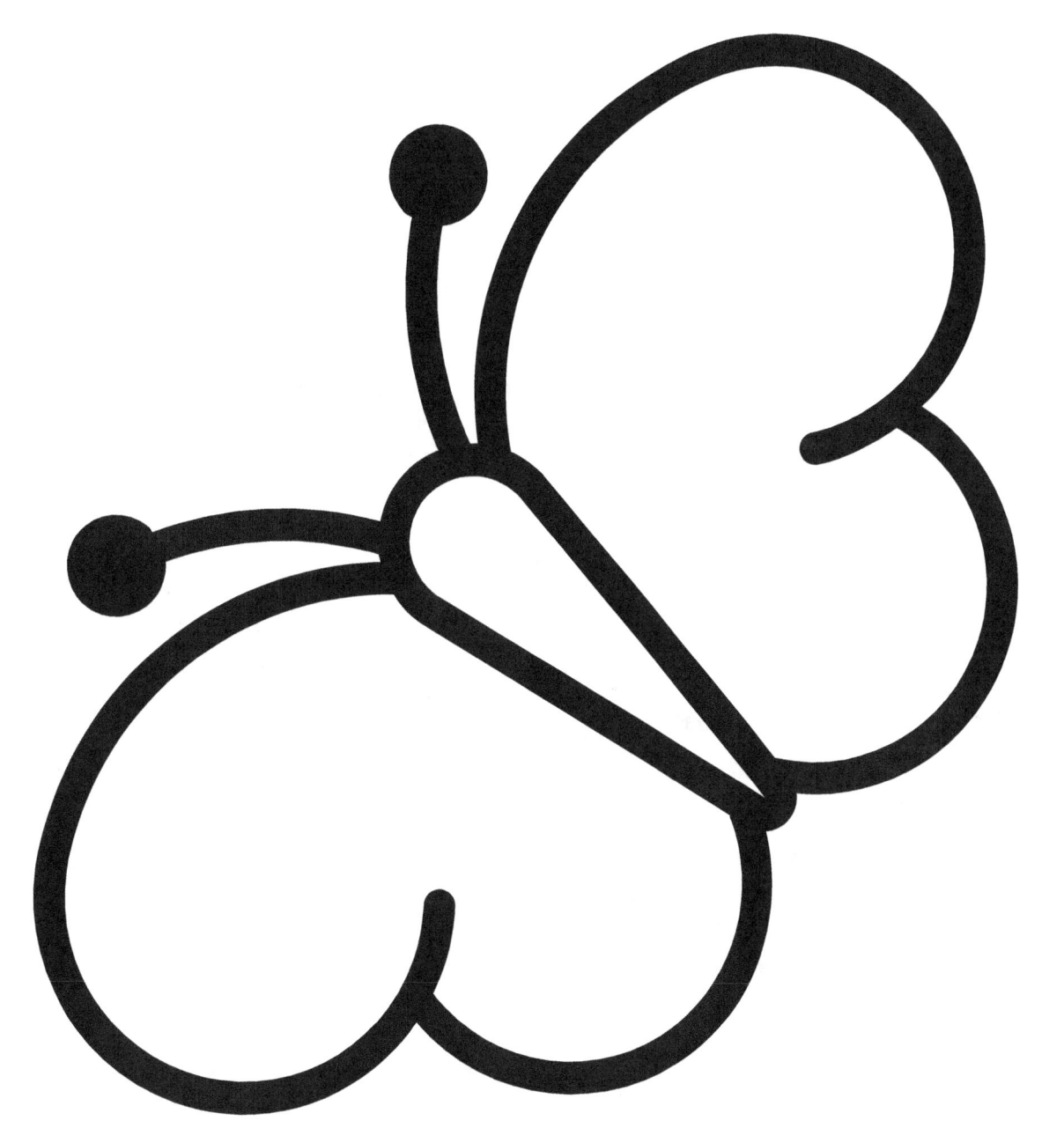

butterfly

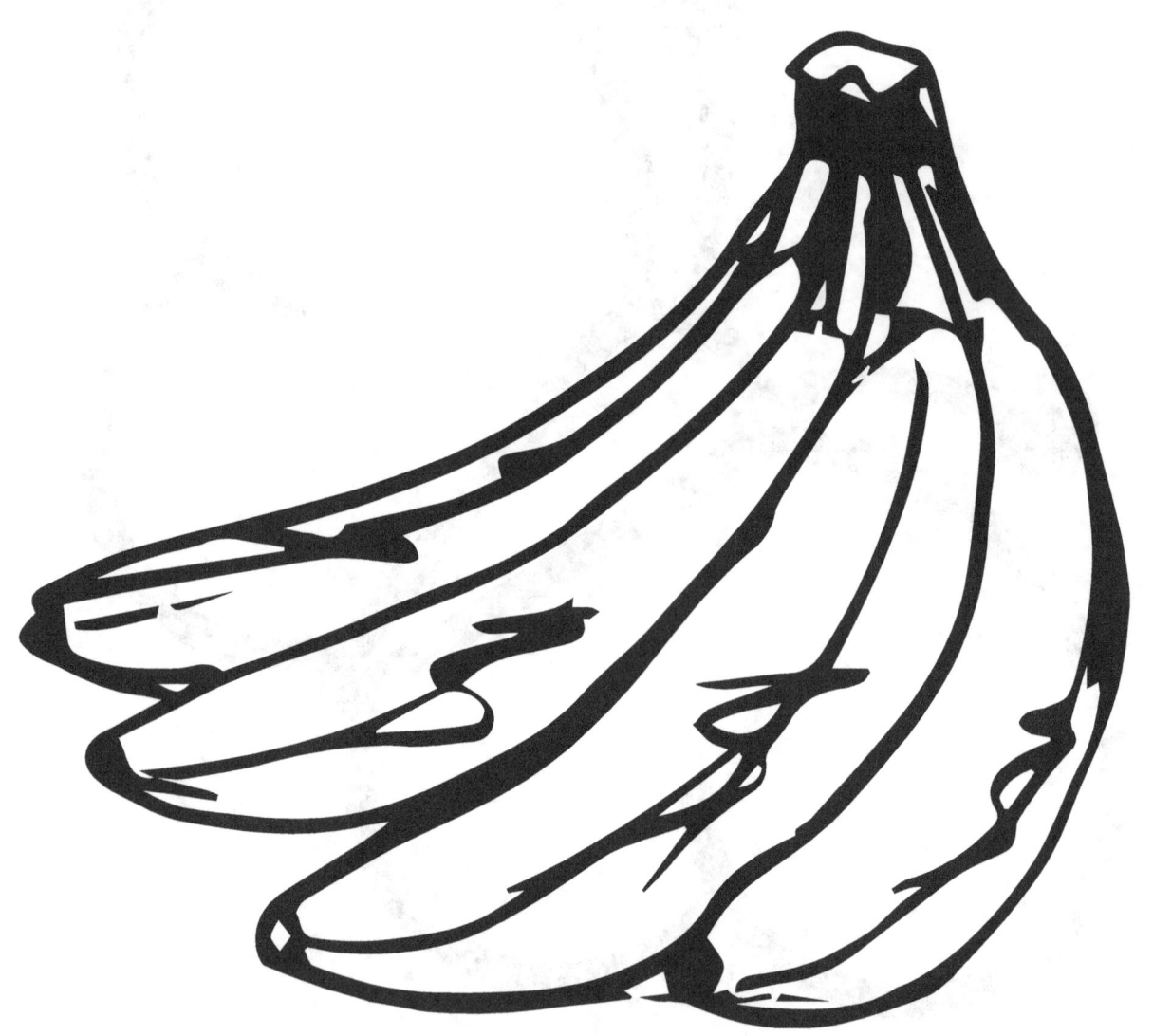

banana

Name:

Bb Bb Bb Bb Bb

Bb Bb Bb Bb Bb

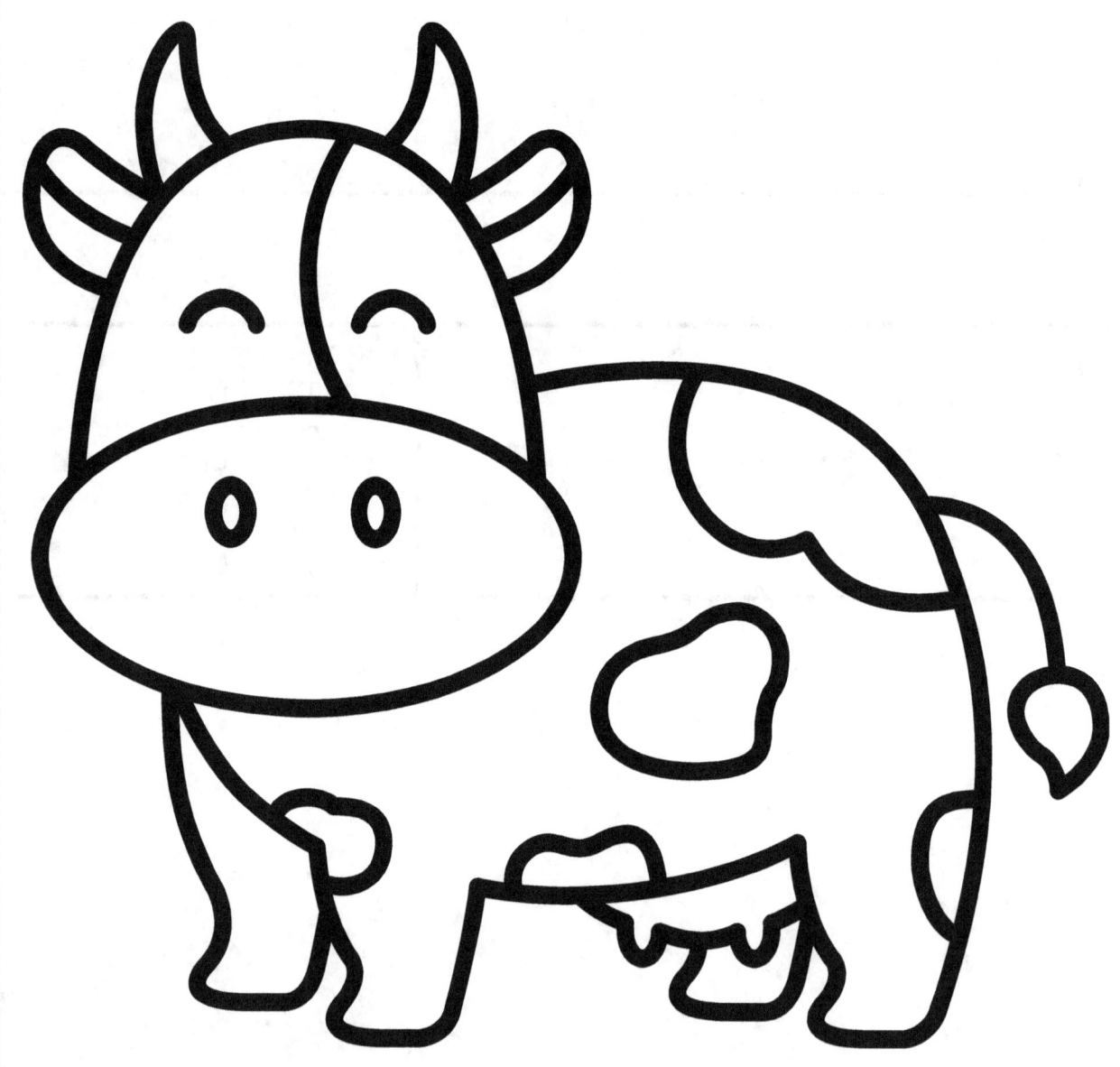

Cow

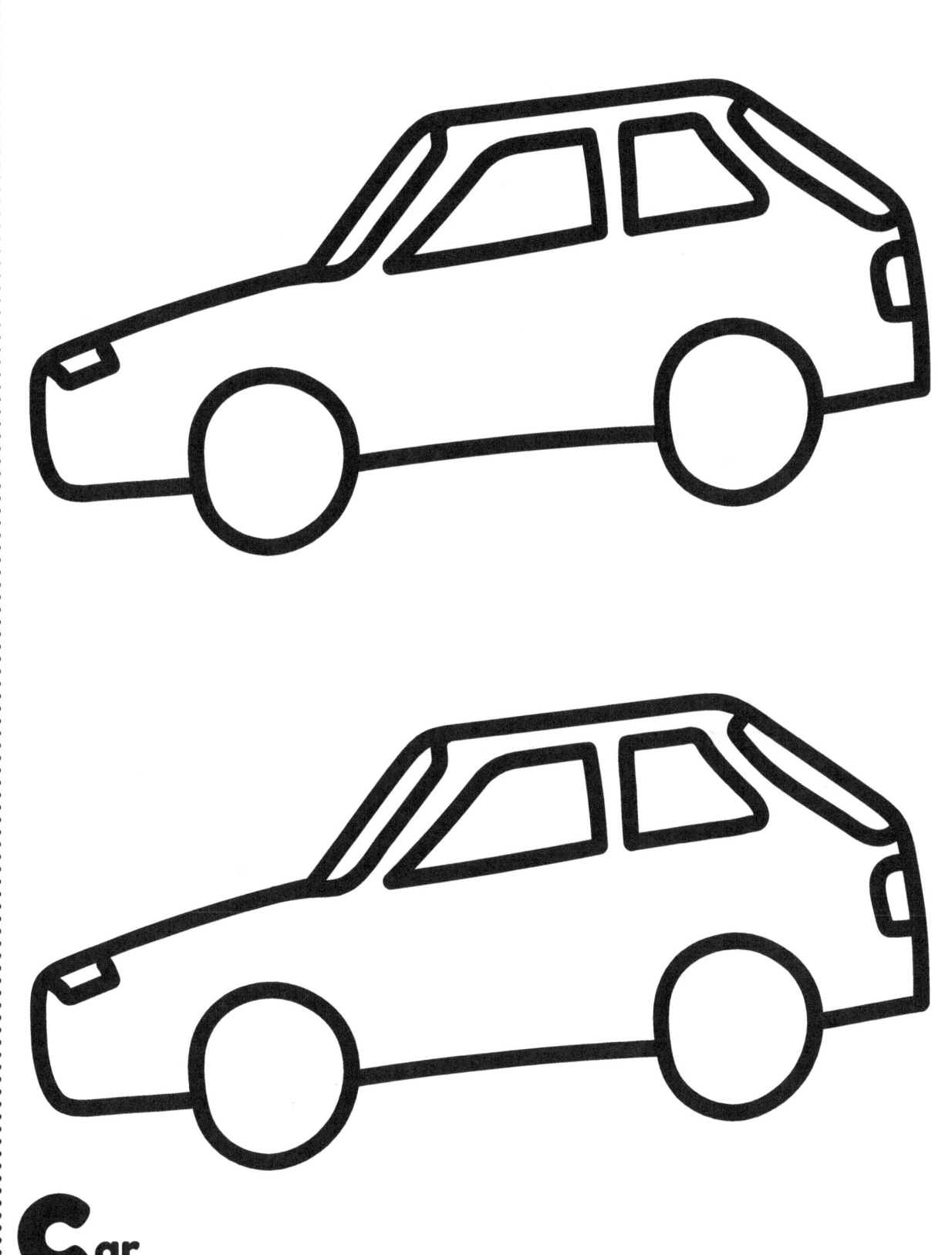

Car

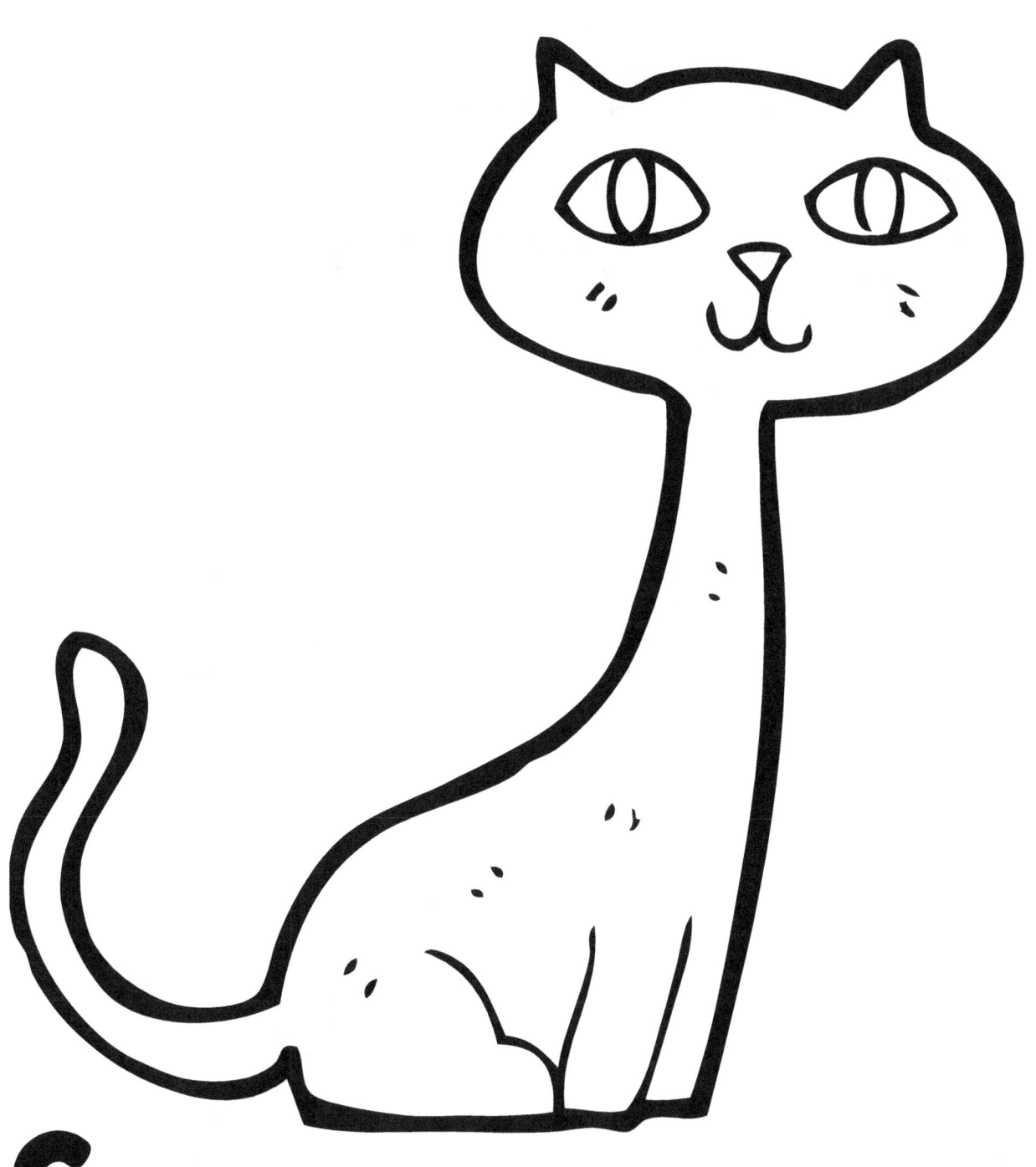

Cat

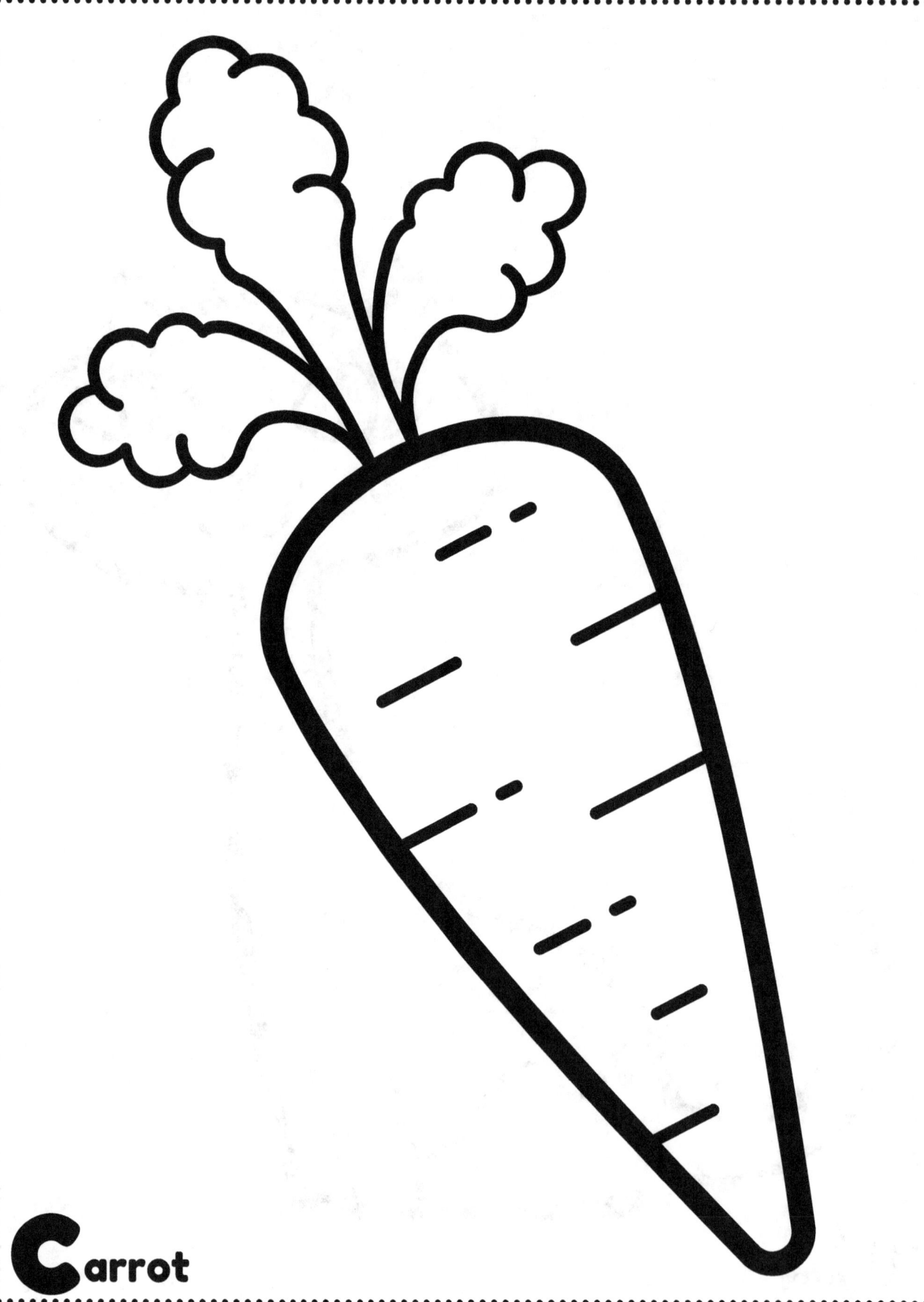

Name:

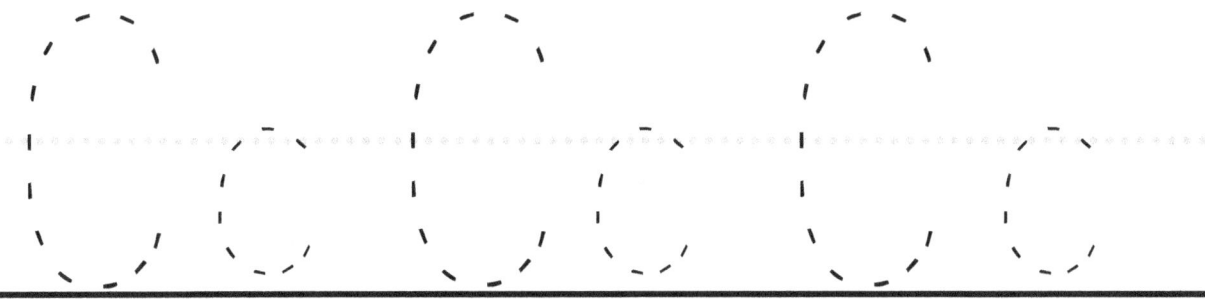

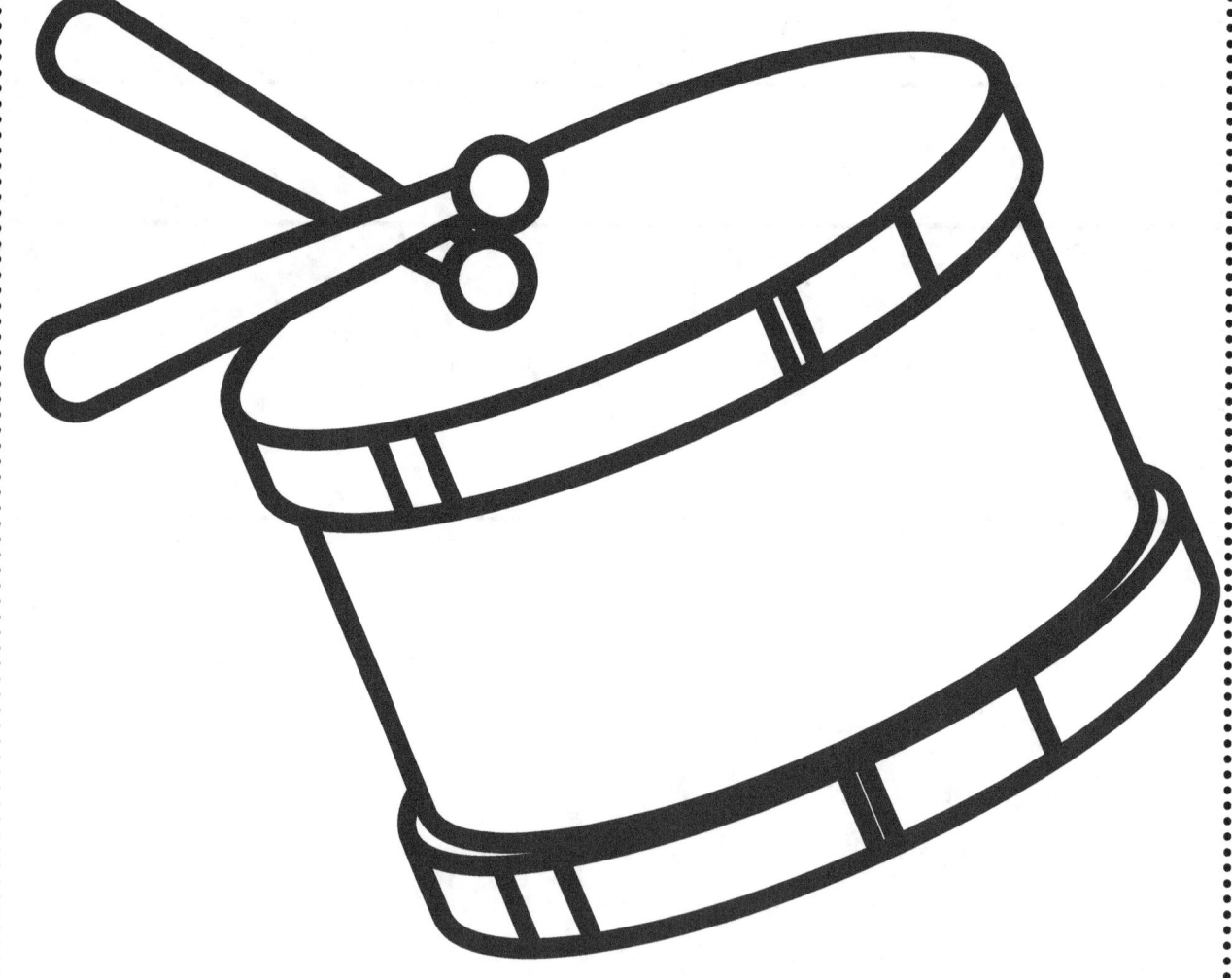

drum

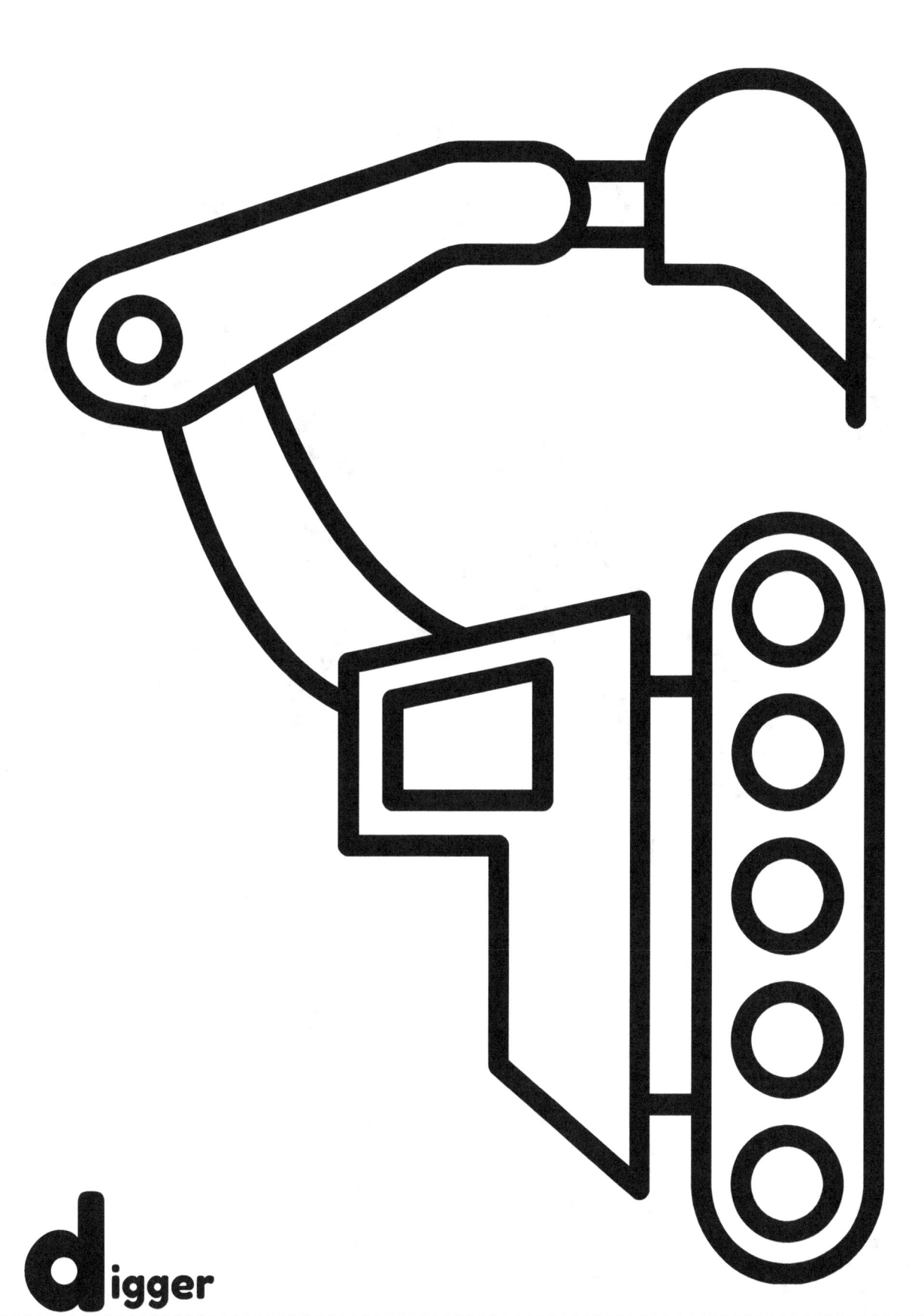

digger

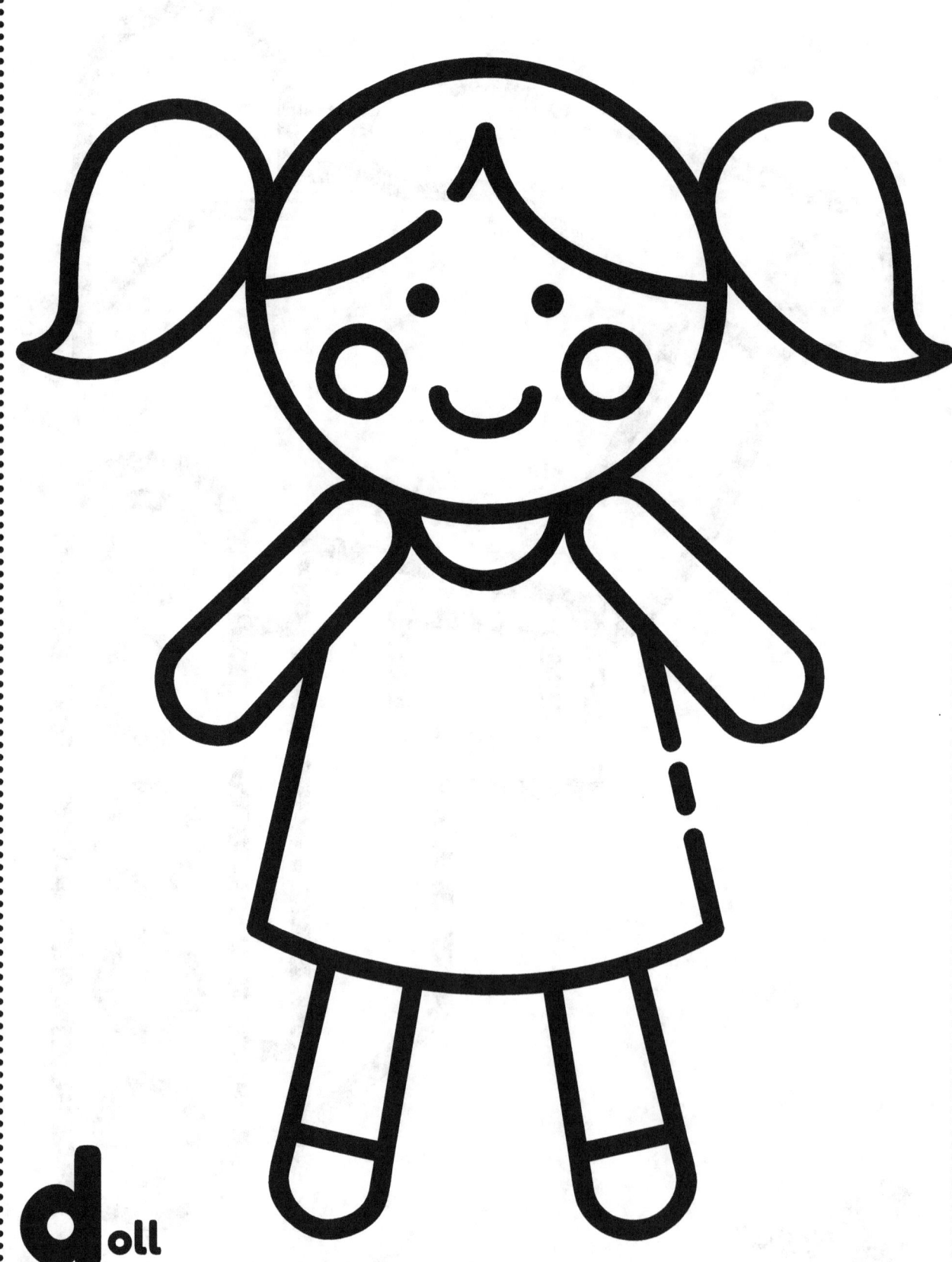

doll

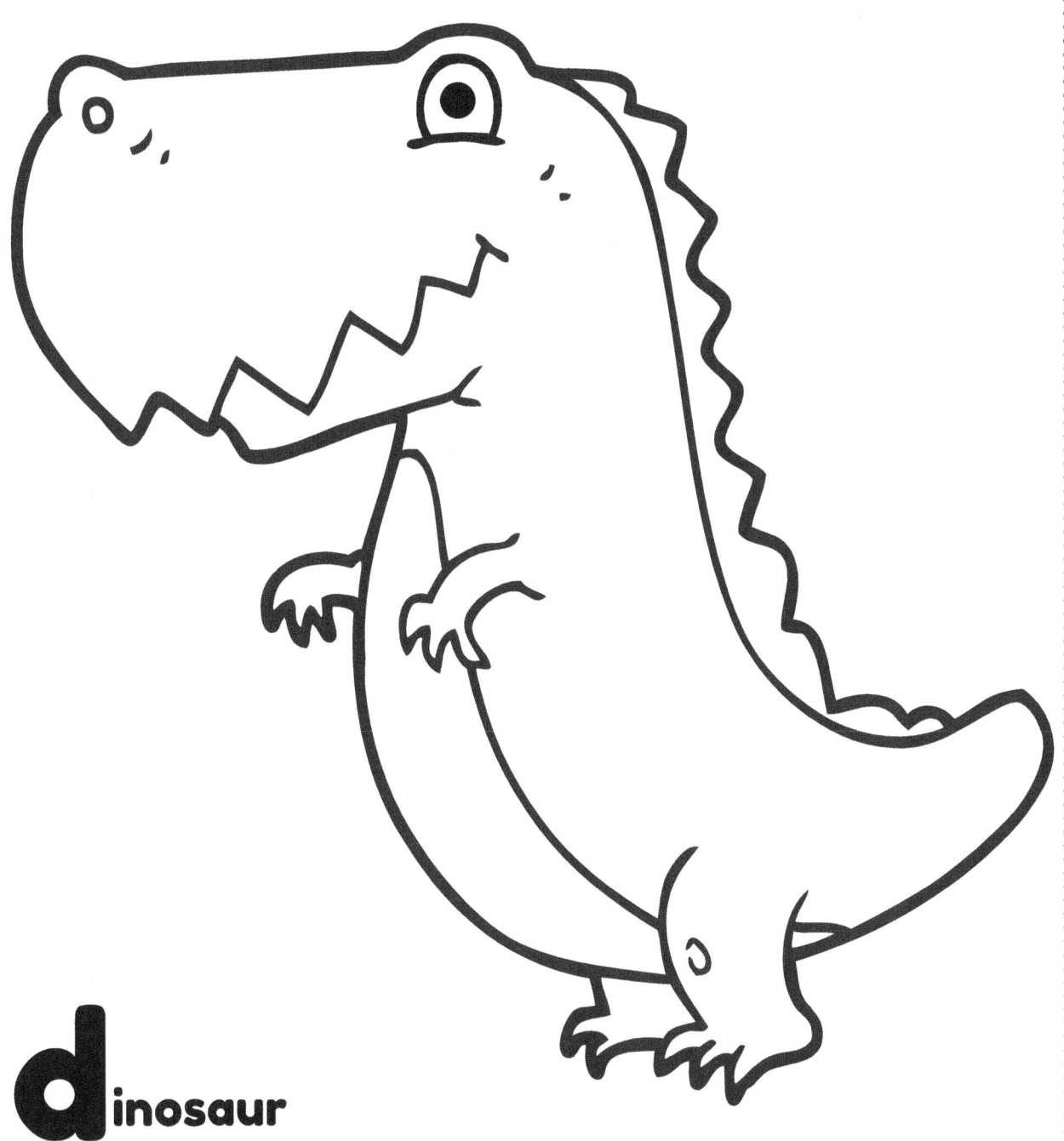

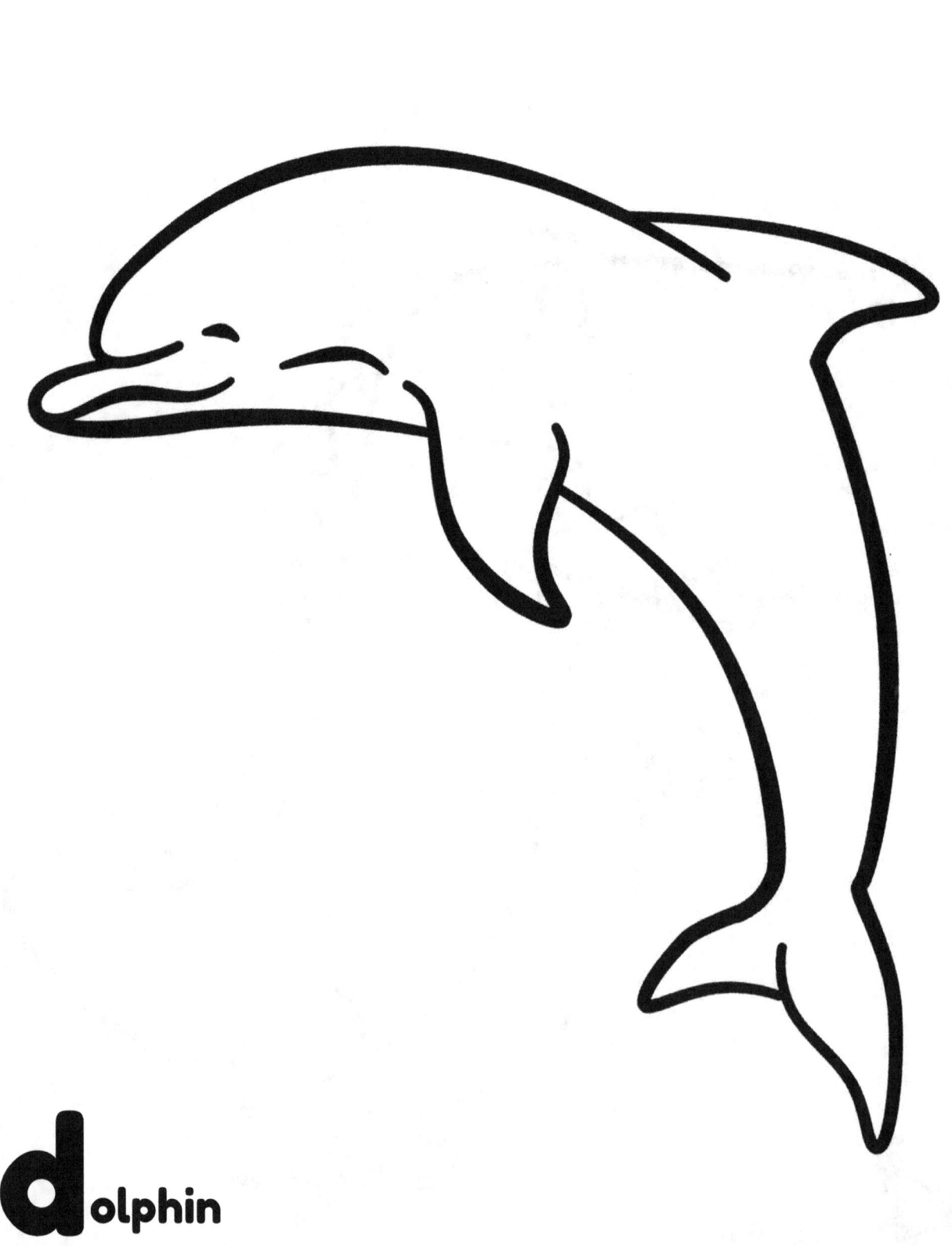

dolphin

Name:

Dd Dd Dd

Dd Dd Dd

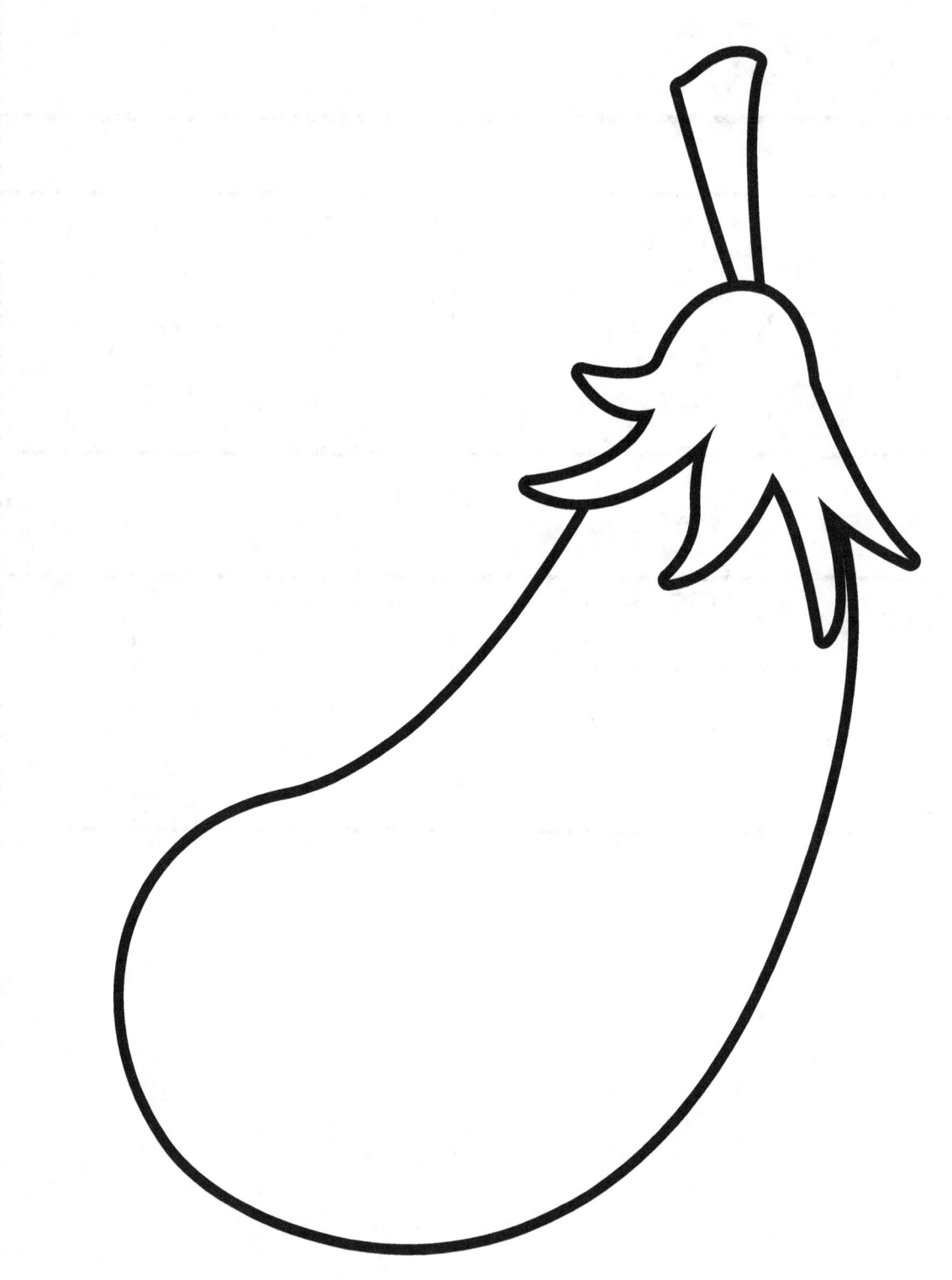

eggplant

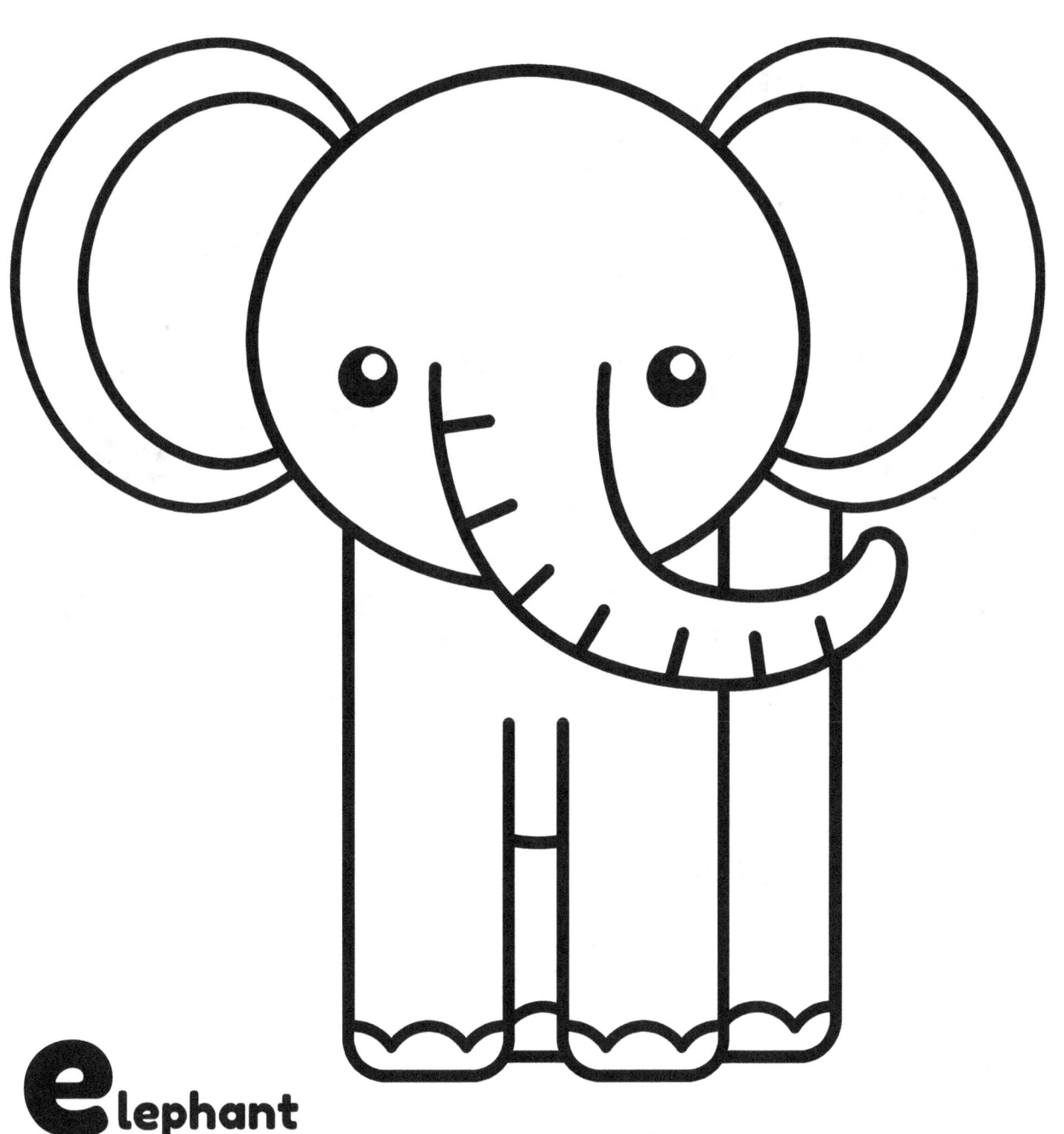

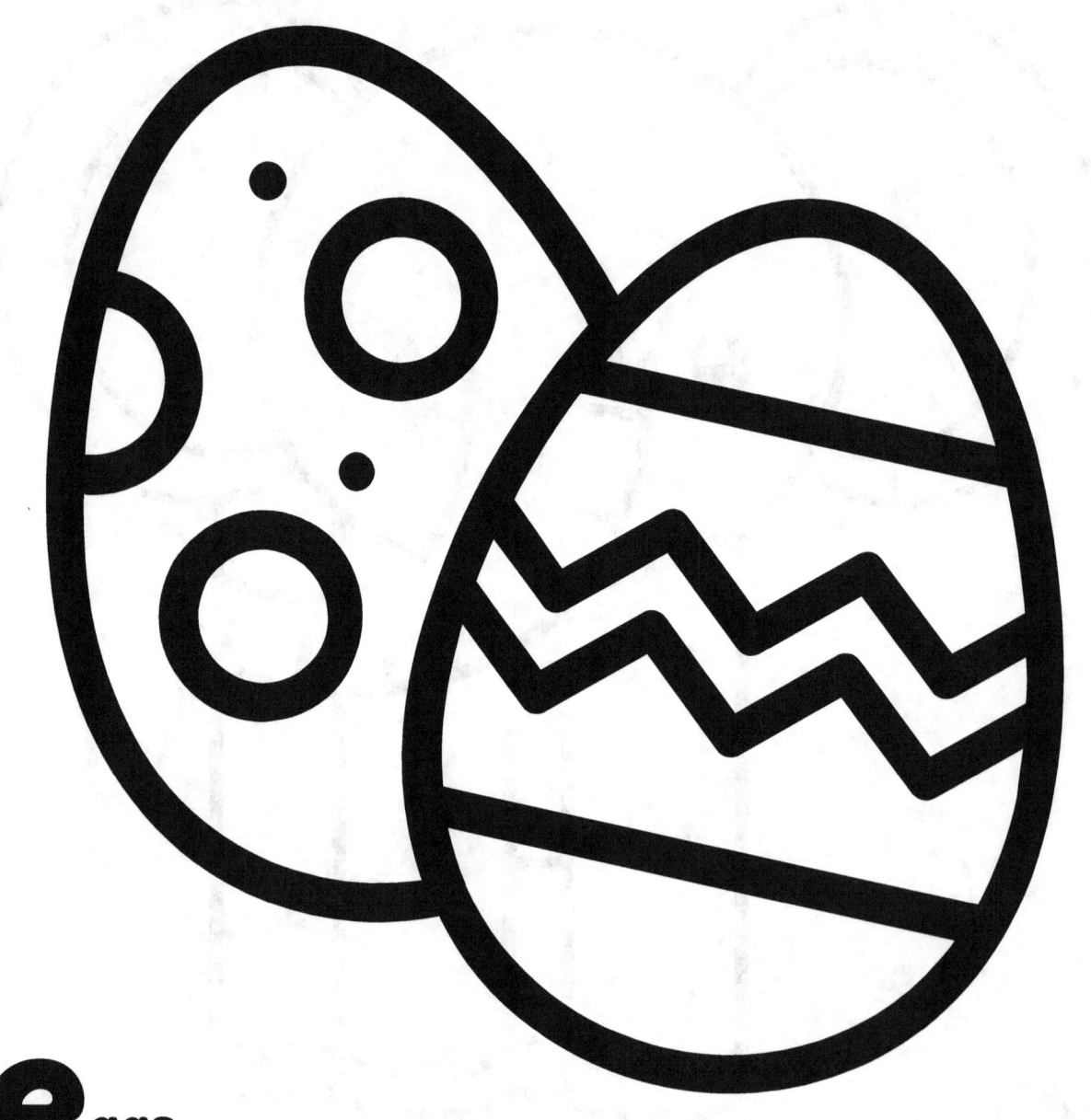

eggs

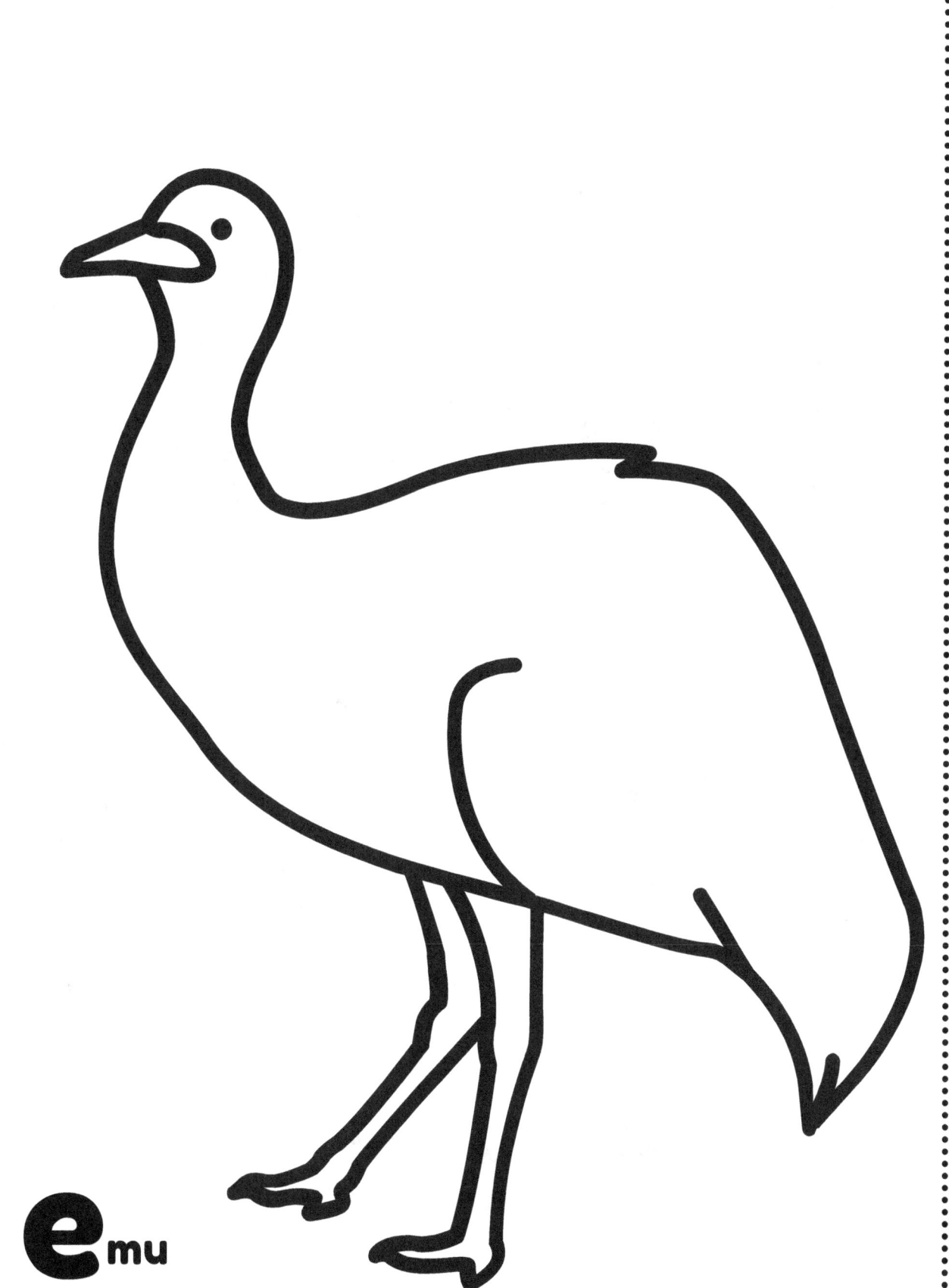

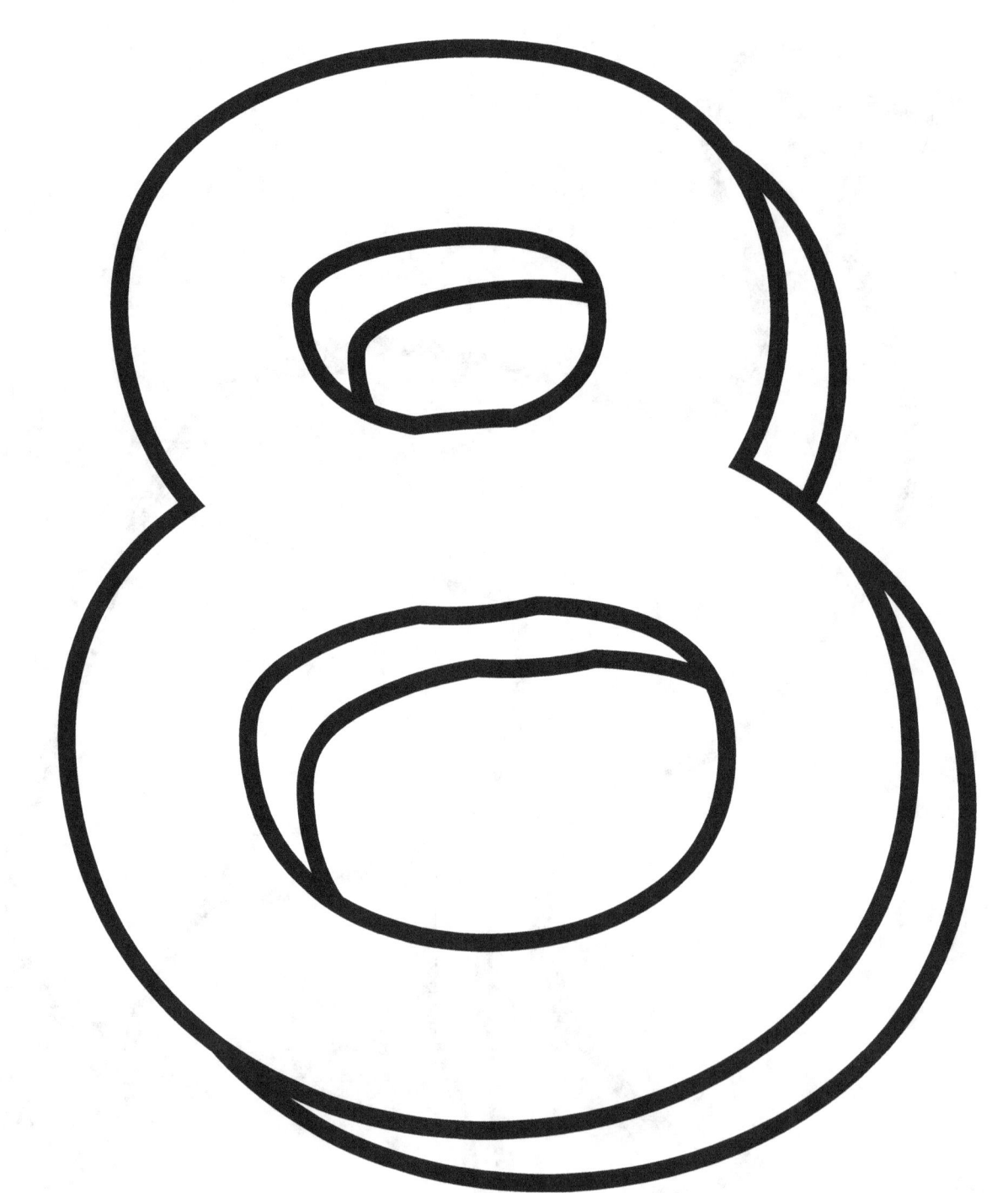

Name:

Fefefe

Fefefe

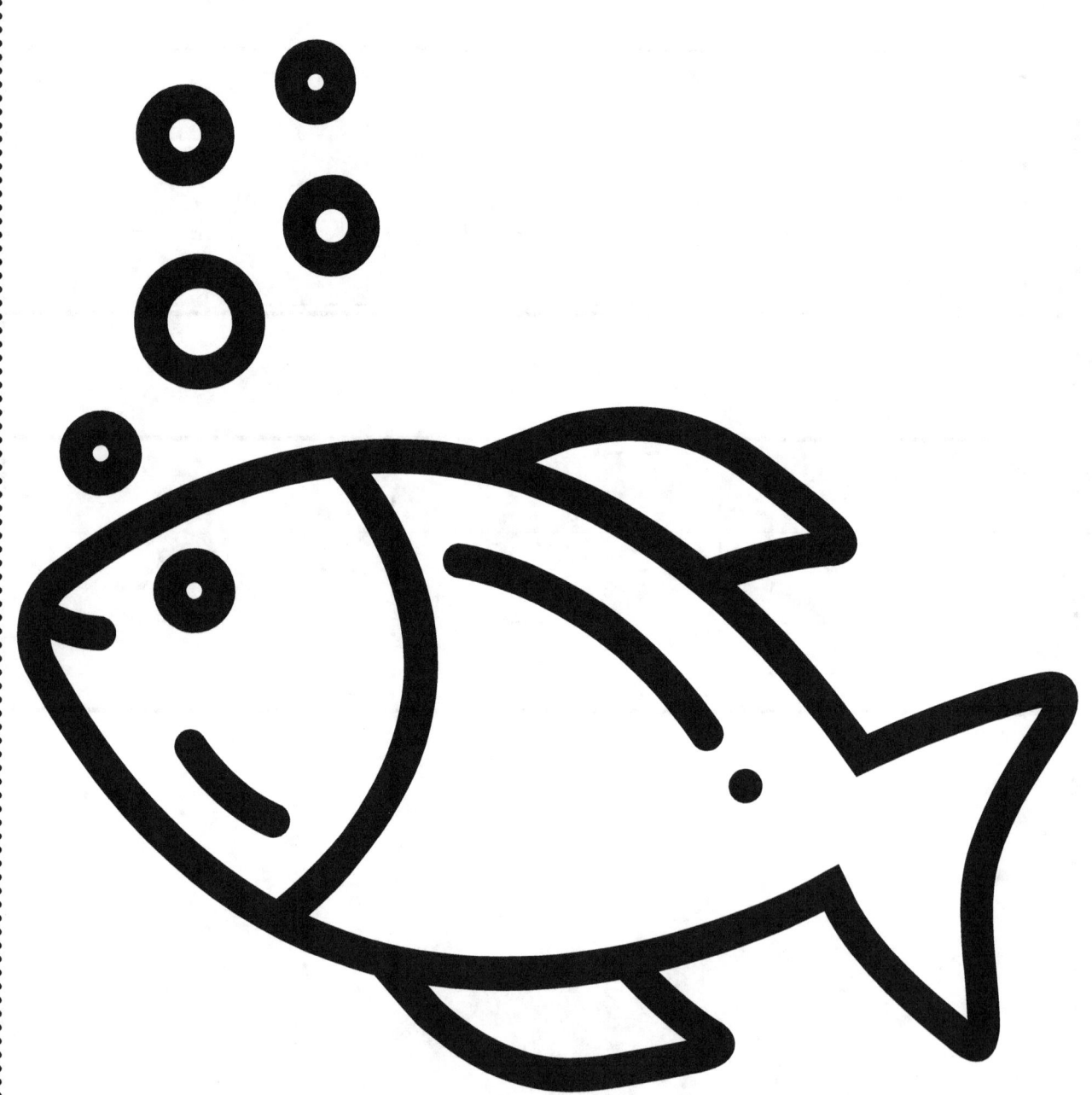

fish

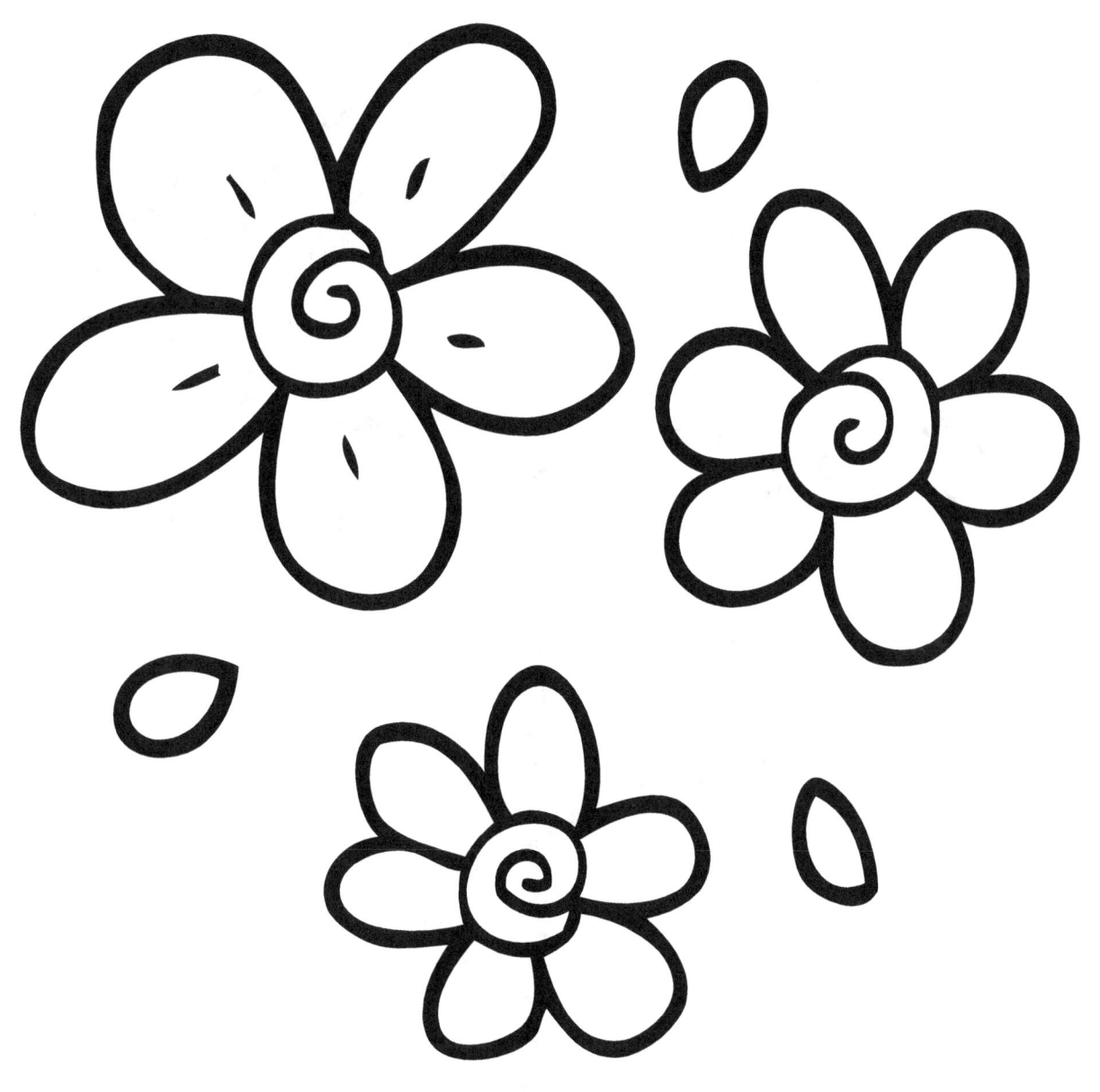

f lowers

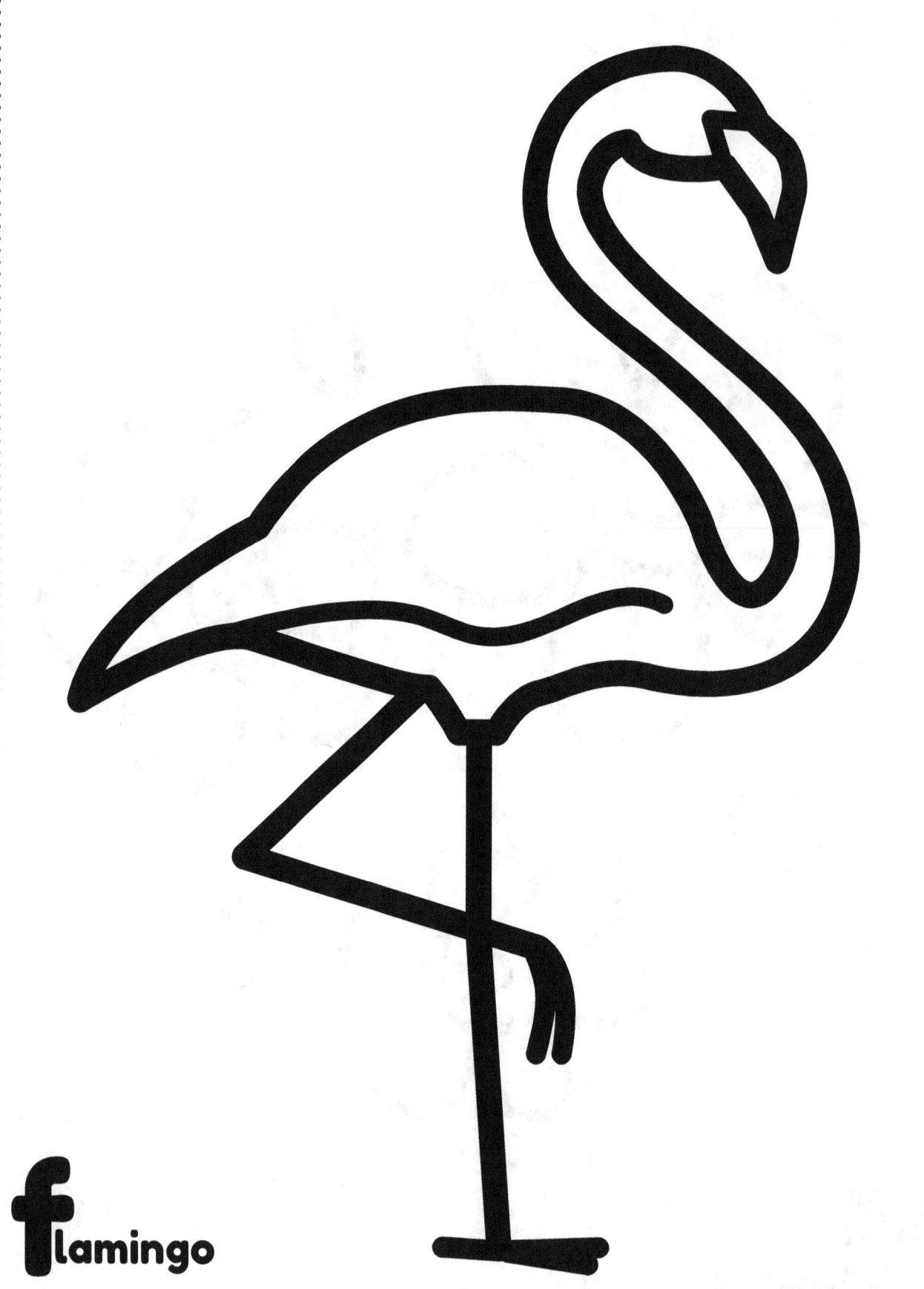

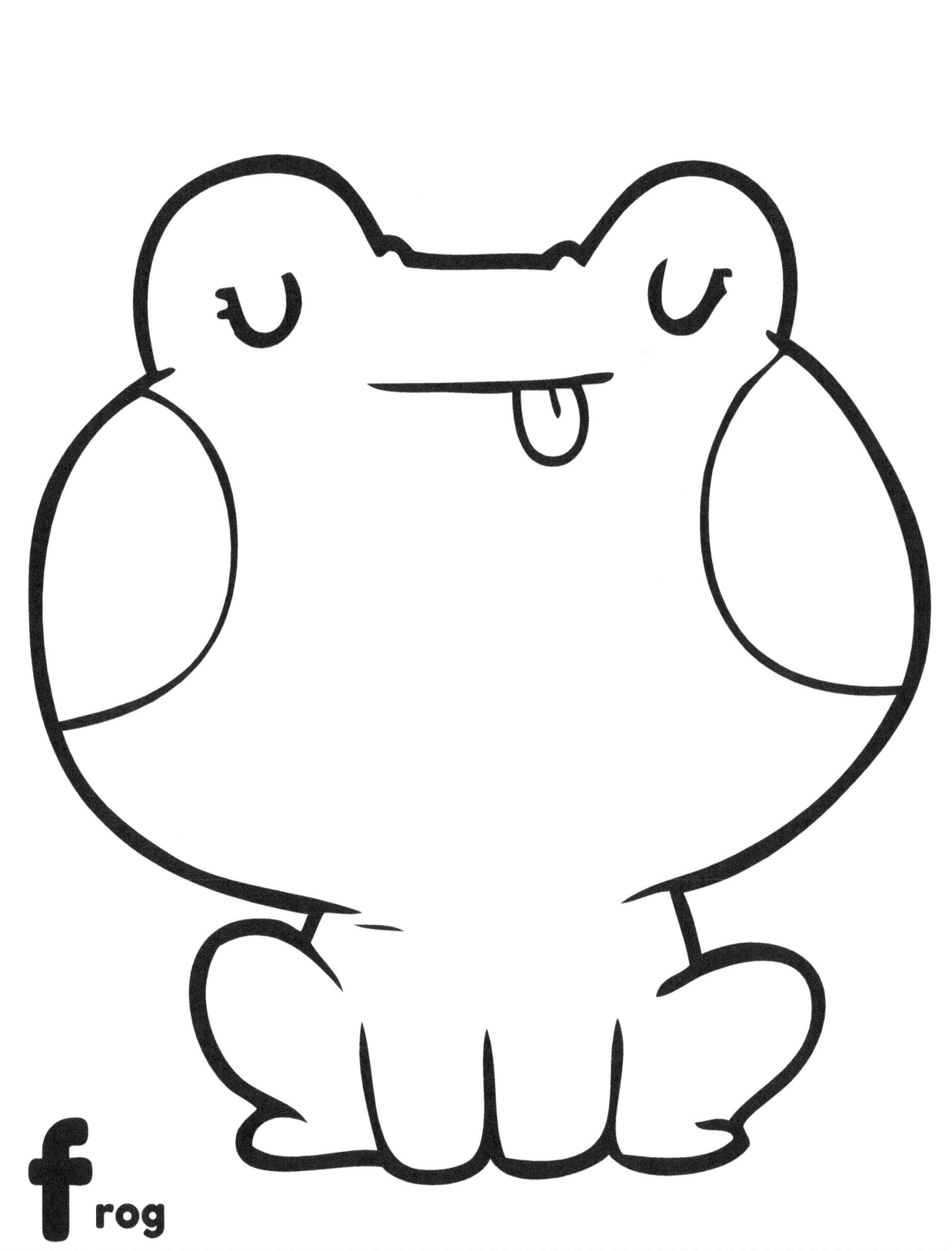

frog

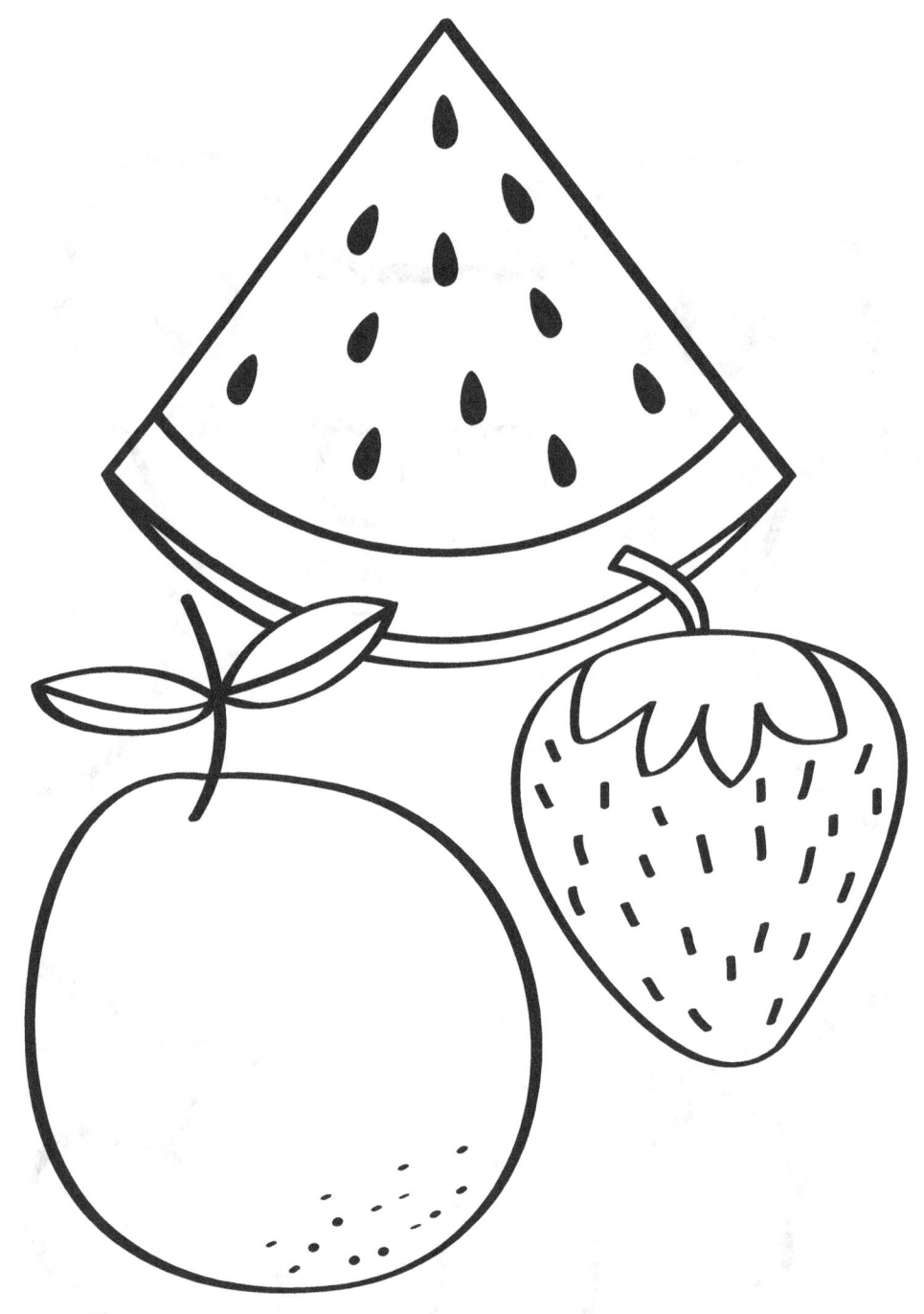

fruits

Name:

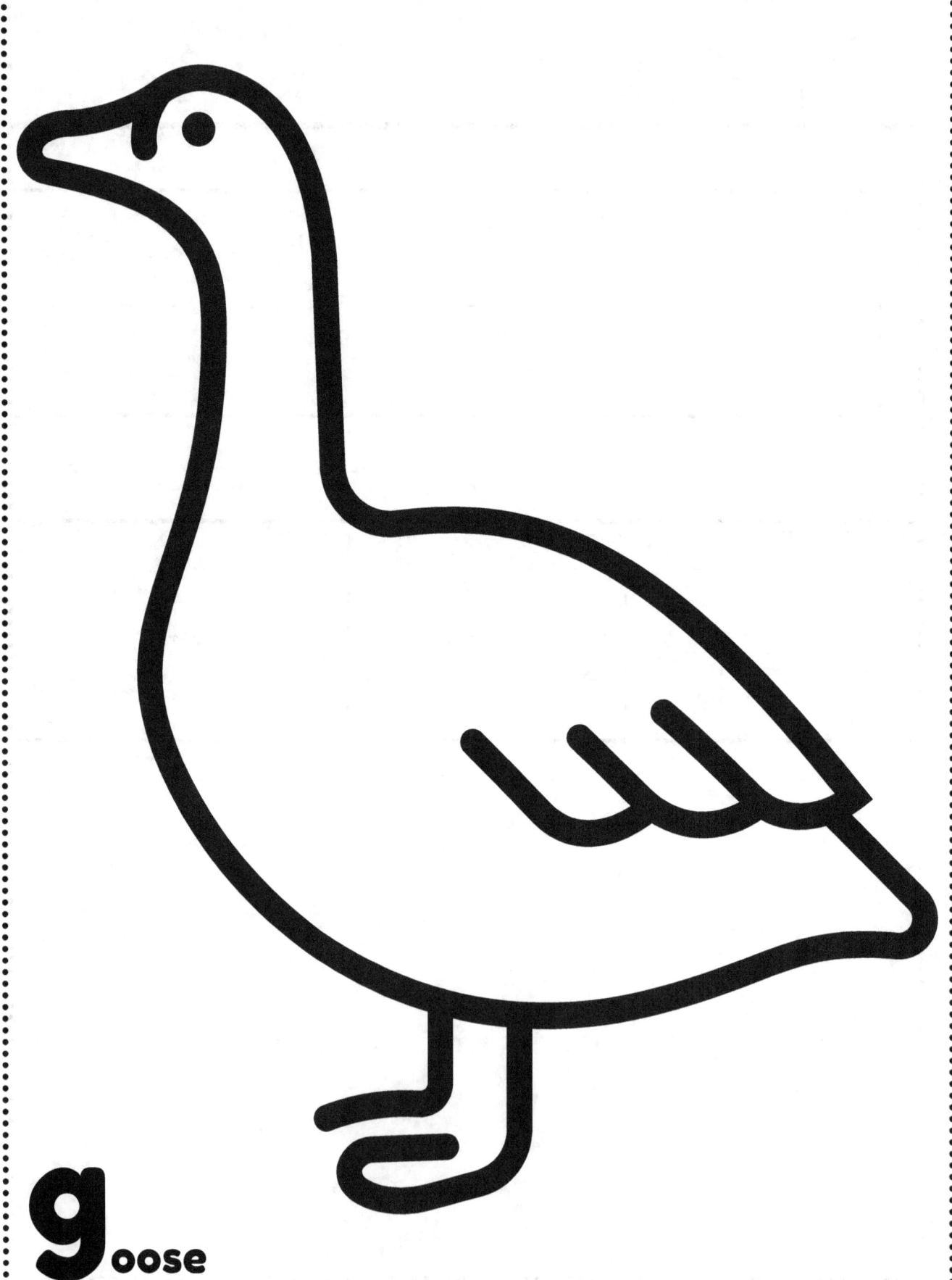

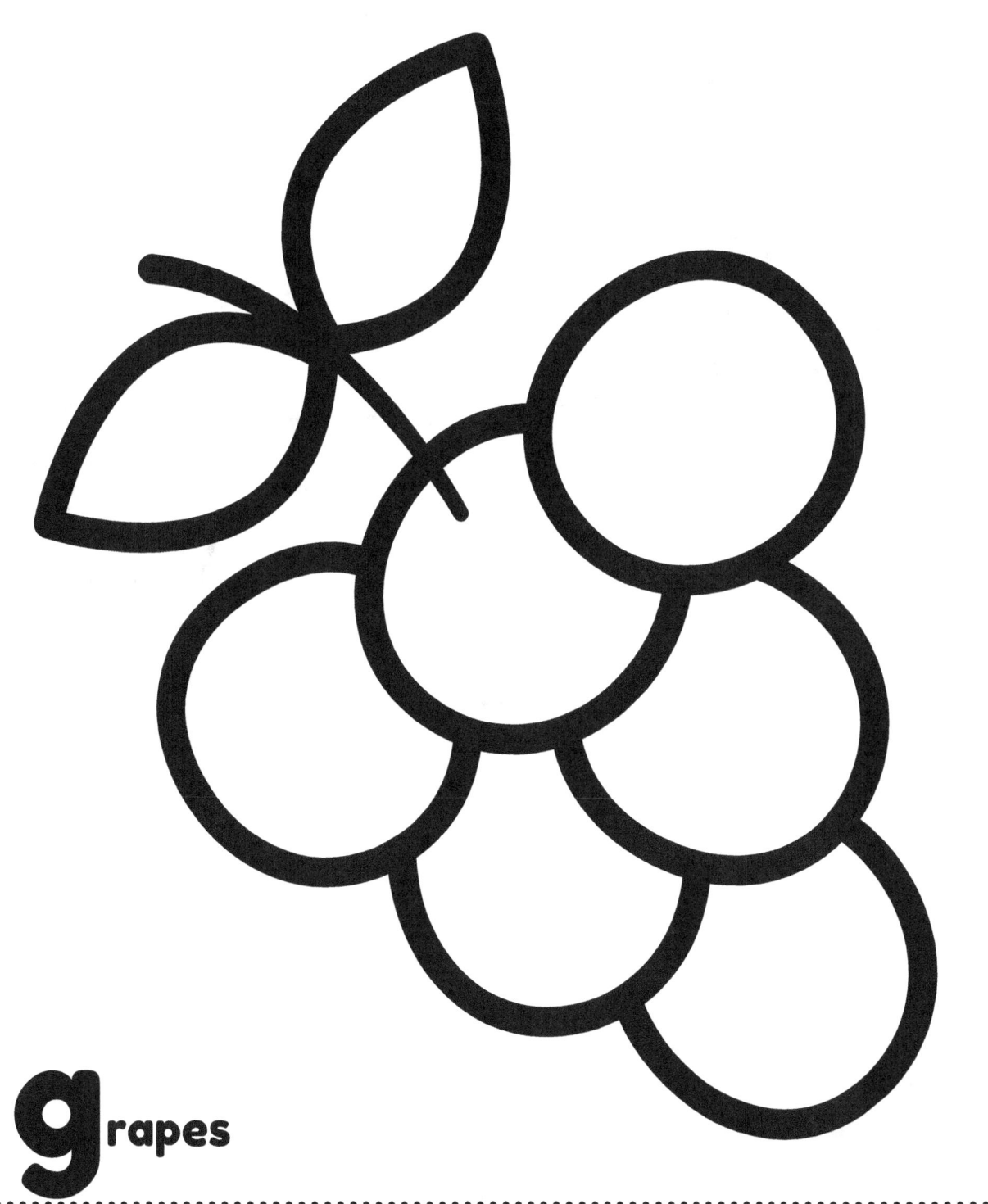

grapes

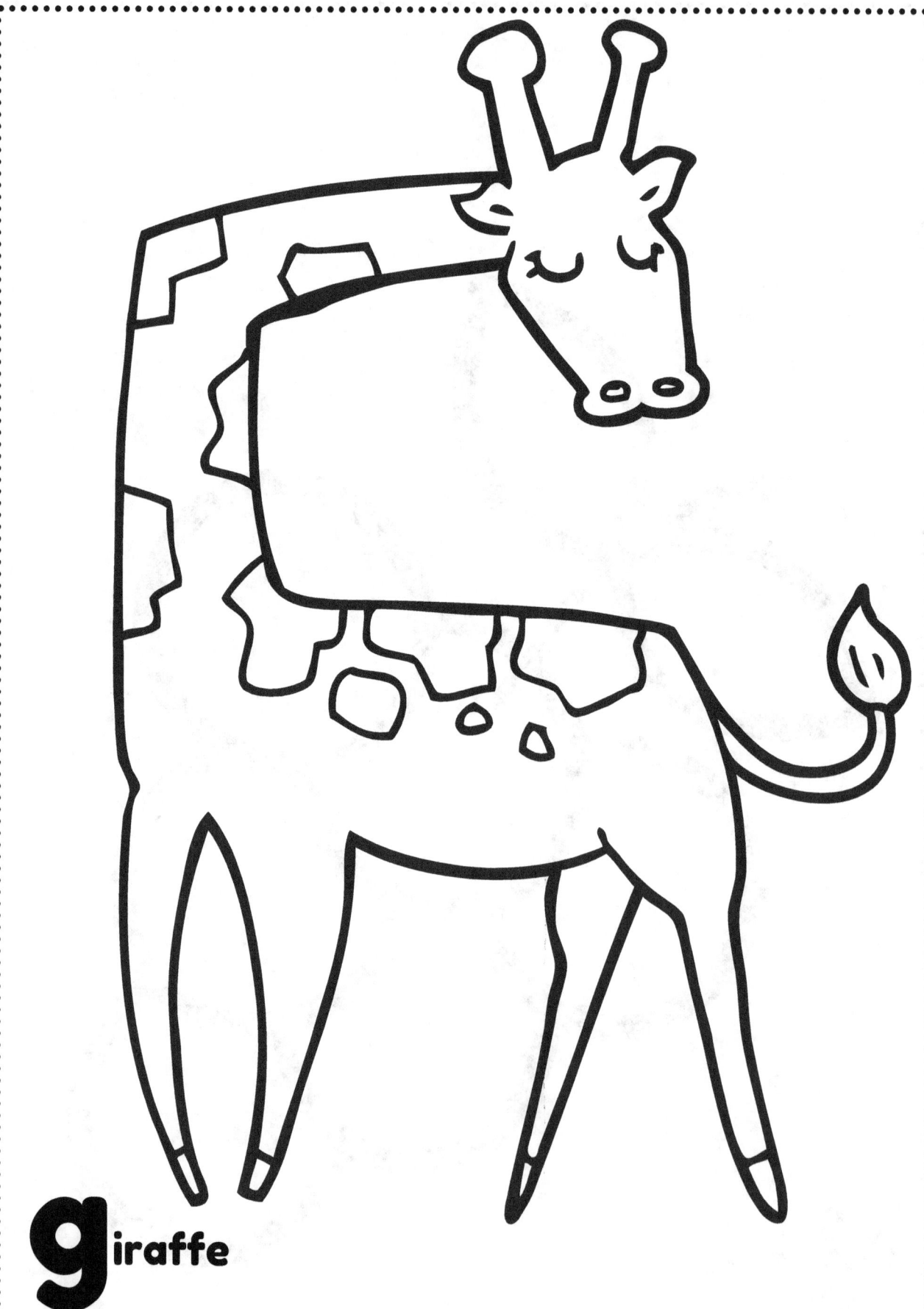

giraffe

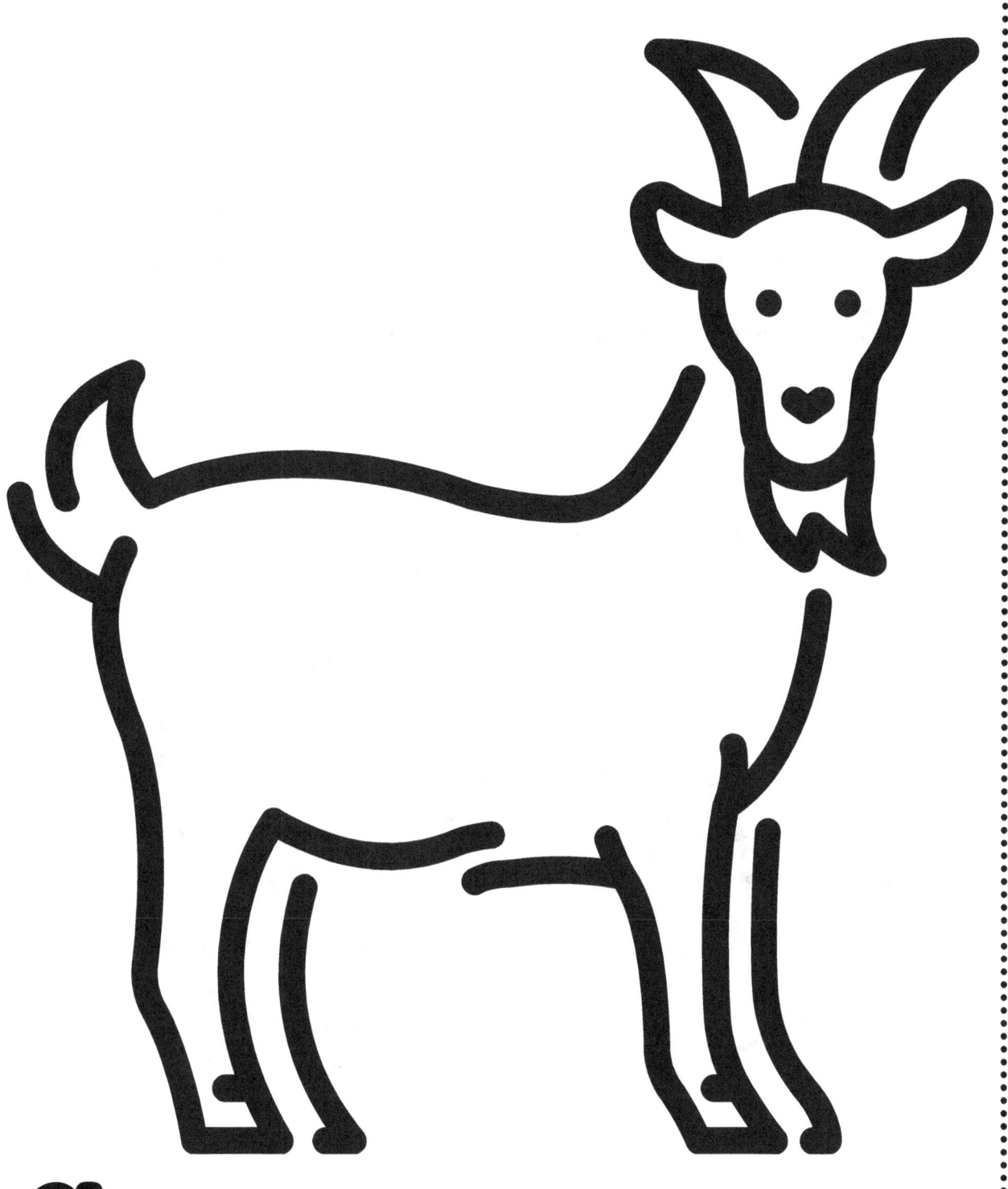

goat

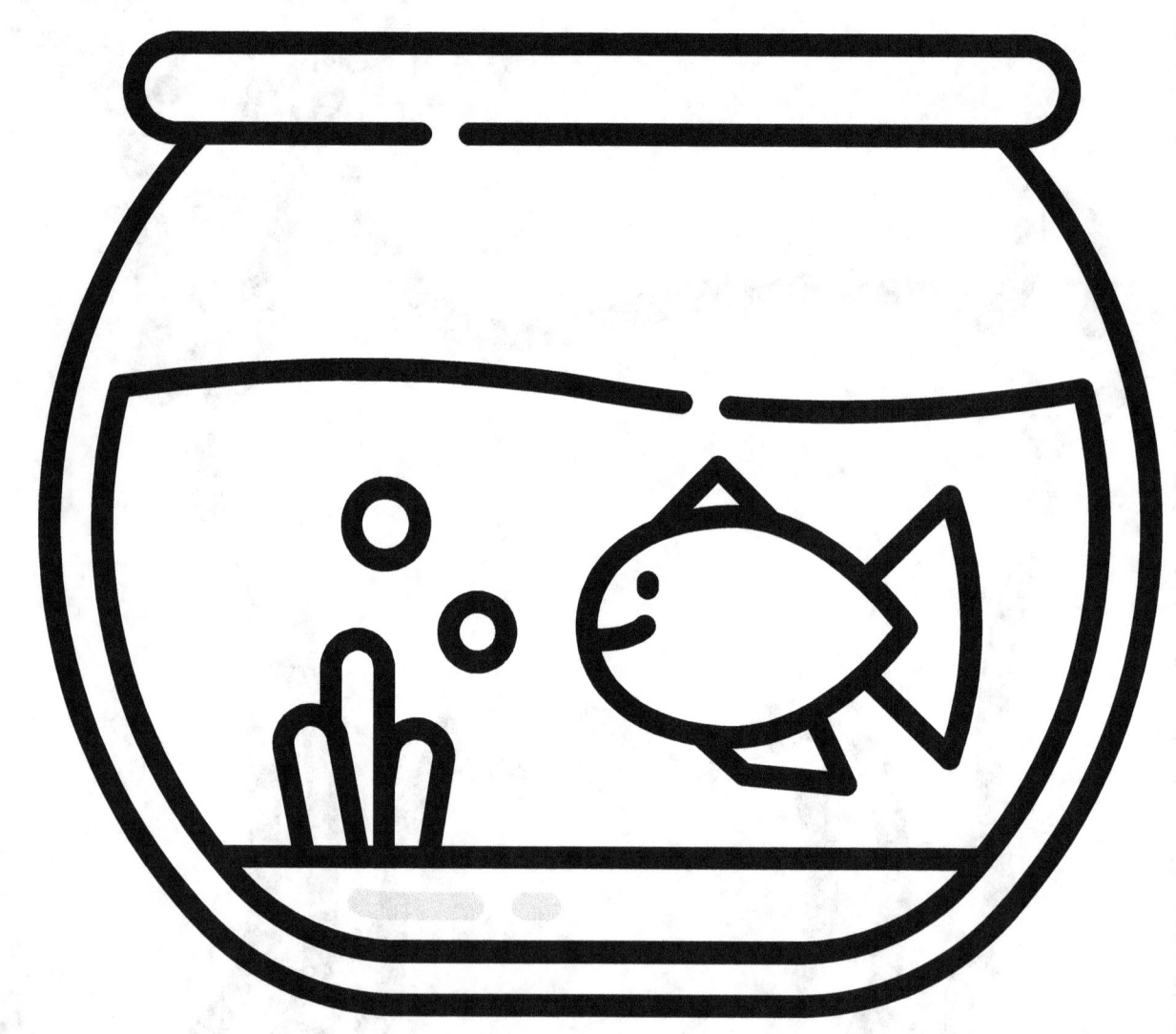

goldfish

Name:

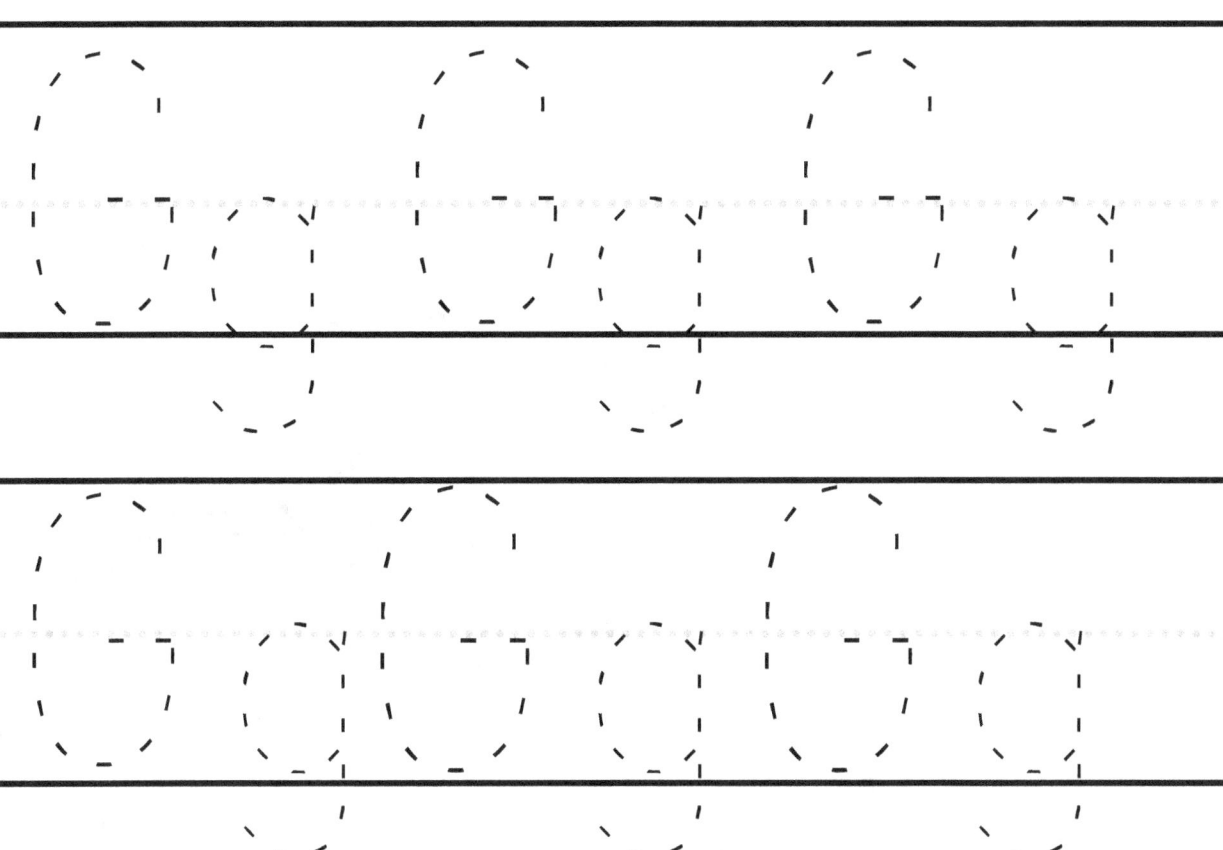

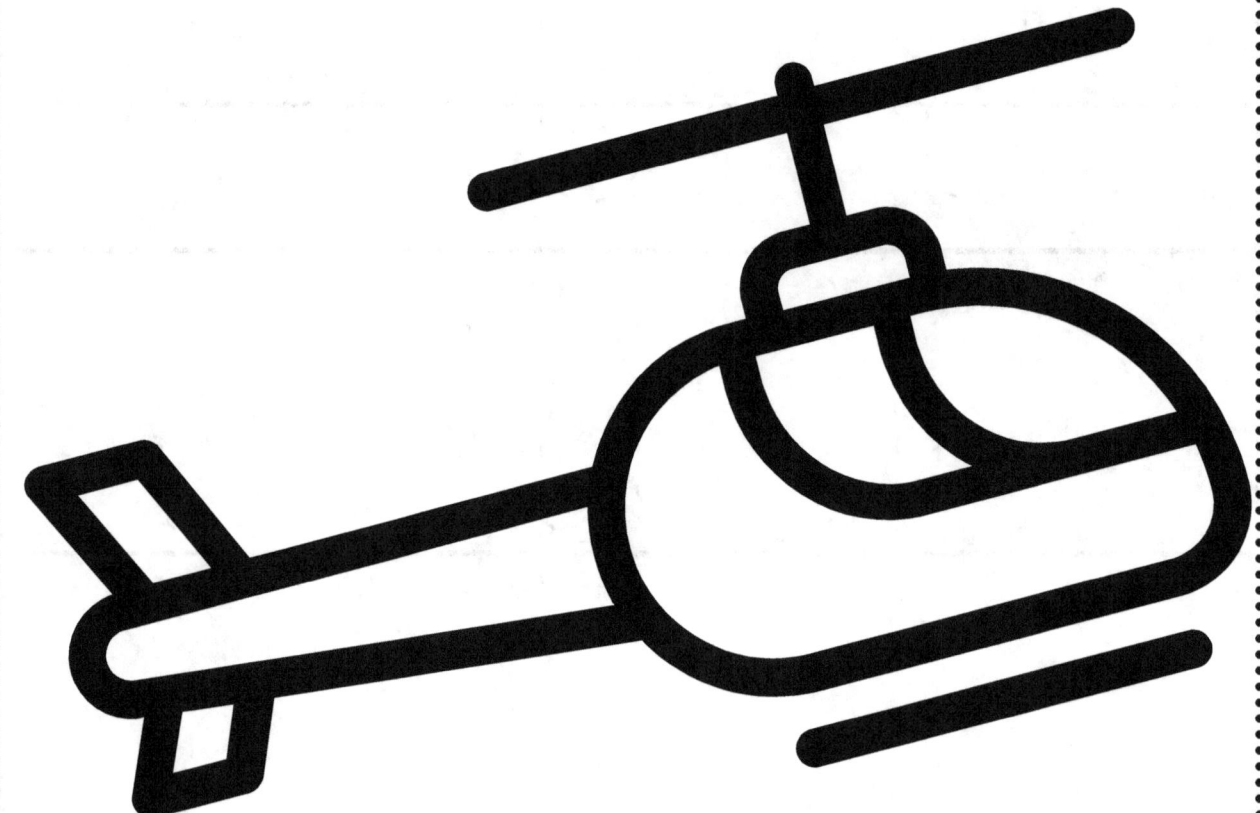

helicopter

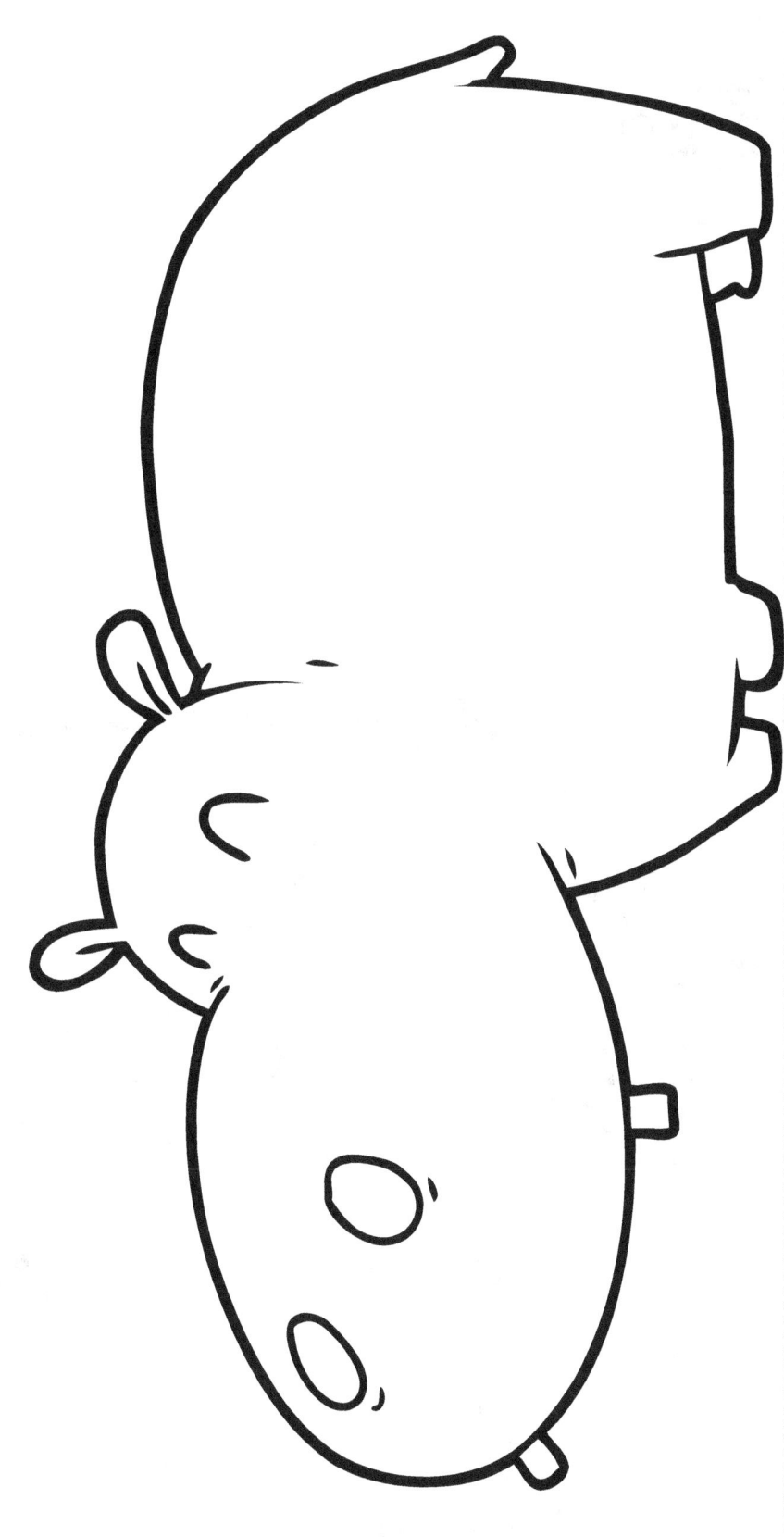

hippo

house

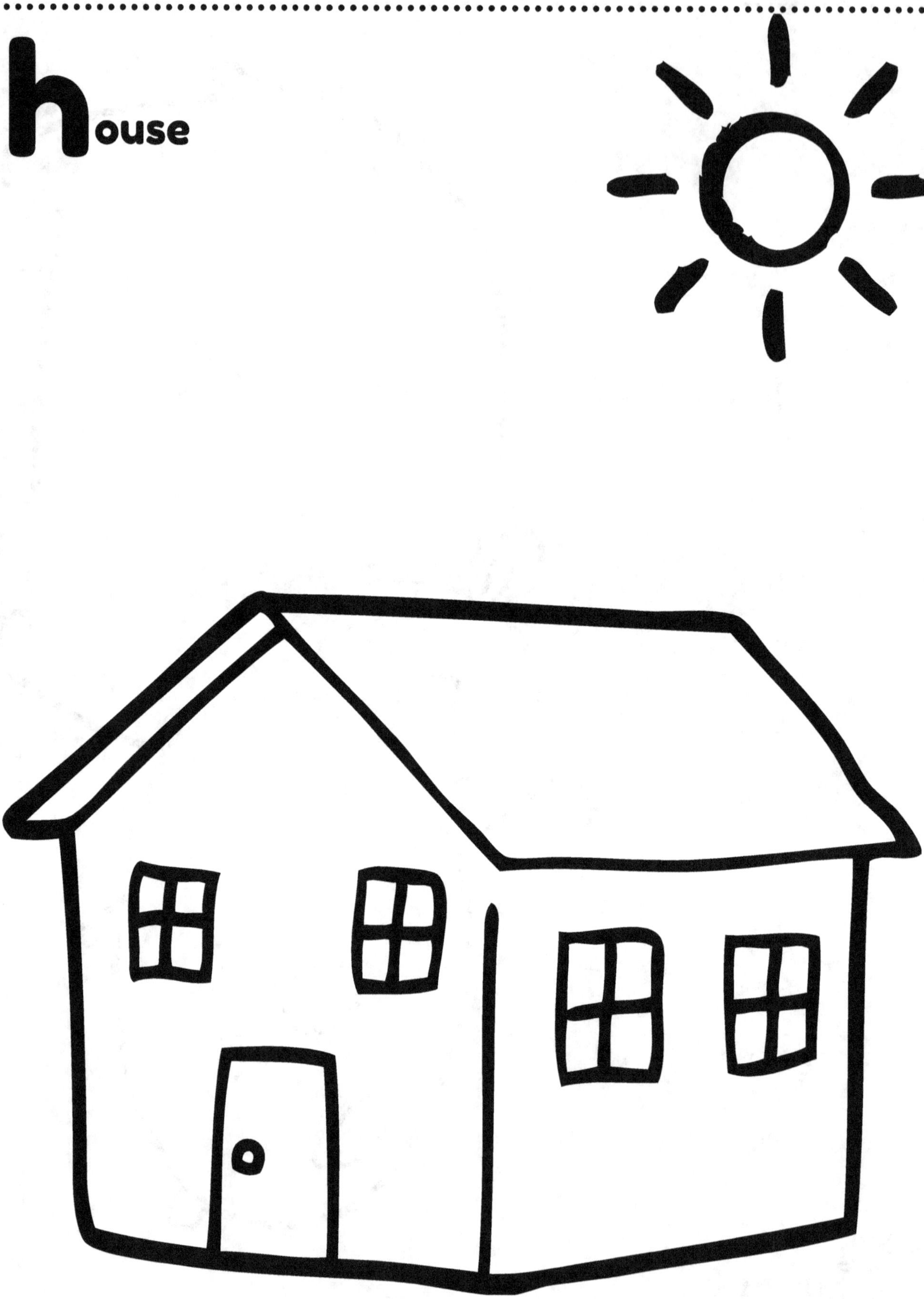

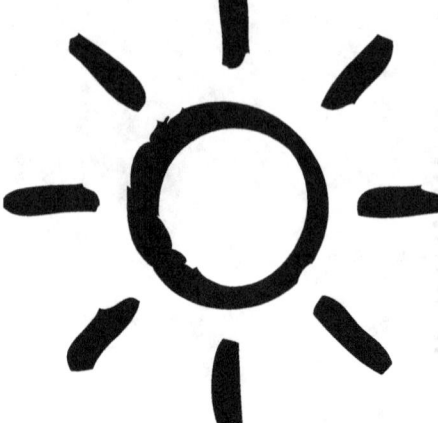

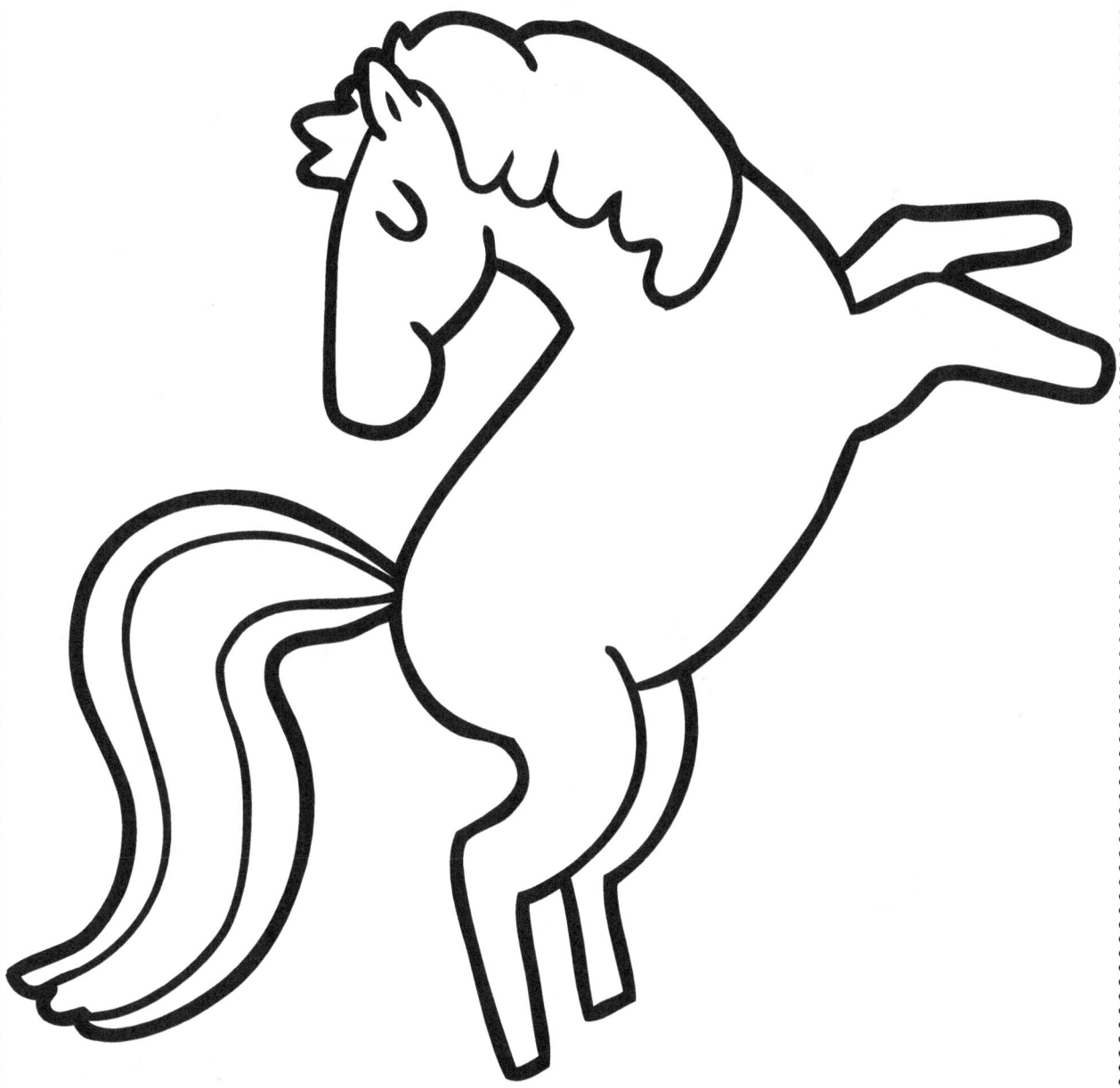

horse

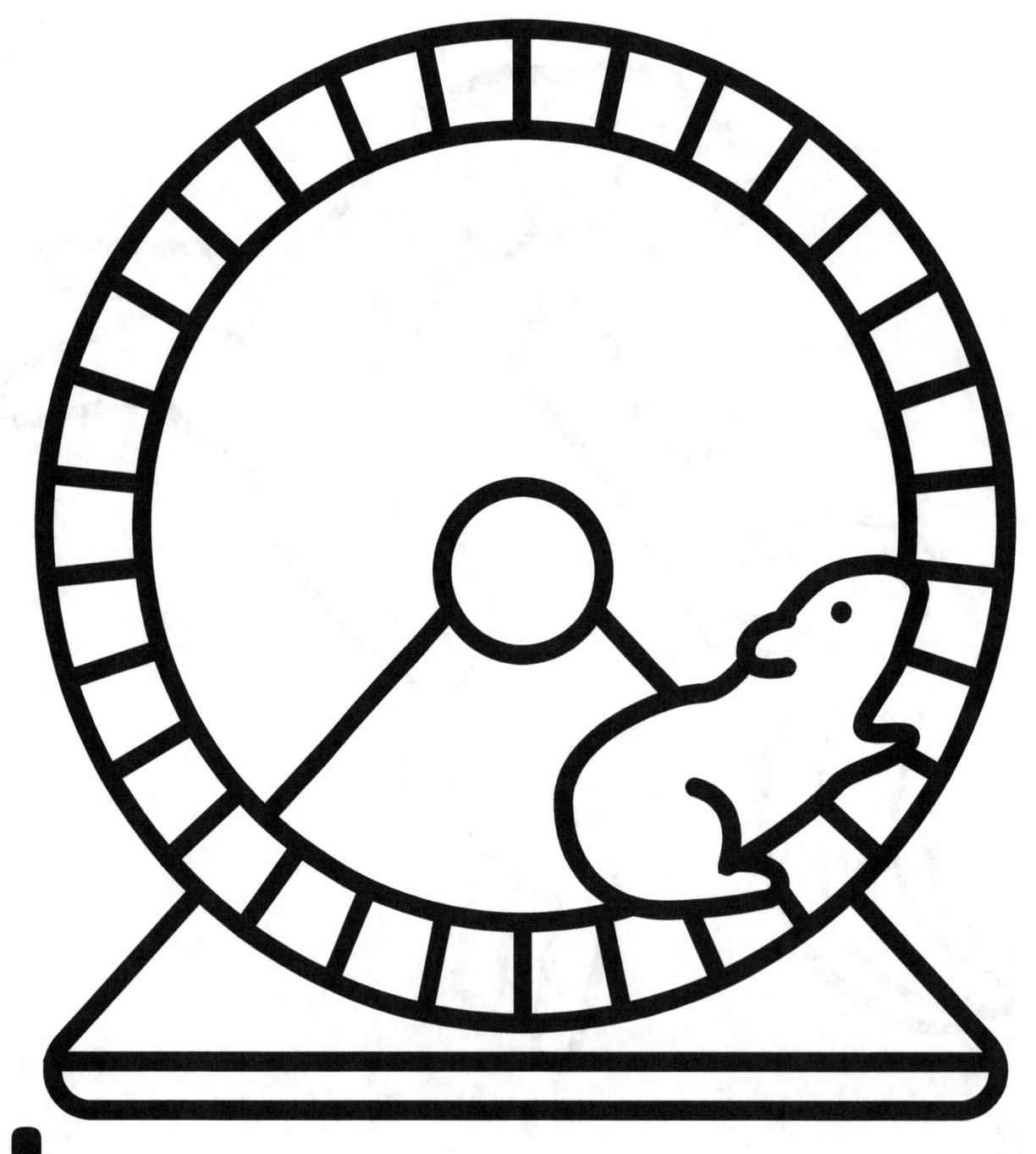

hamster

Name:

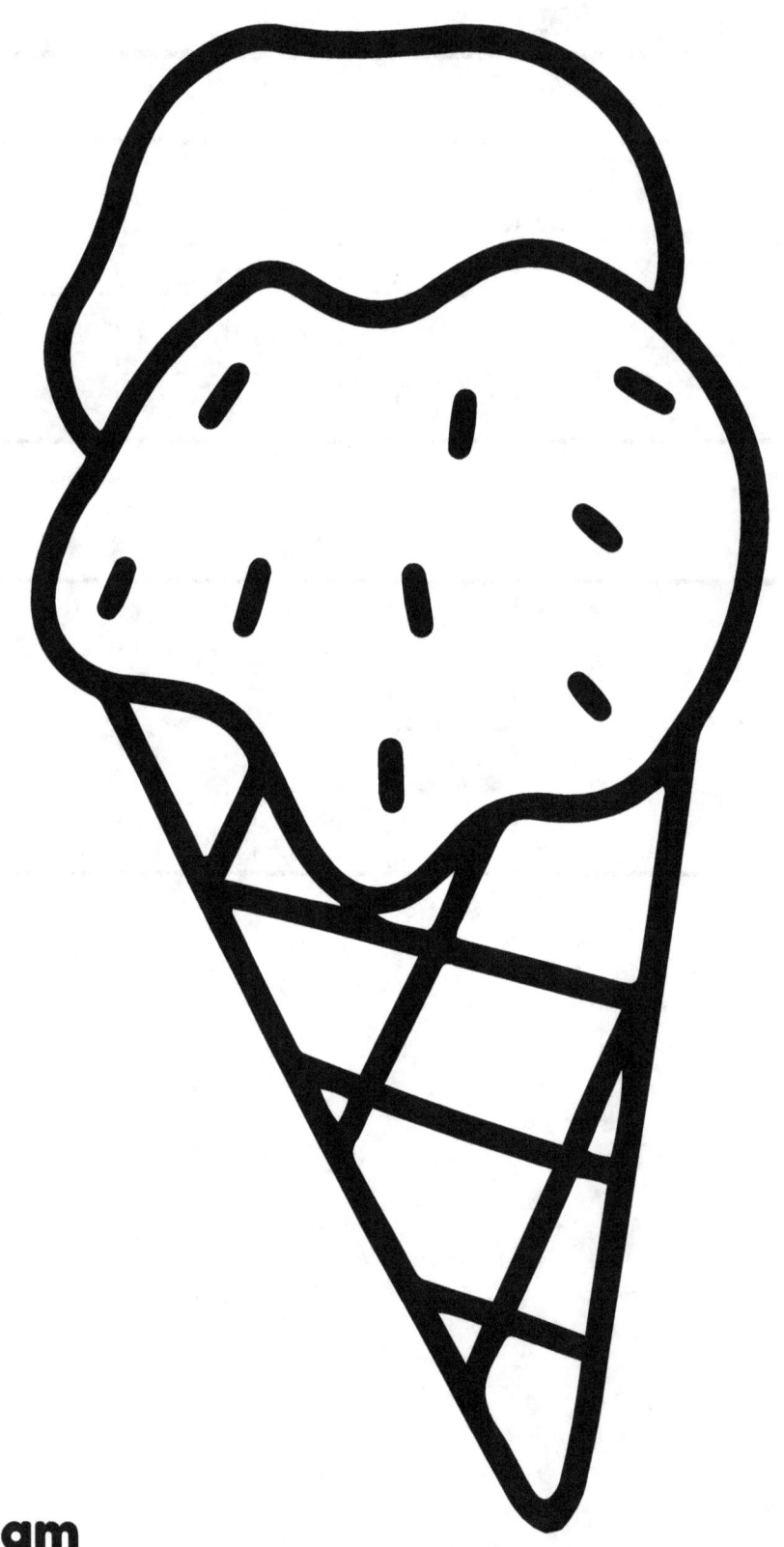

ice cream

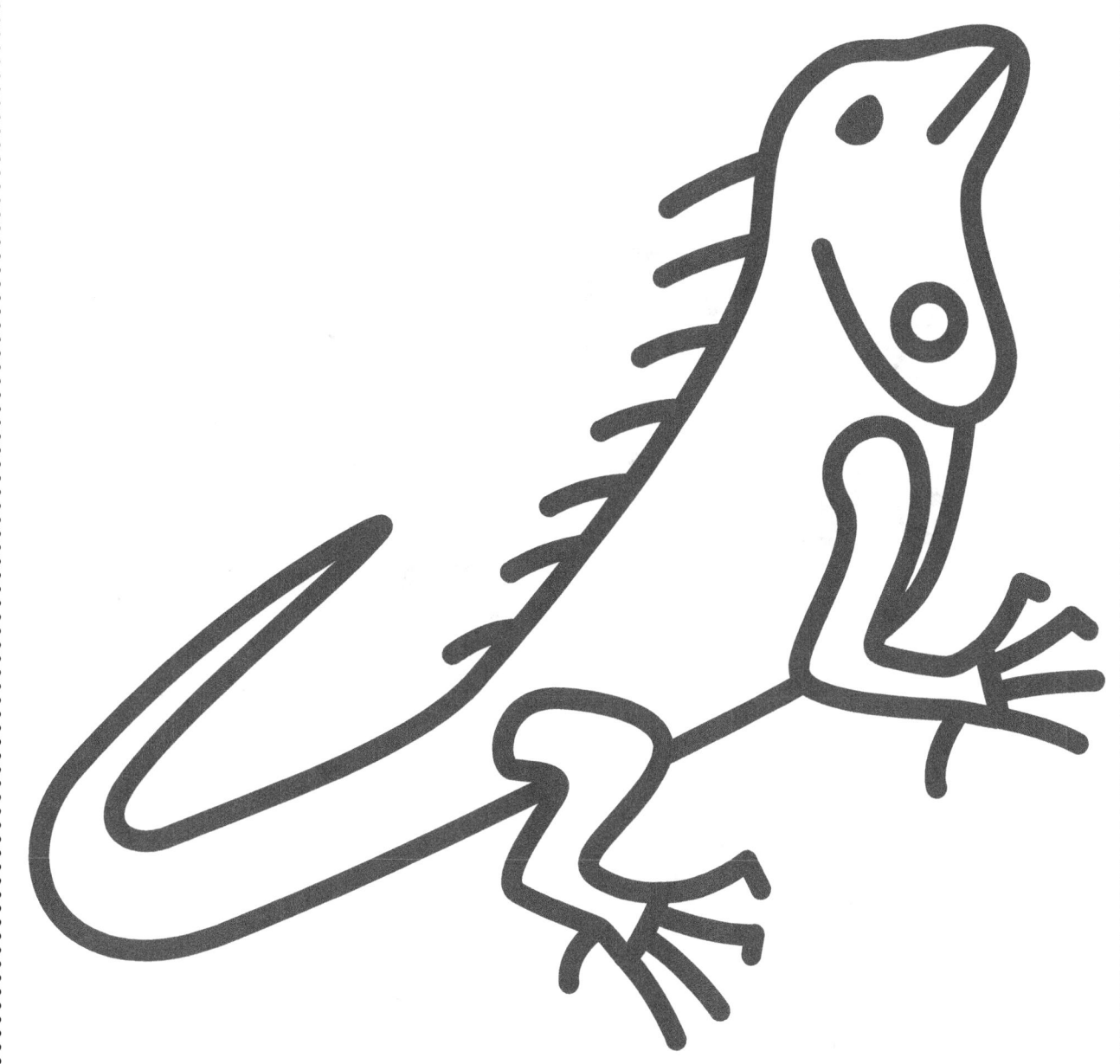

i guana

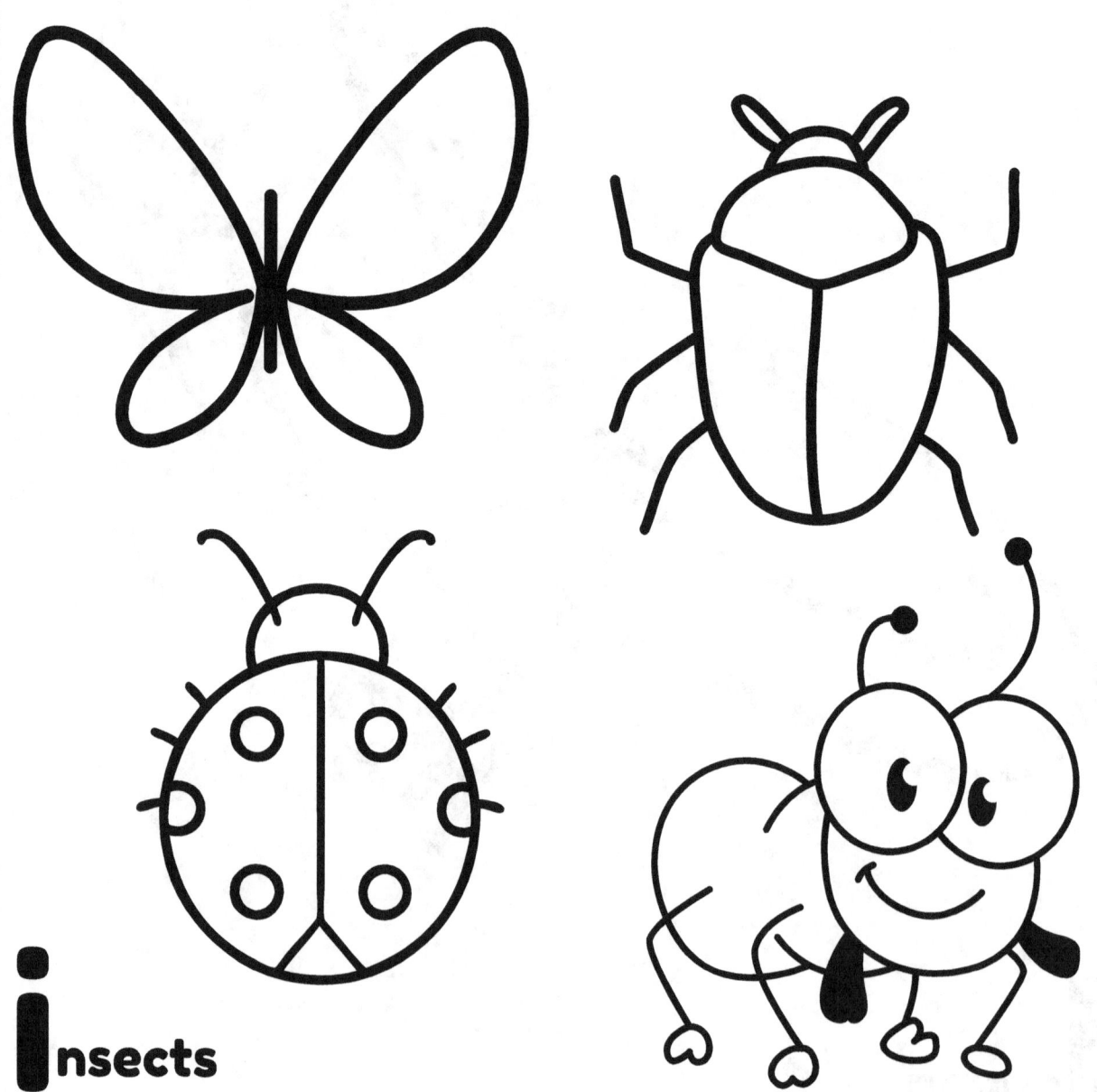

insects

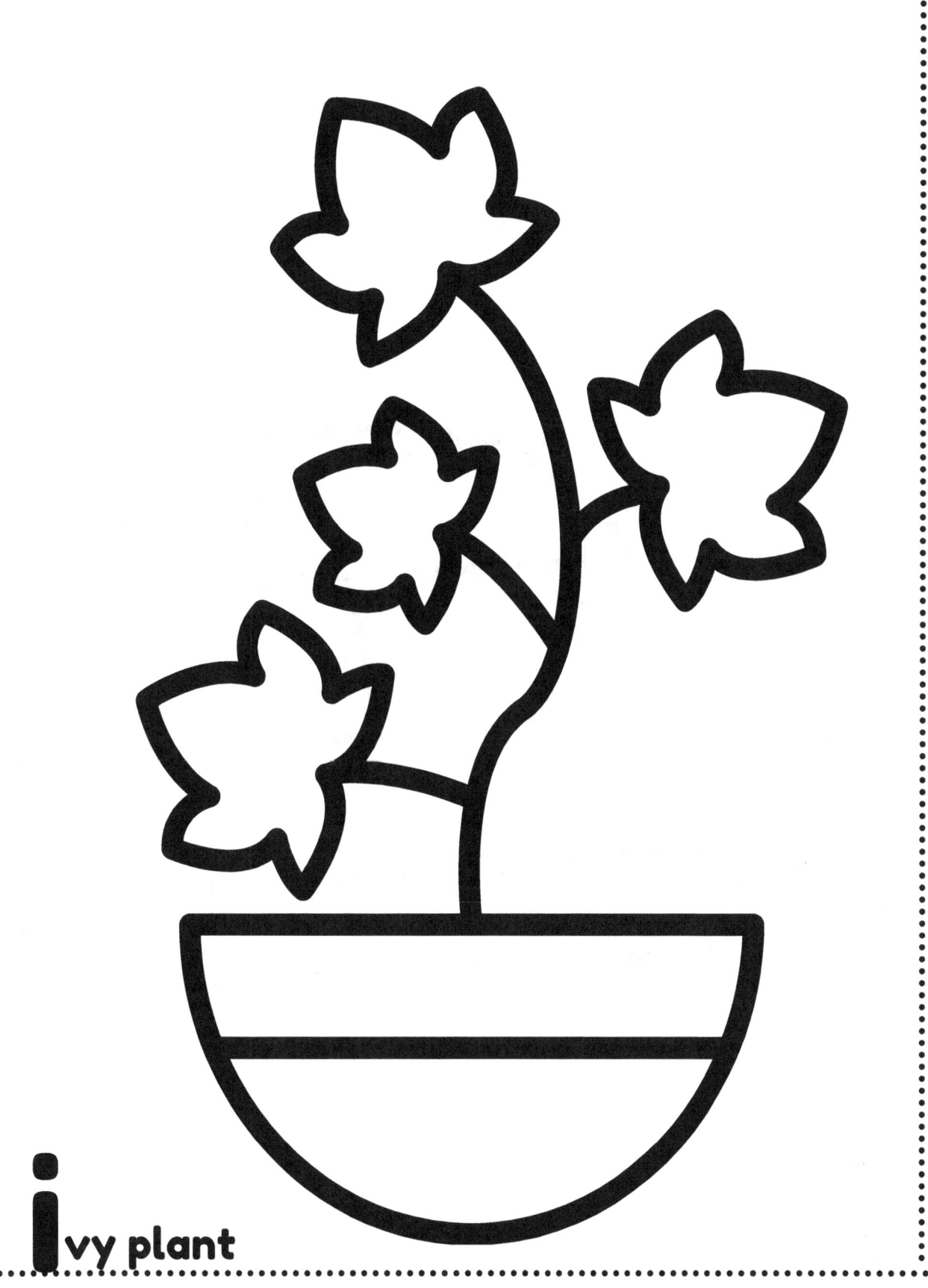

i vy plant

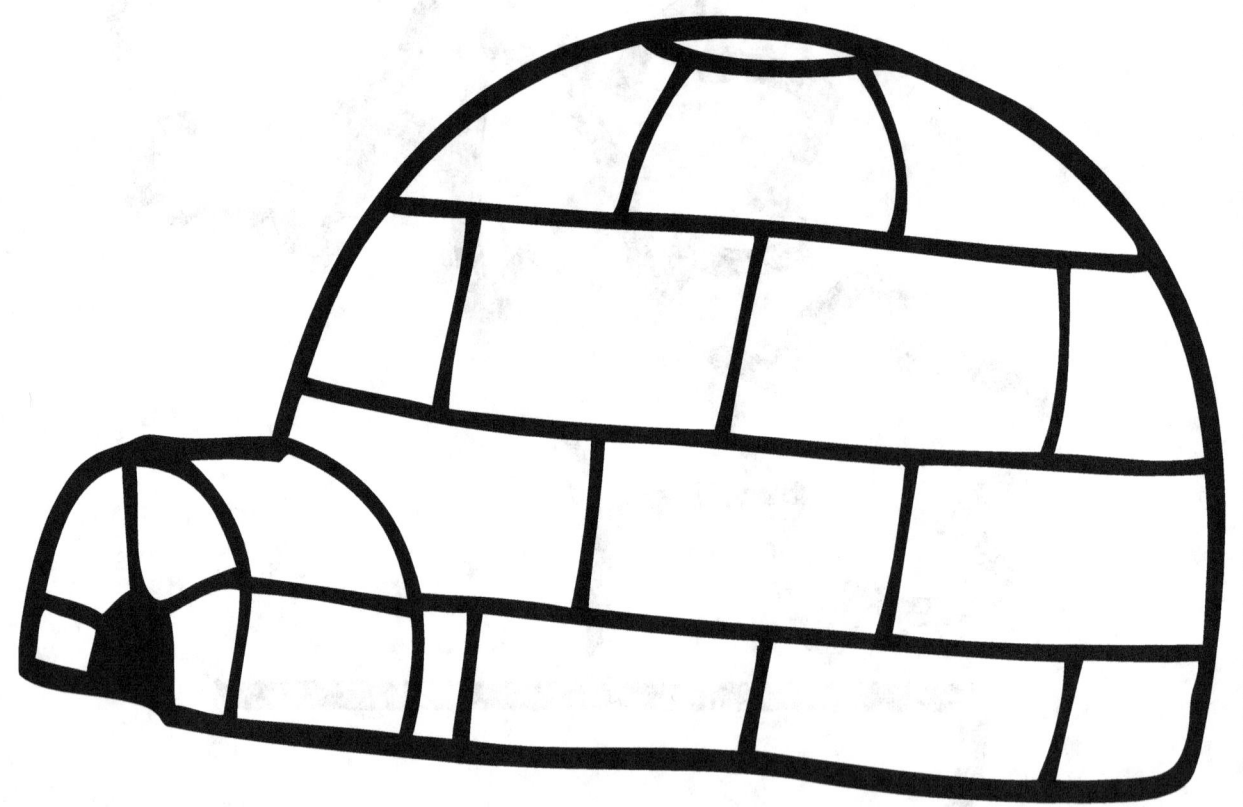

igloo

Name:

I   I   I

I   I   I

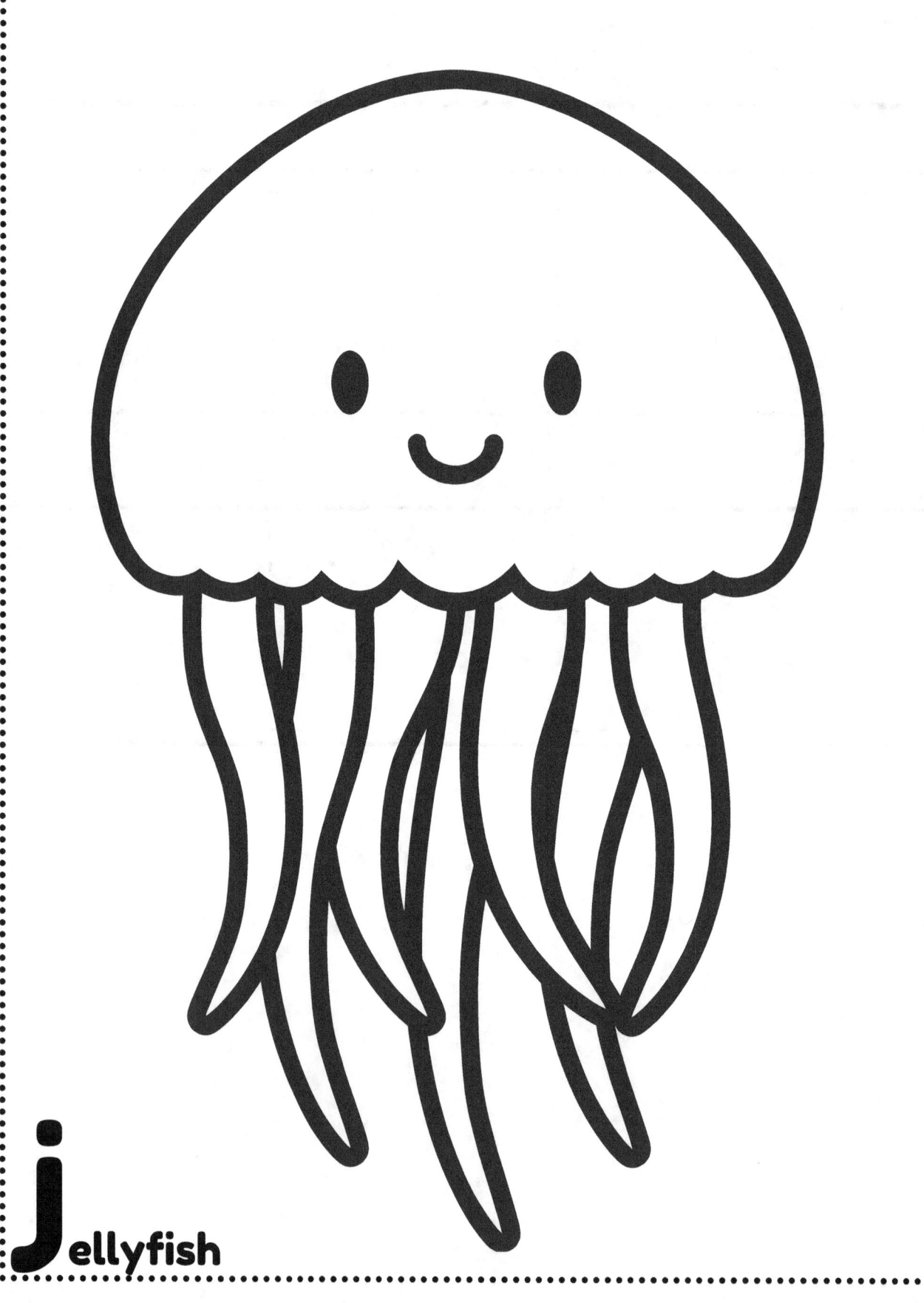

jellyfish

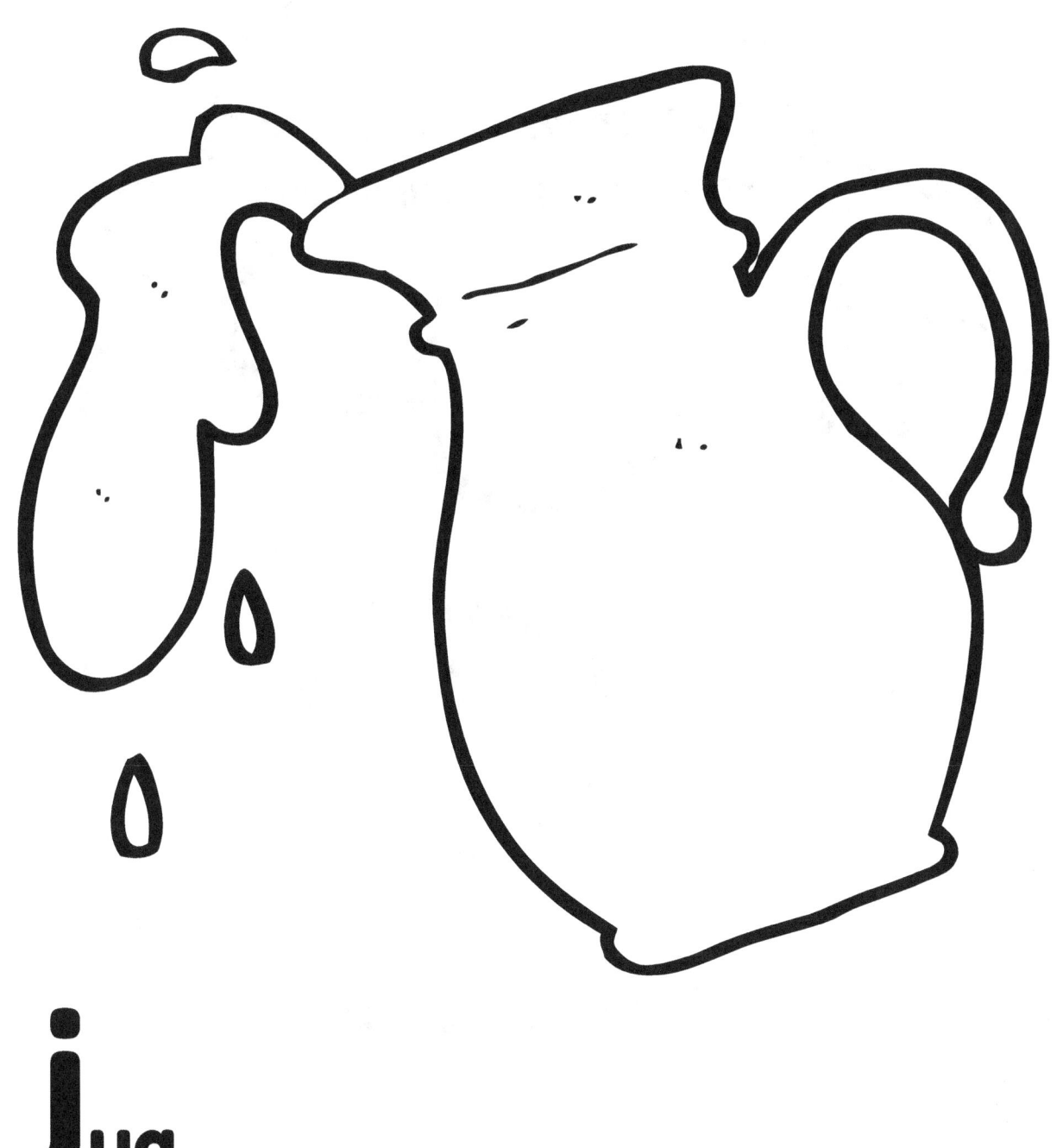

jug

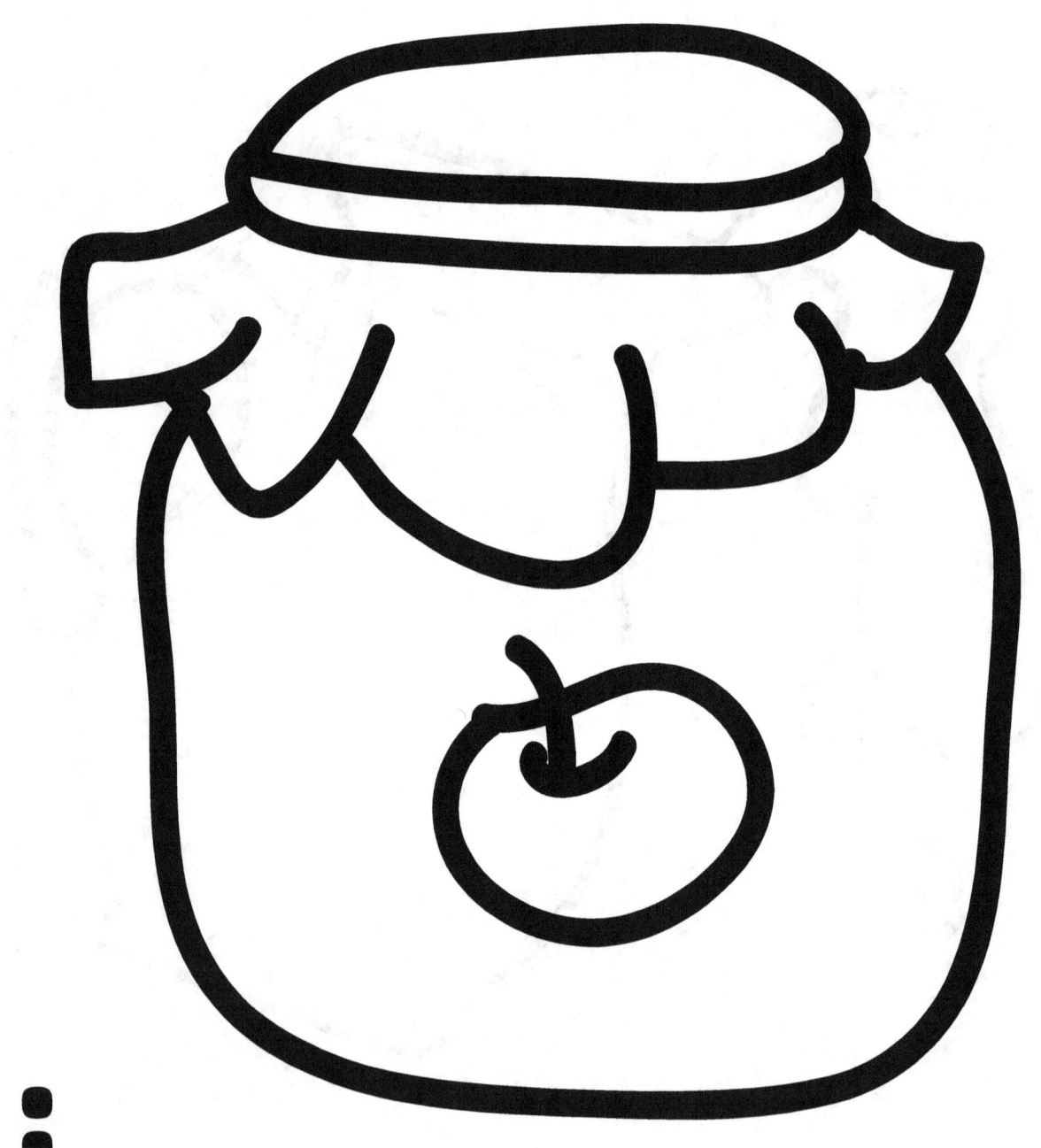

jam

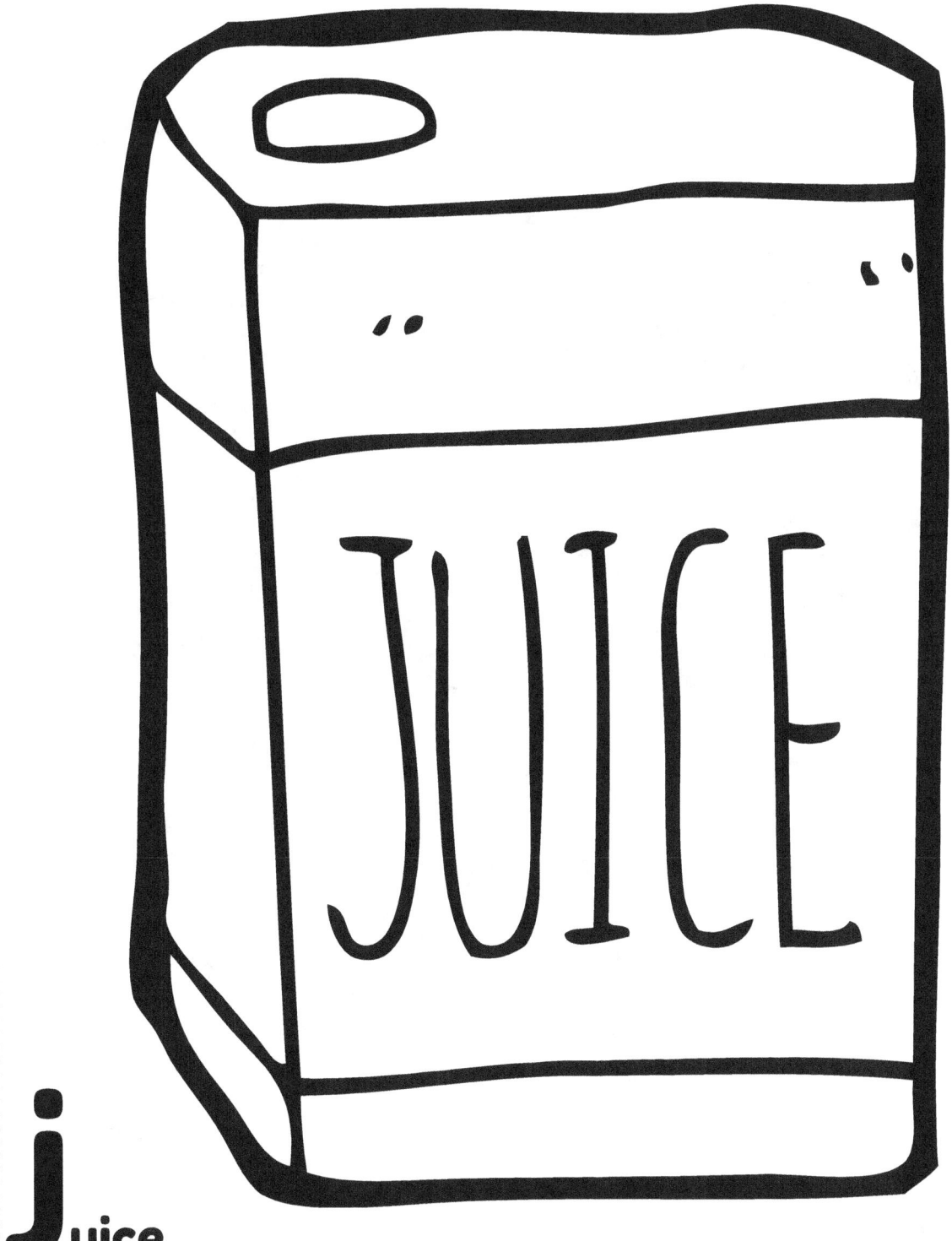

juice

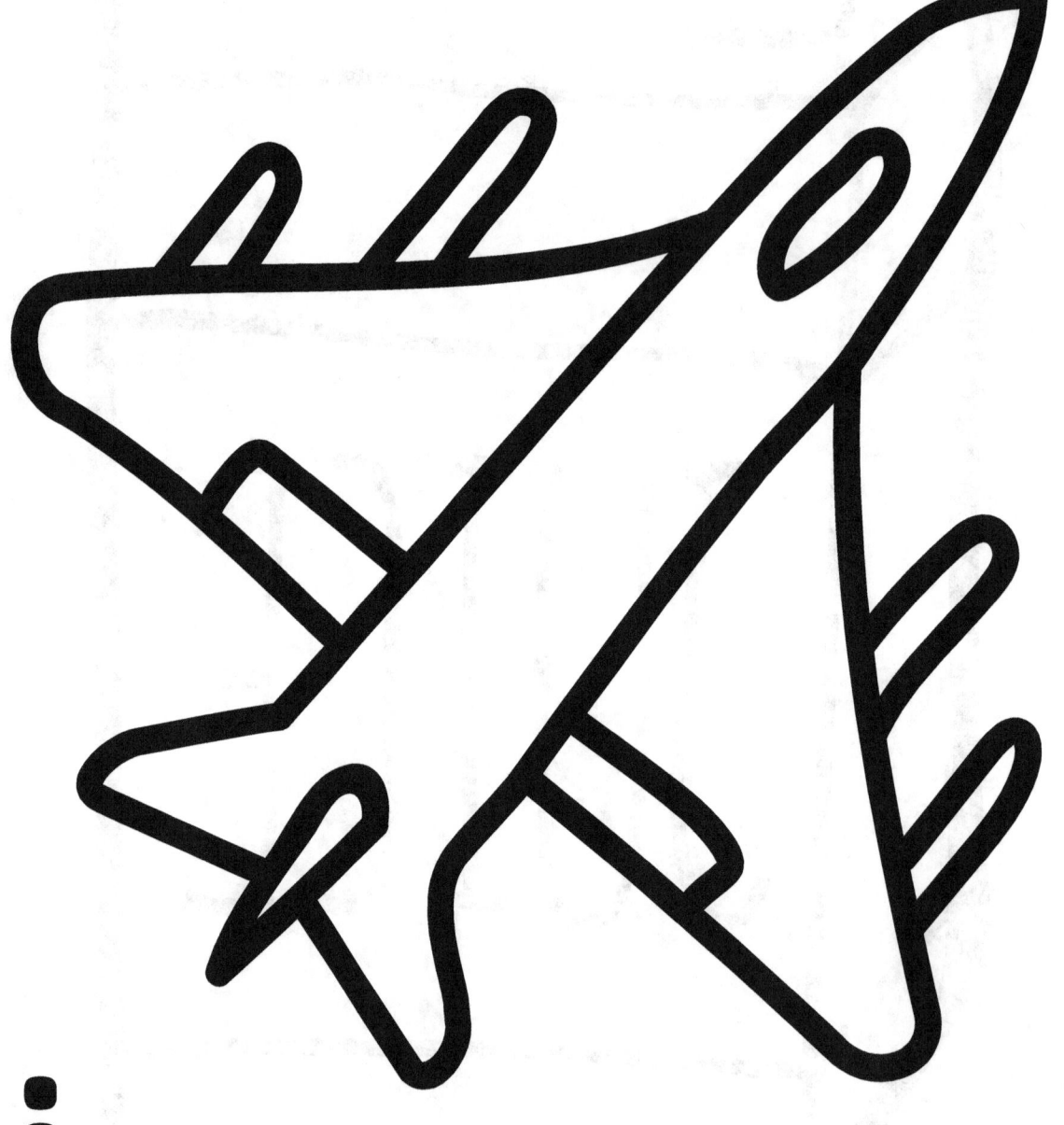

jet

Name:

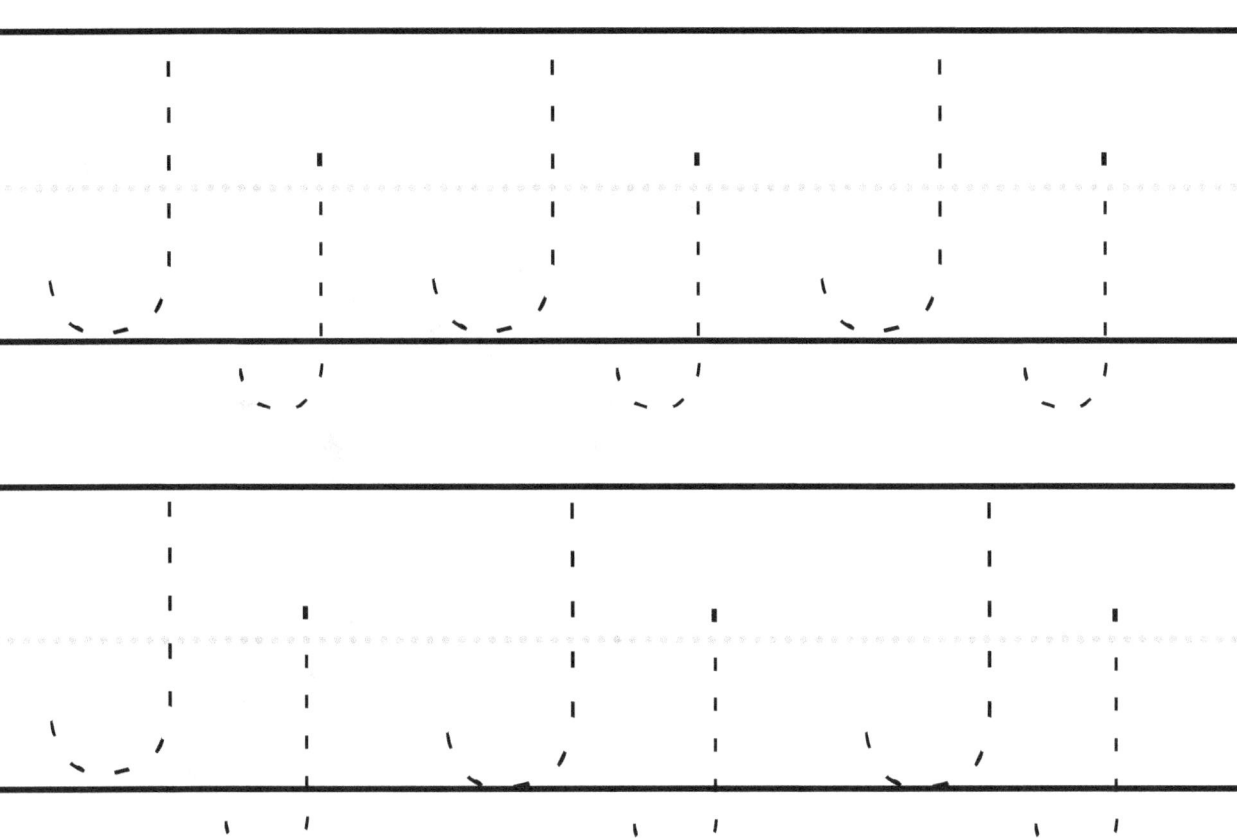

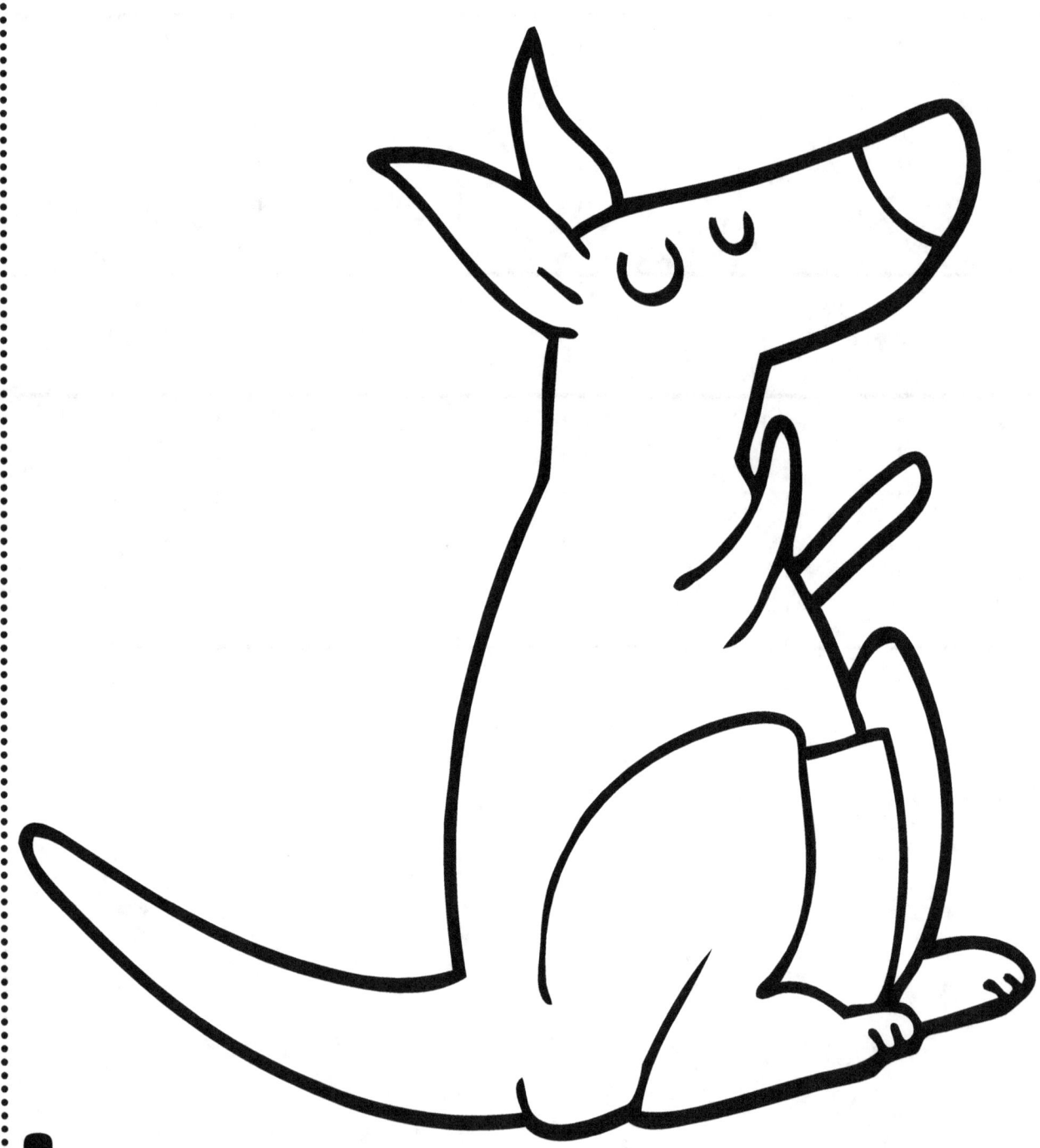

kangaroo

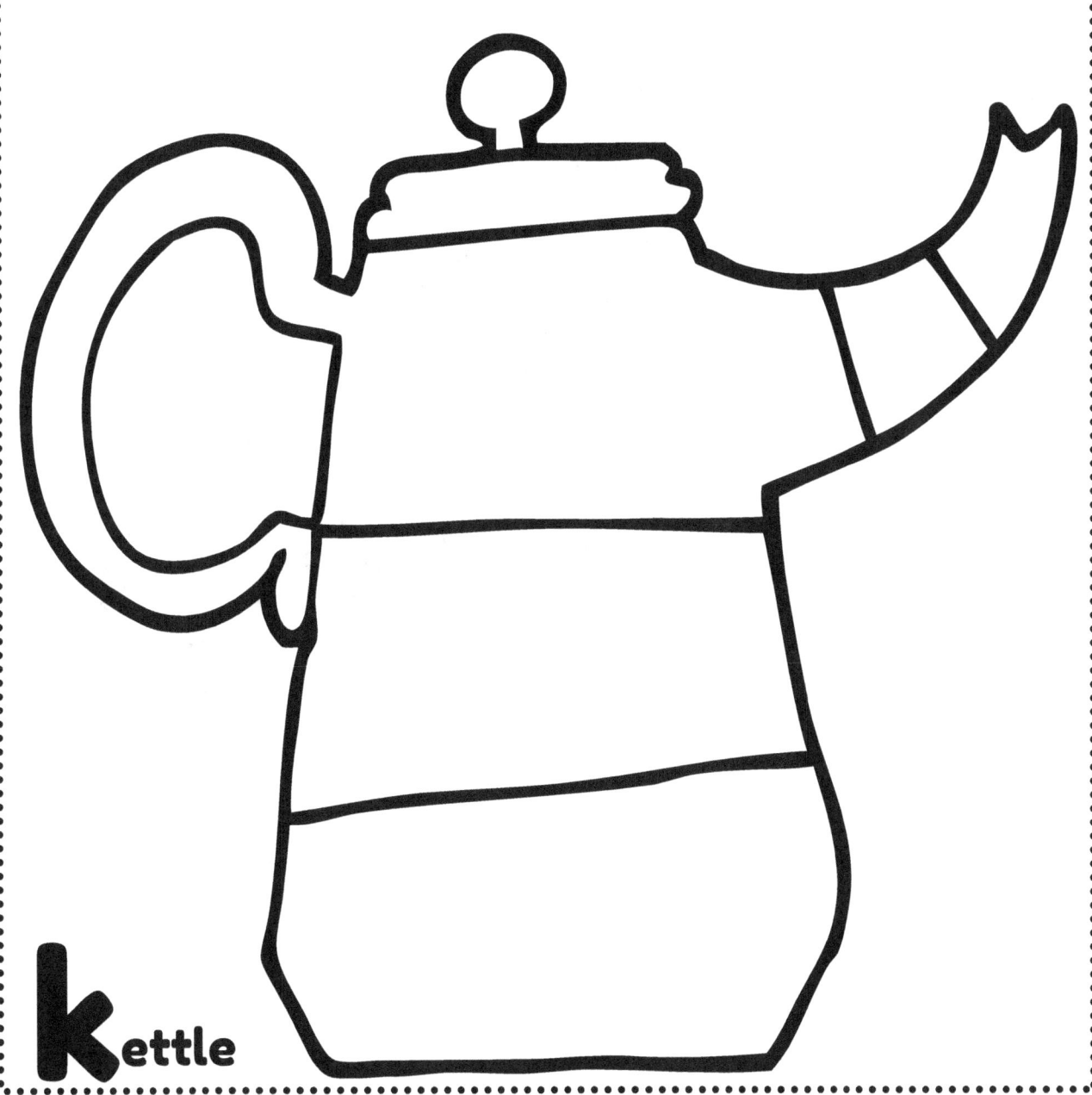

kettle

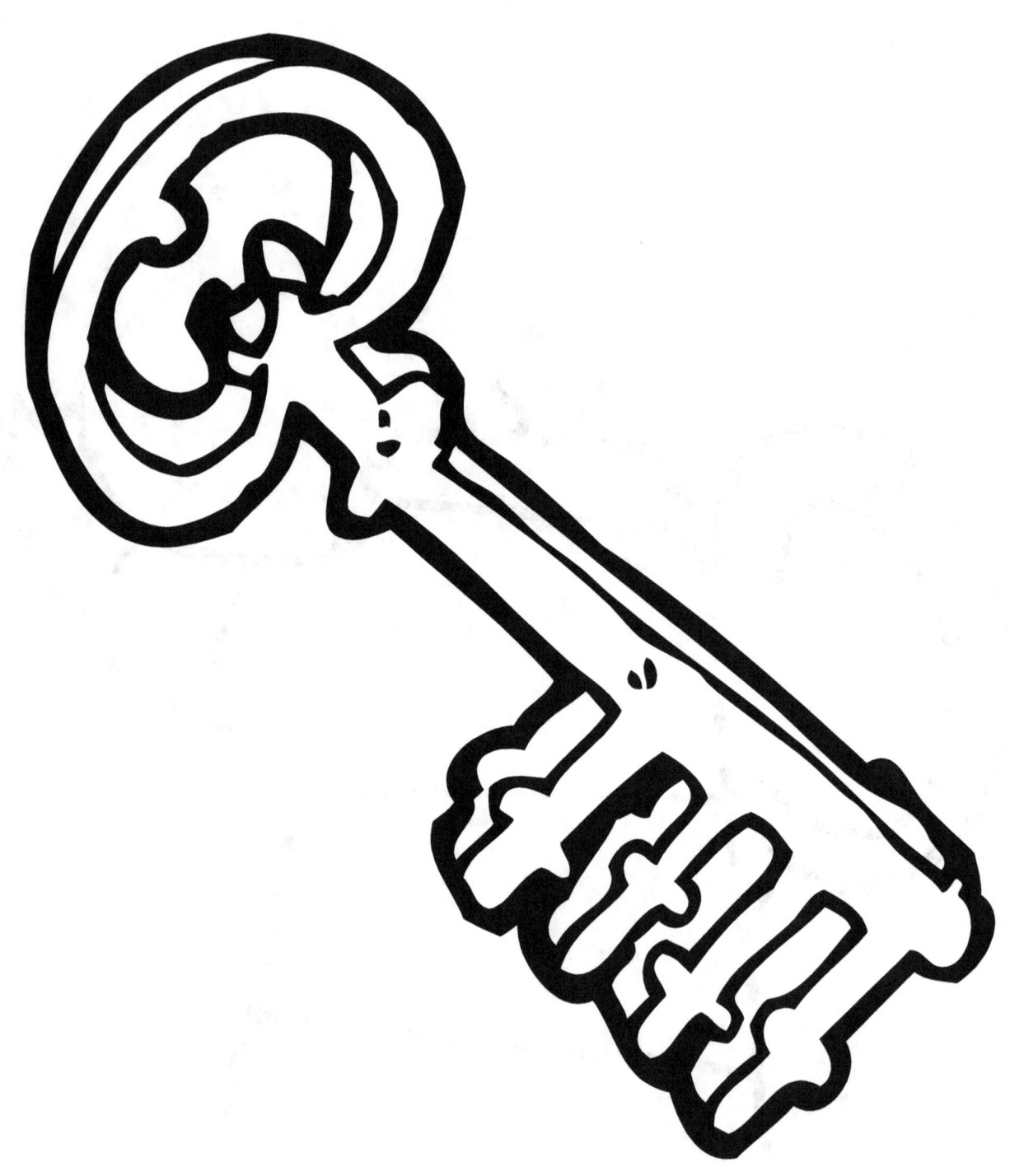

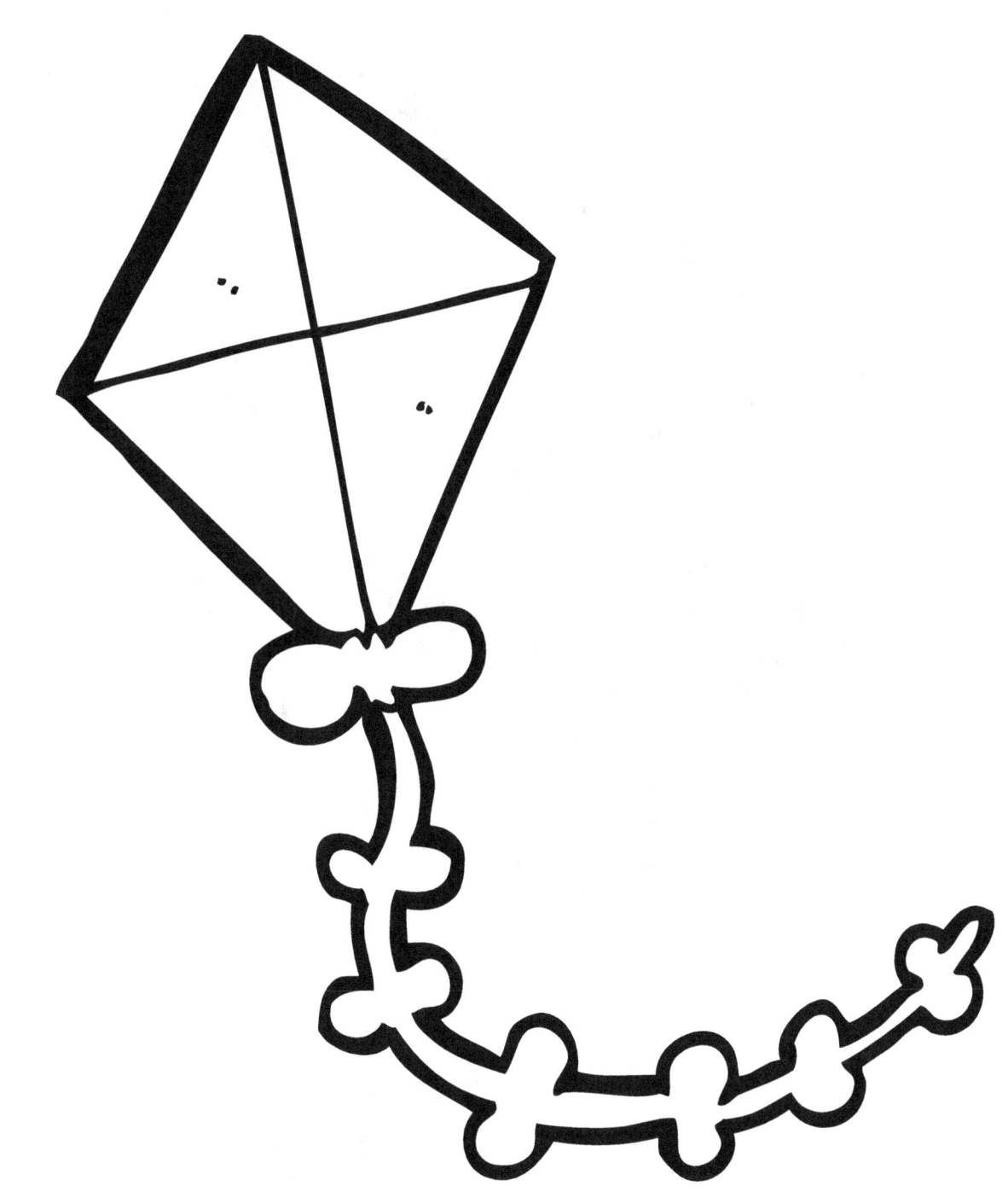

kite

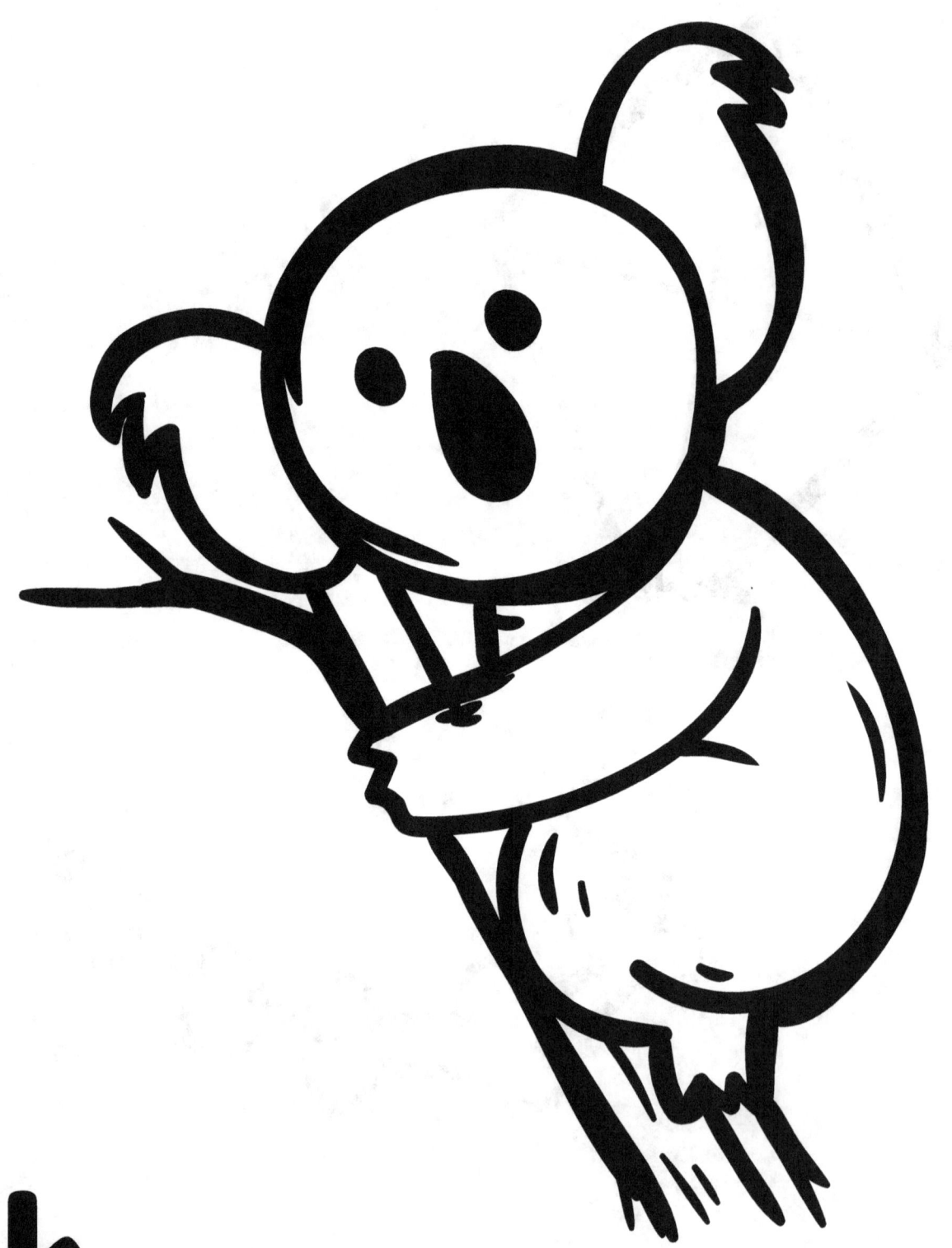
koala

Name:

Kk Kk Kk Kk

Kk Kk Kk Kk

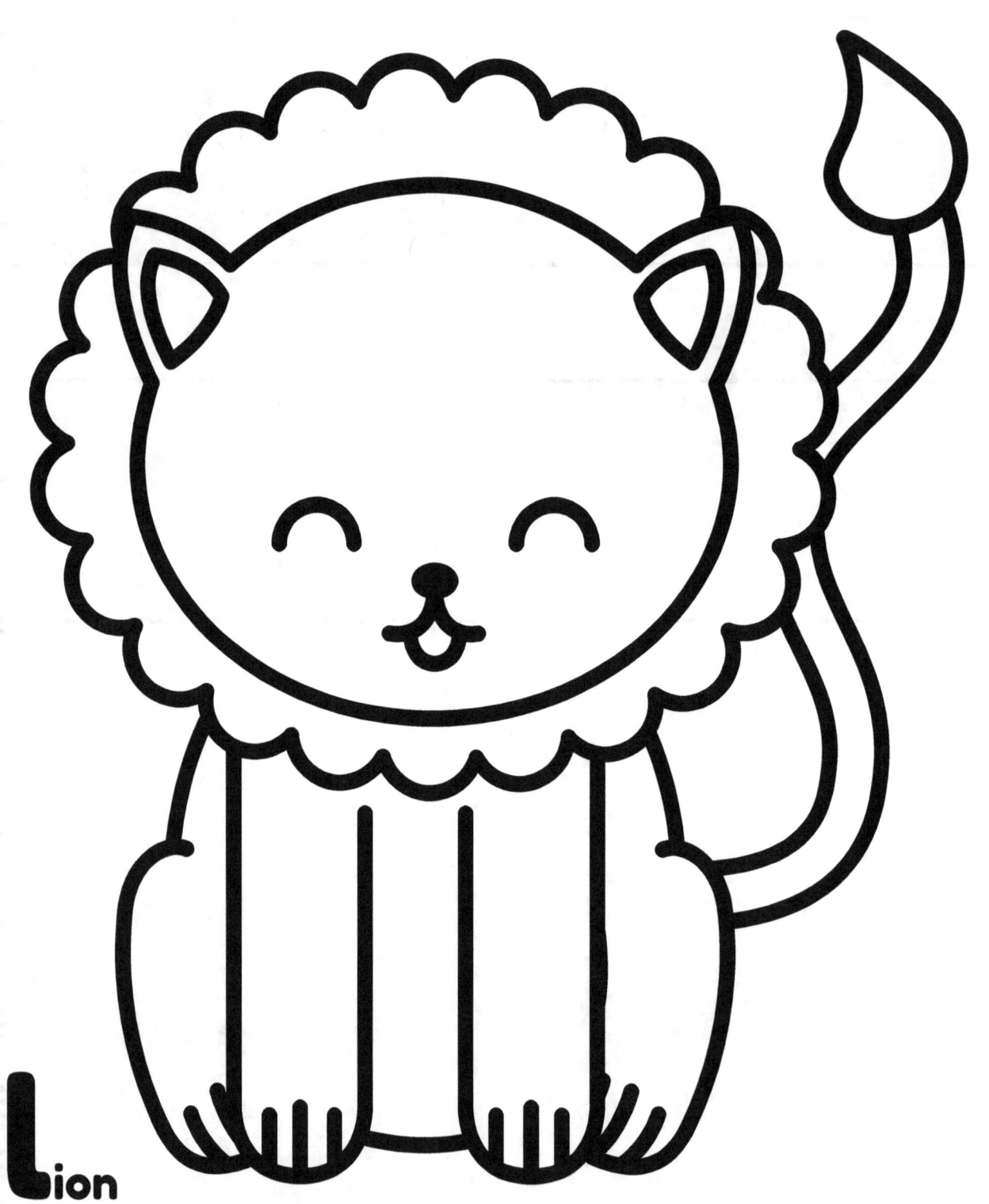

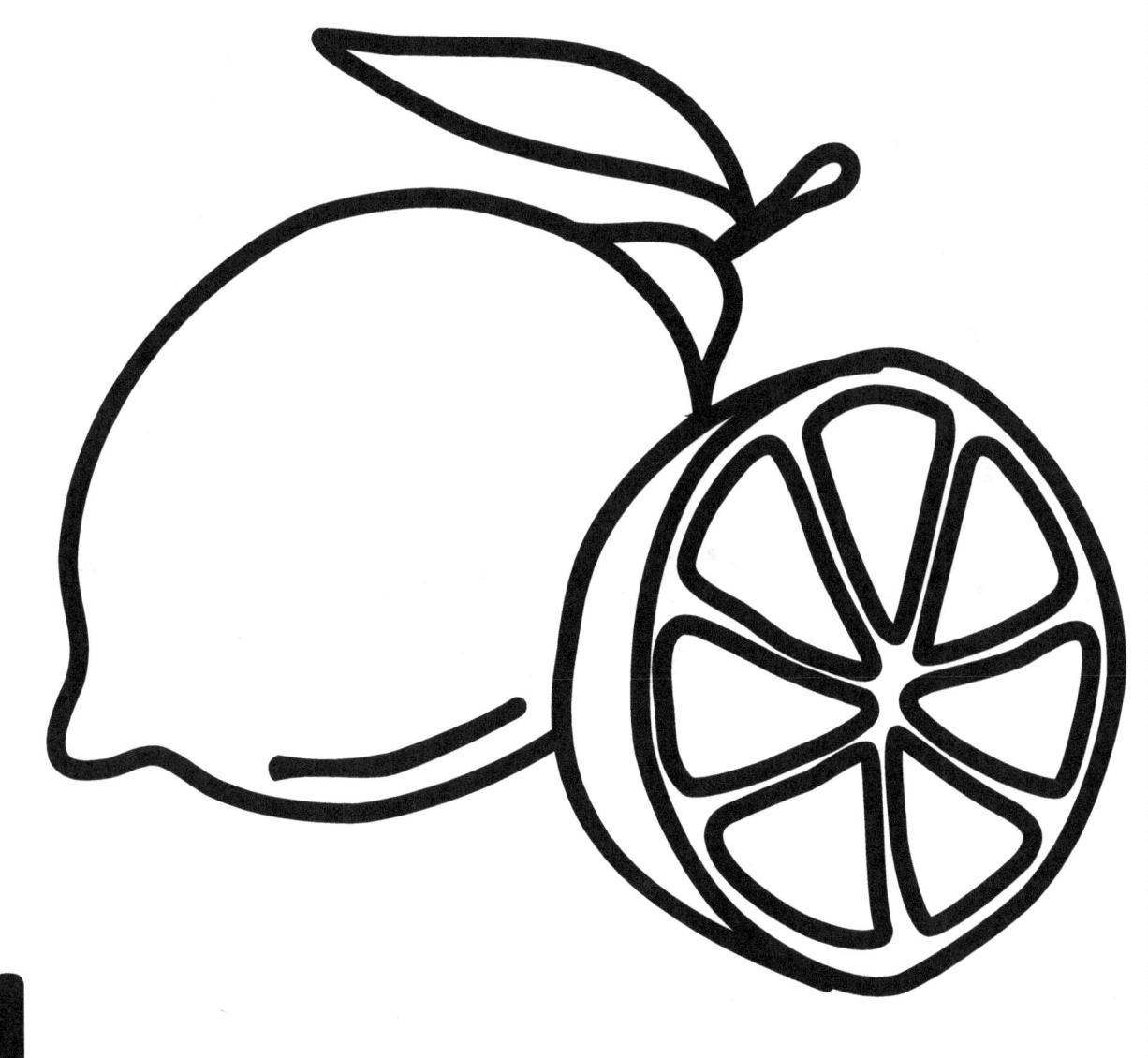

Lemon

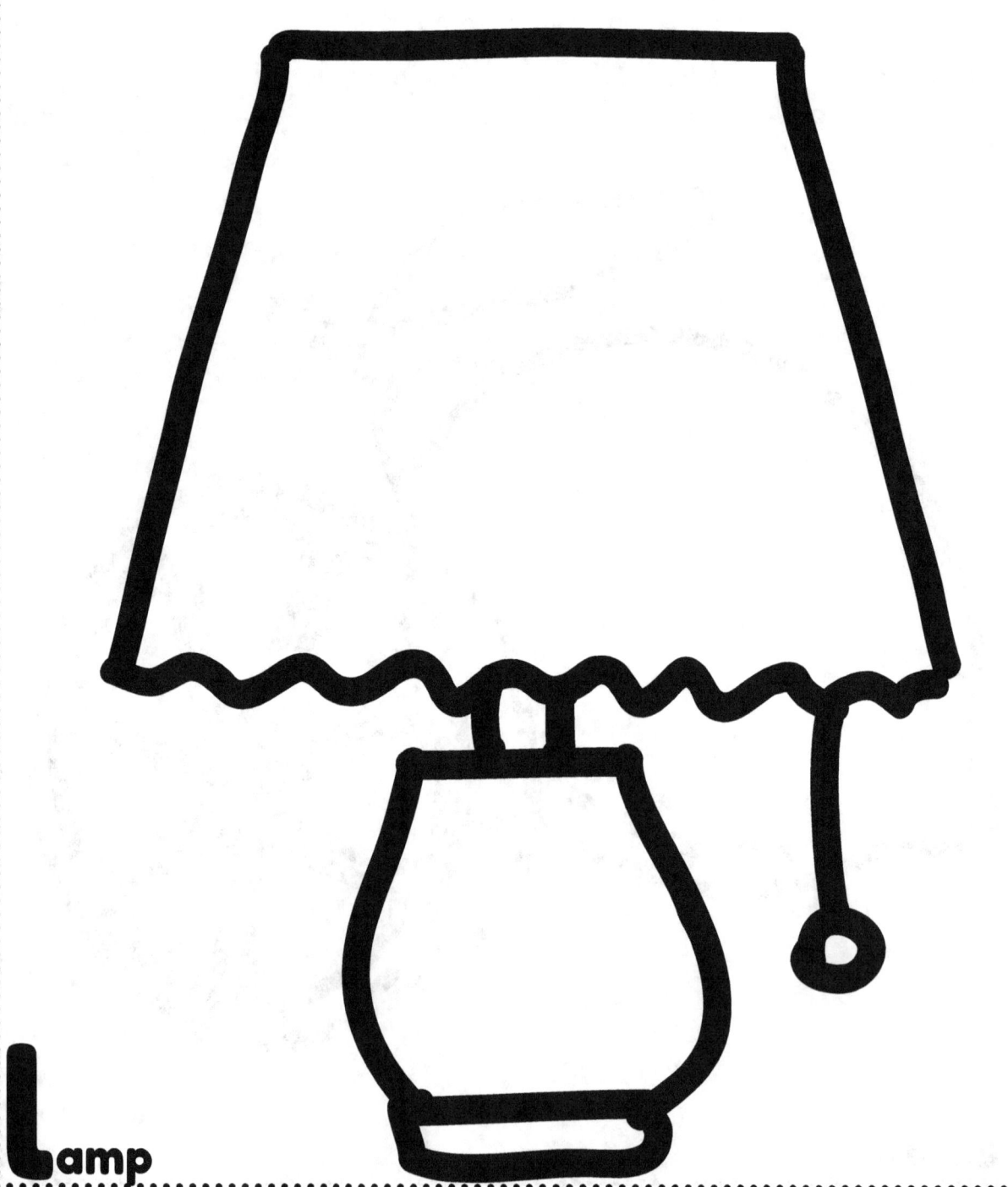

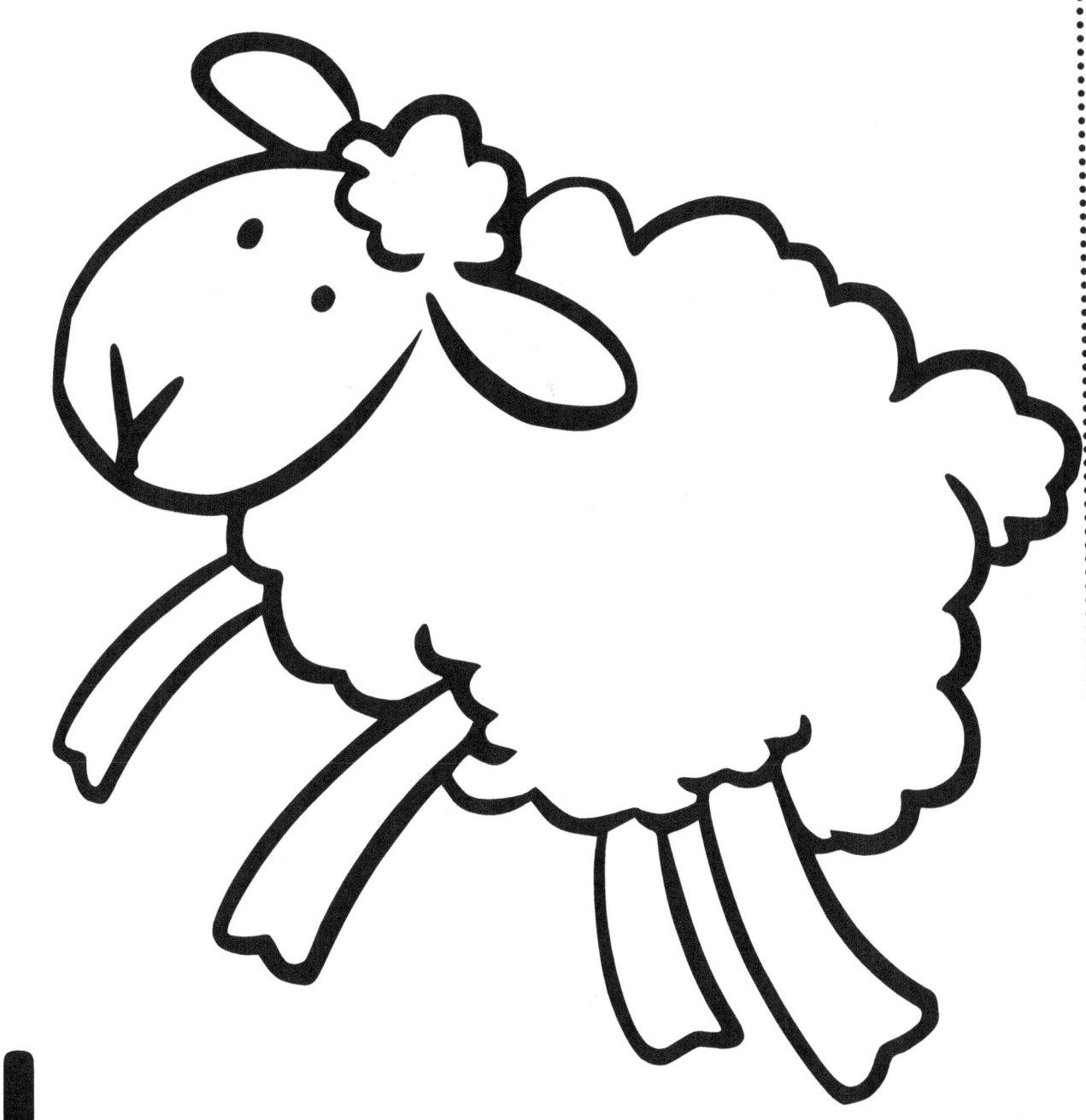

Lamb

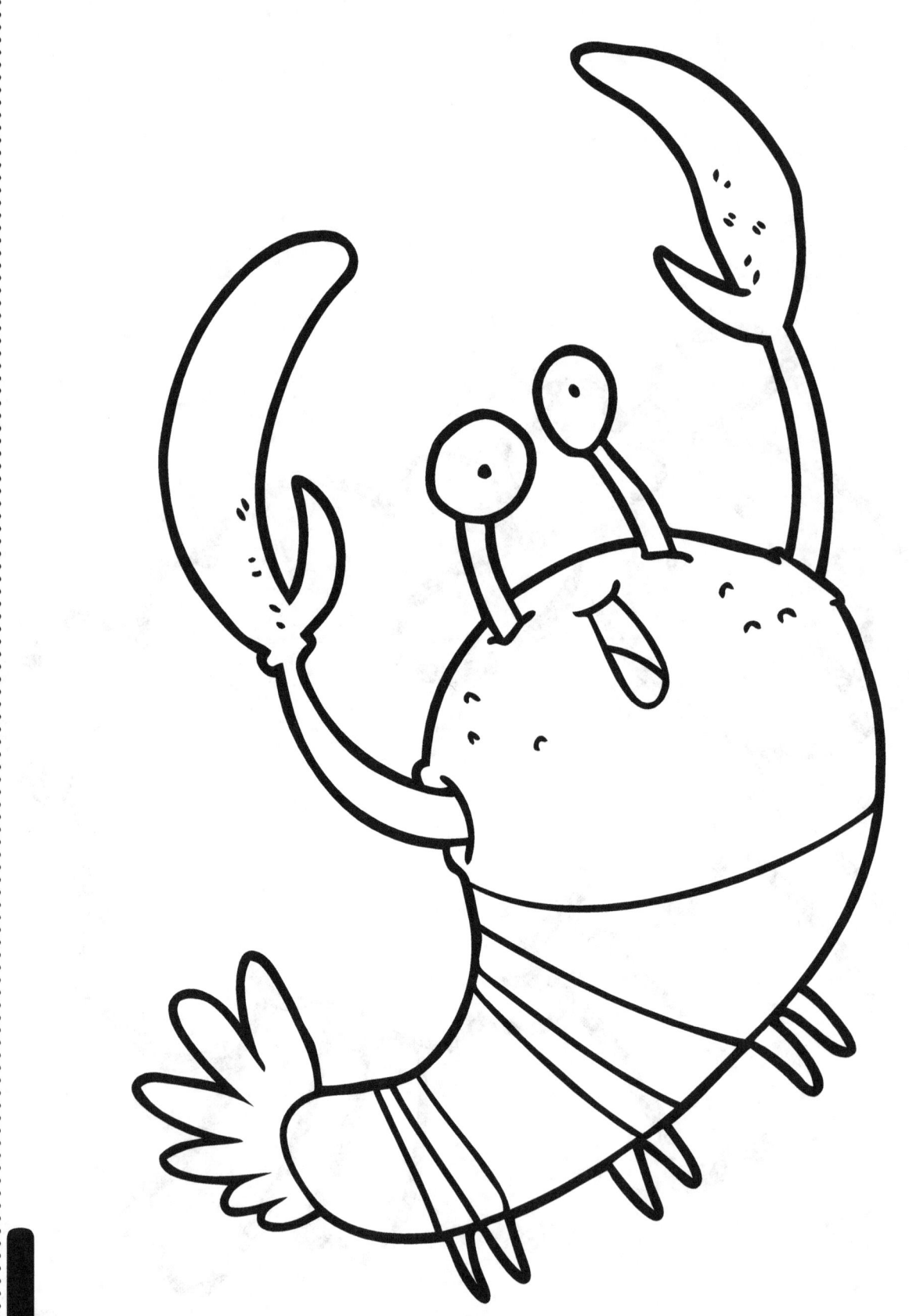

Lobster

Name:

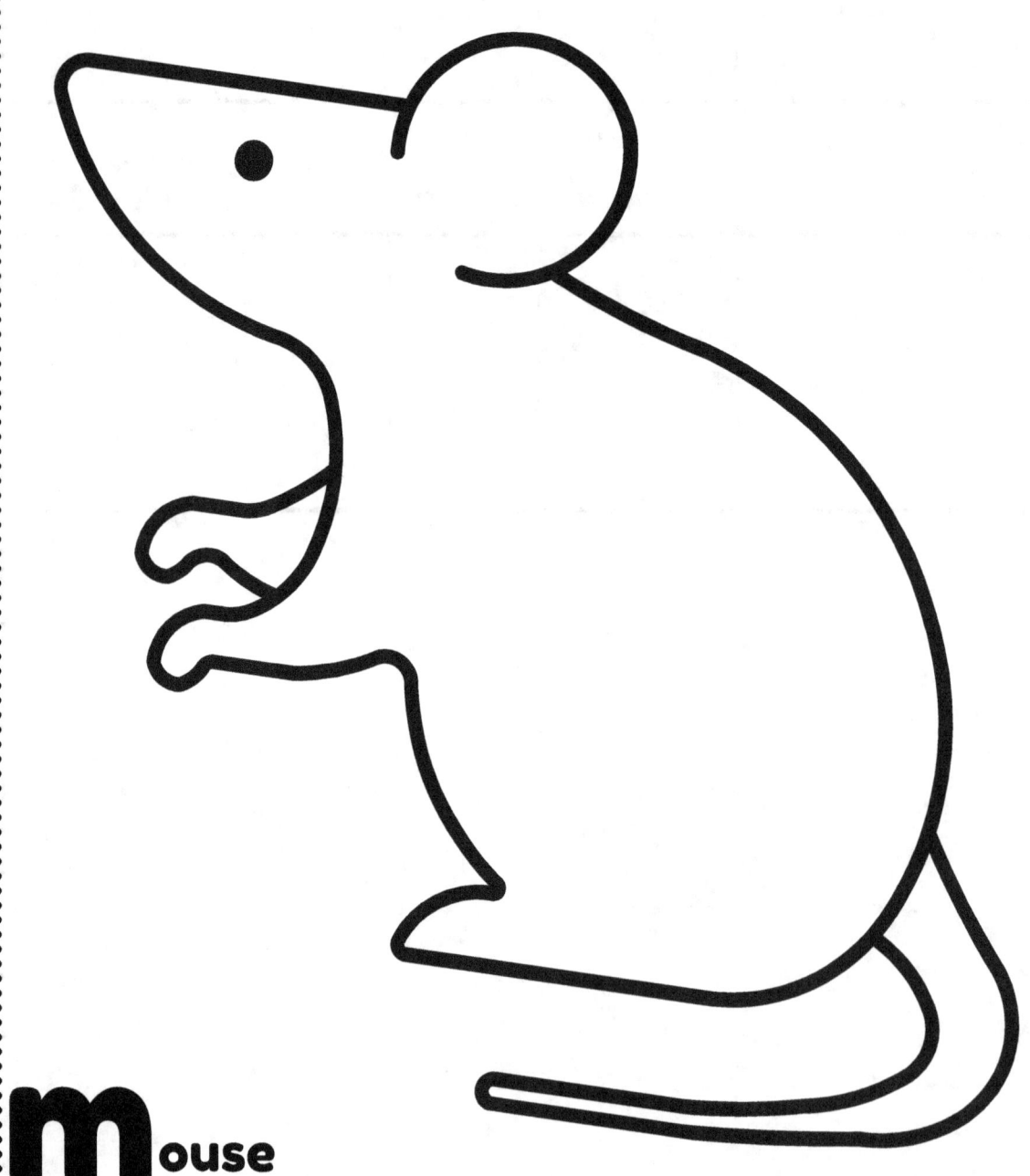

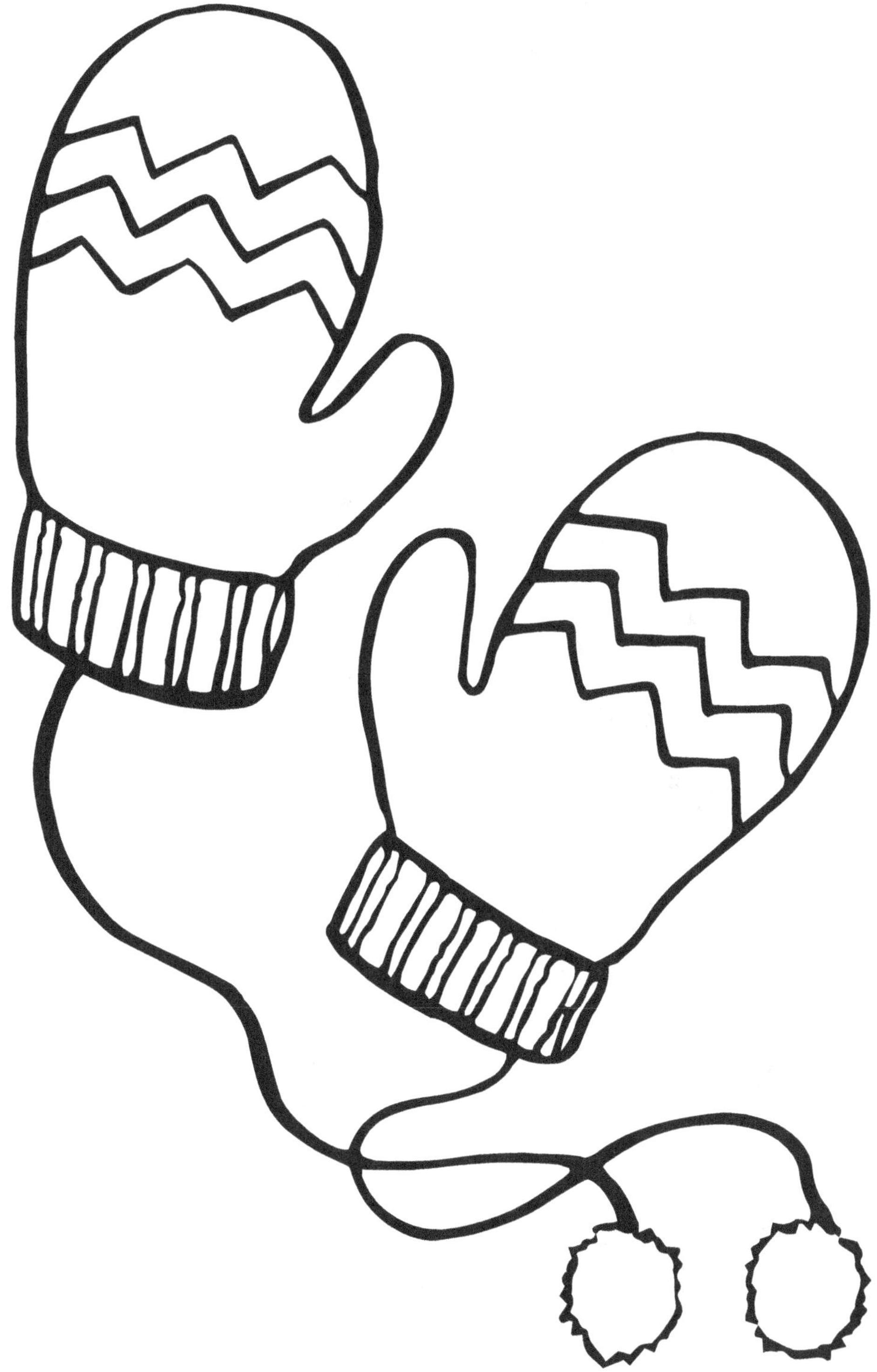

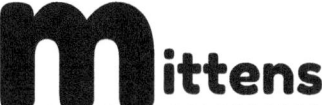

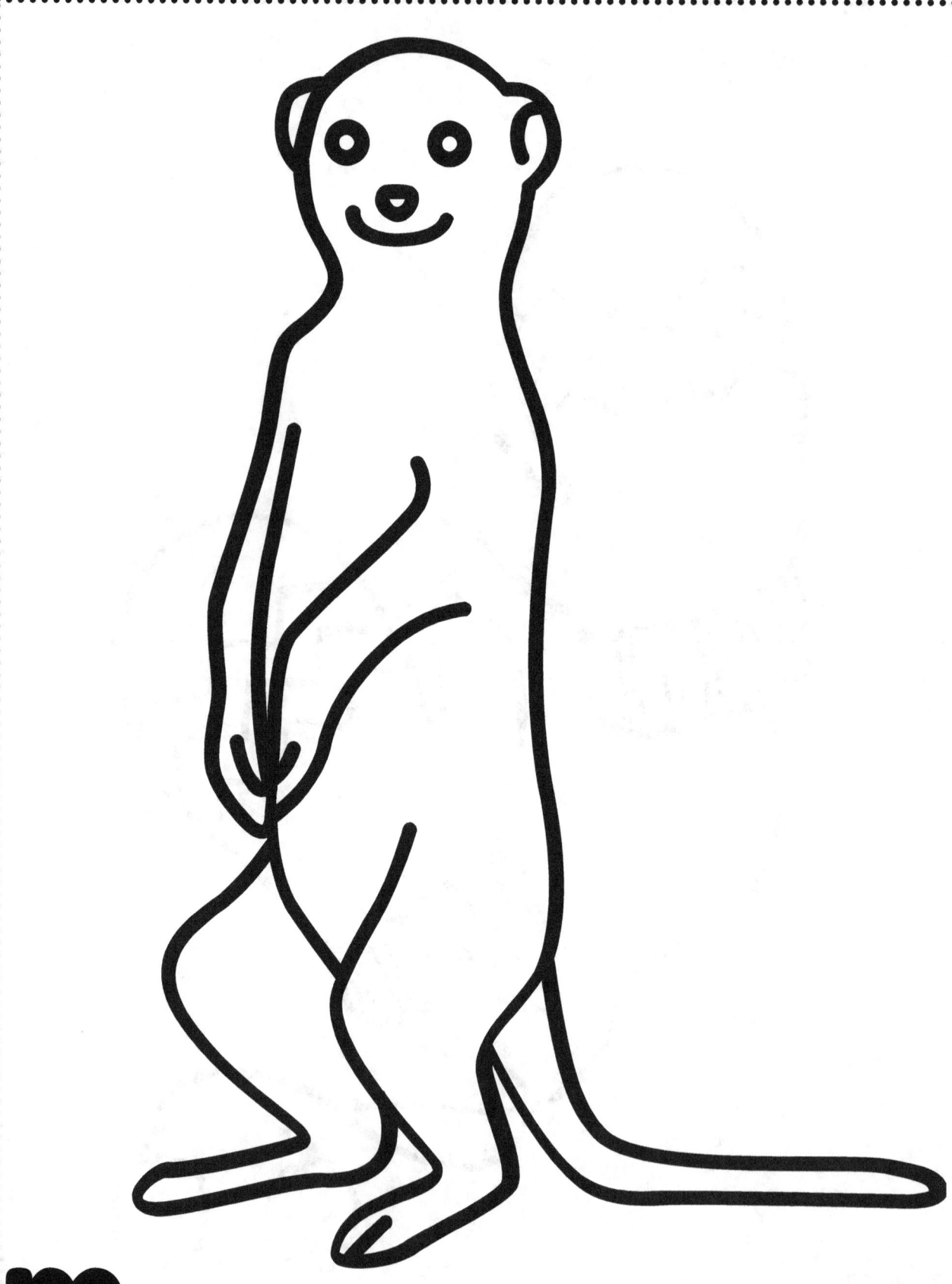

meerkat

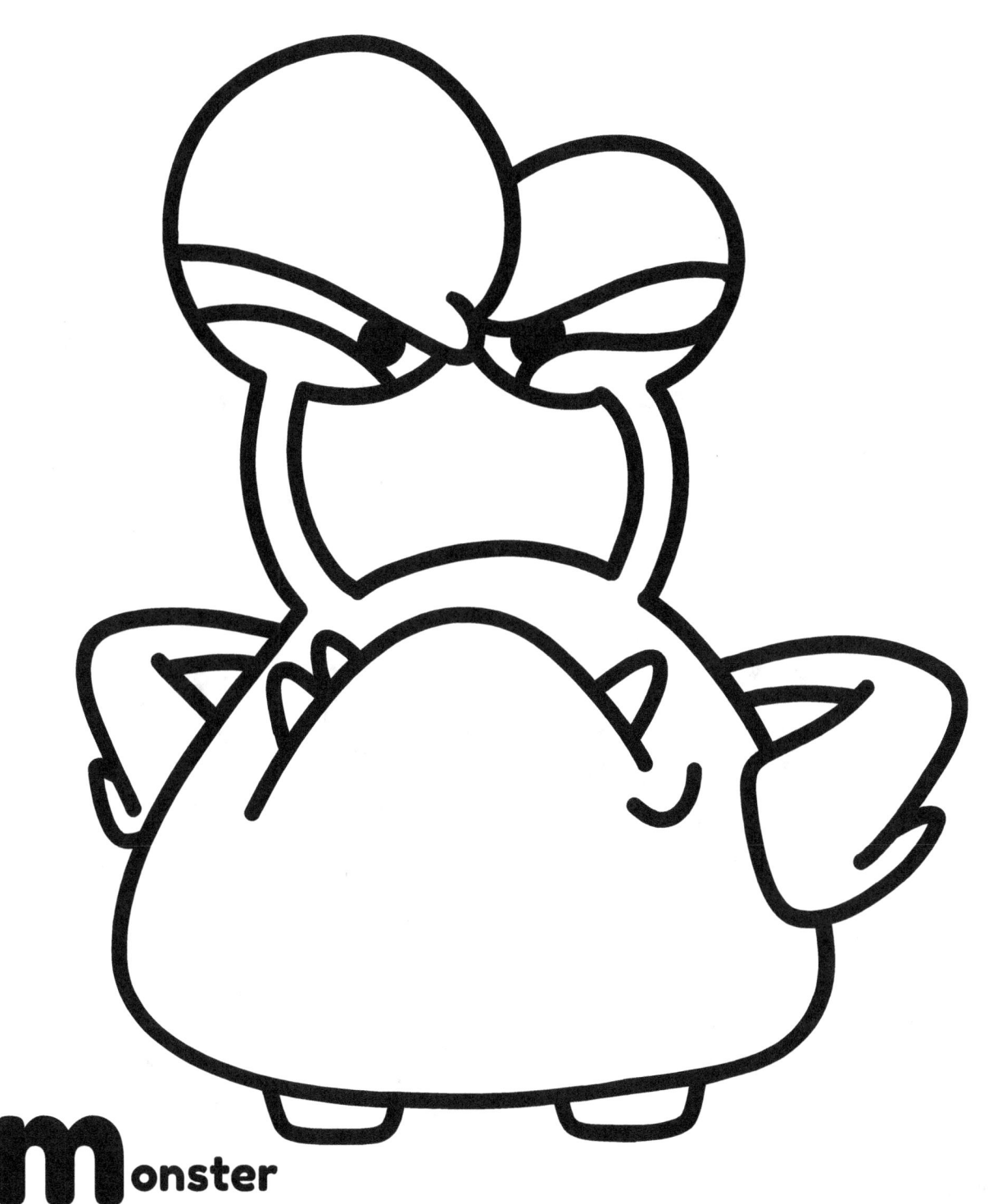

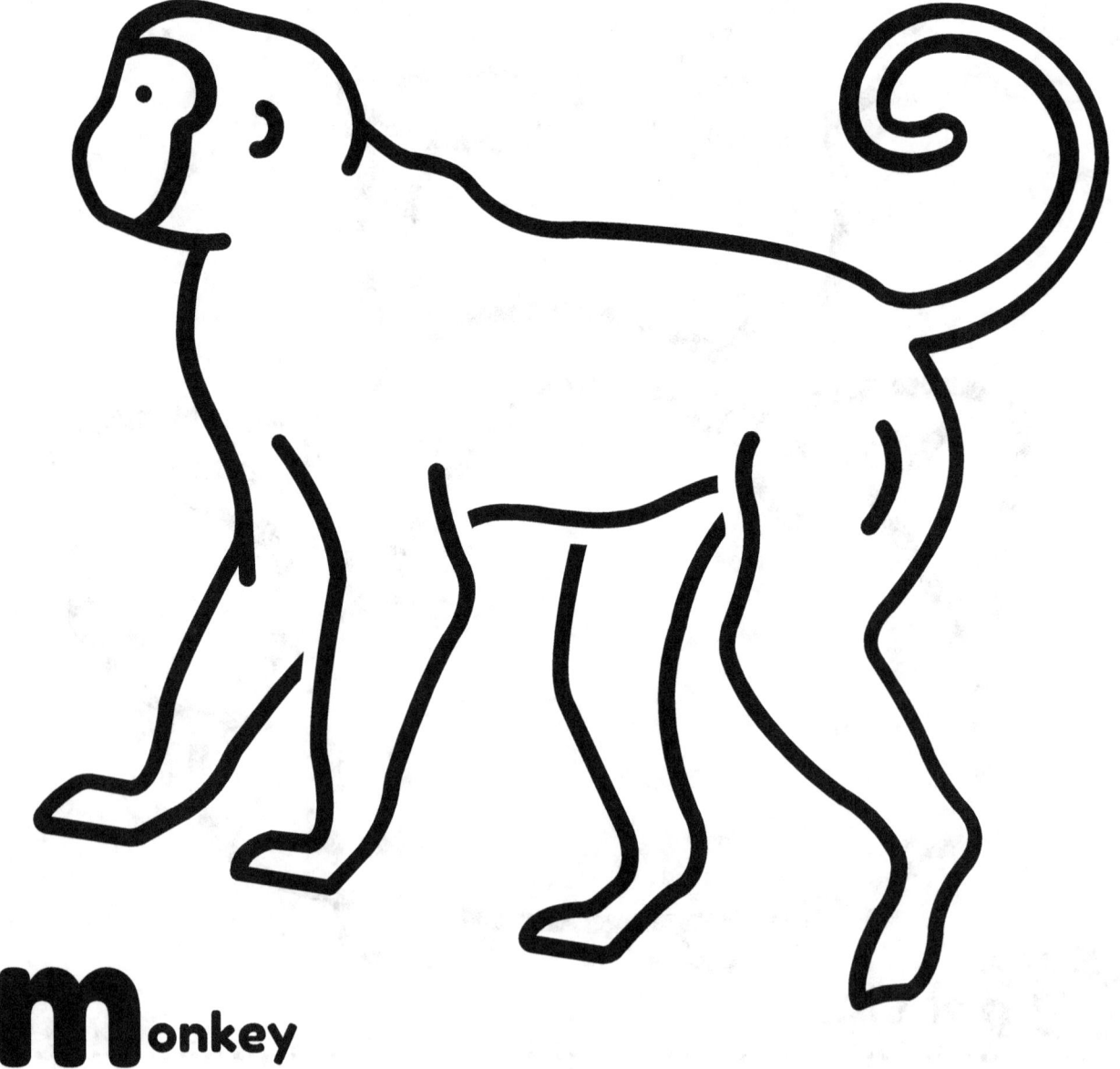

monkey

Name:

Mm Mm Mm

Mm Mm Mm

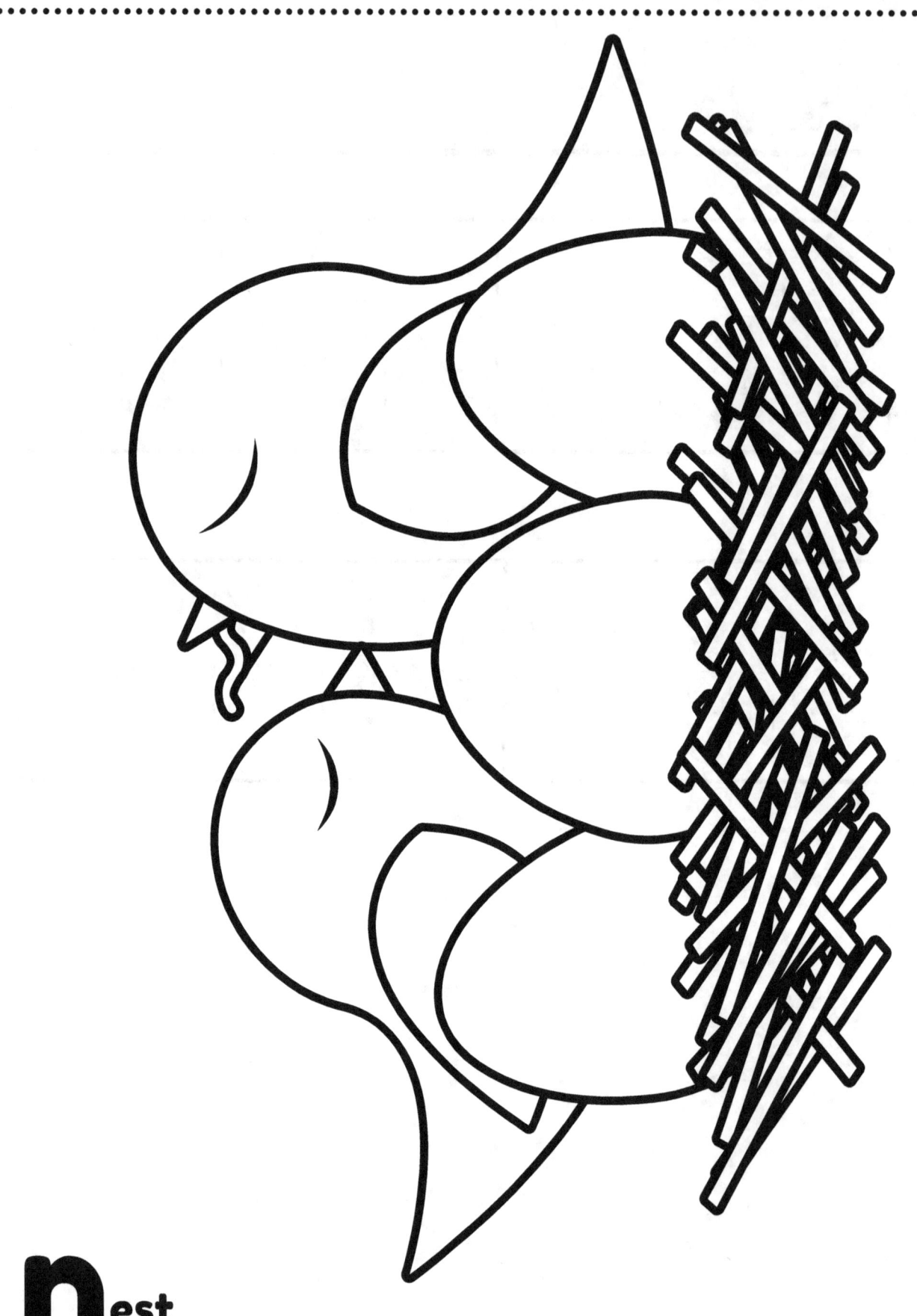

nest

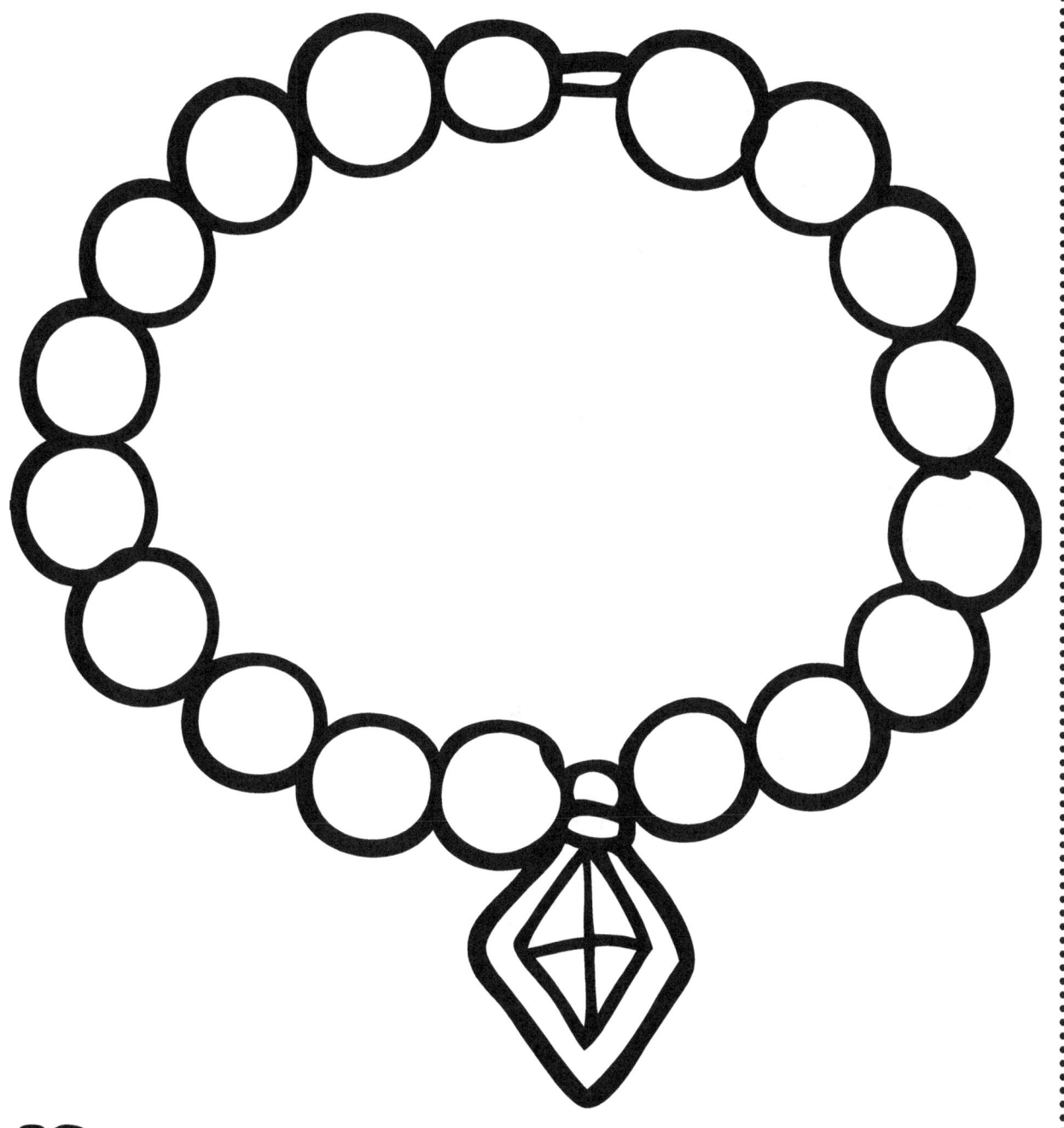

necklace

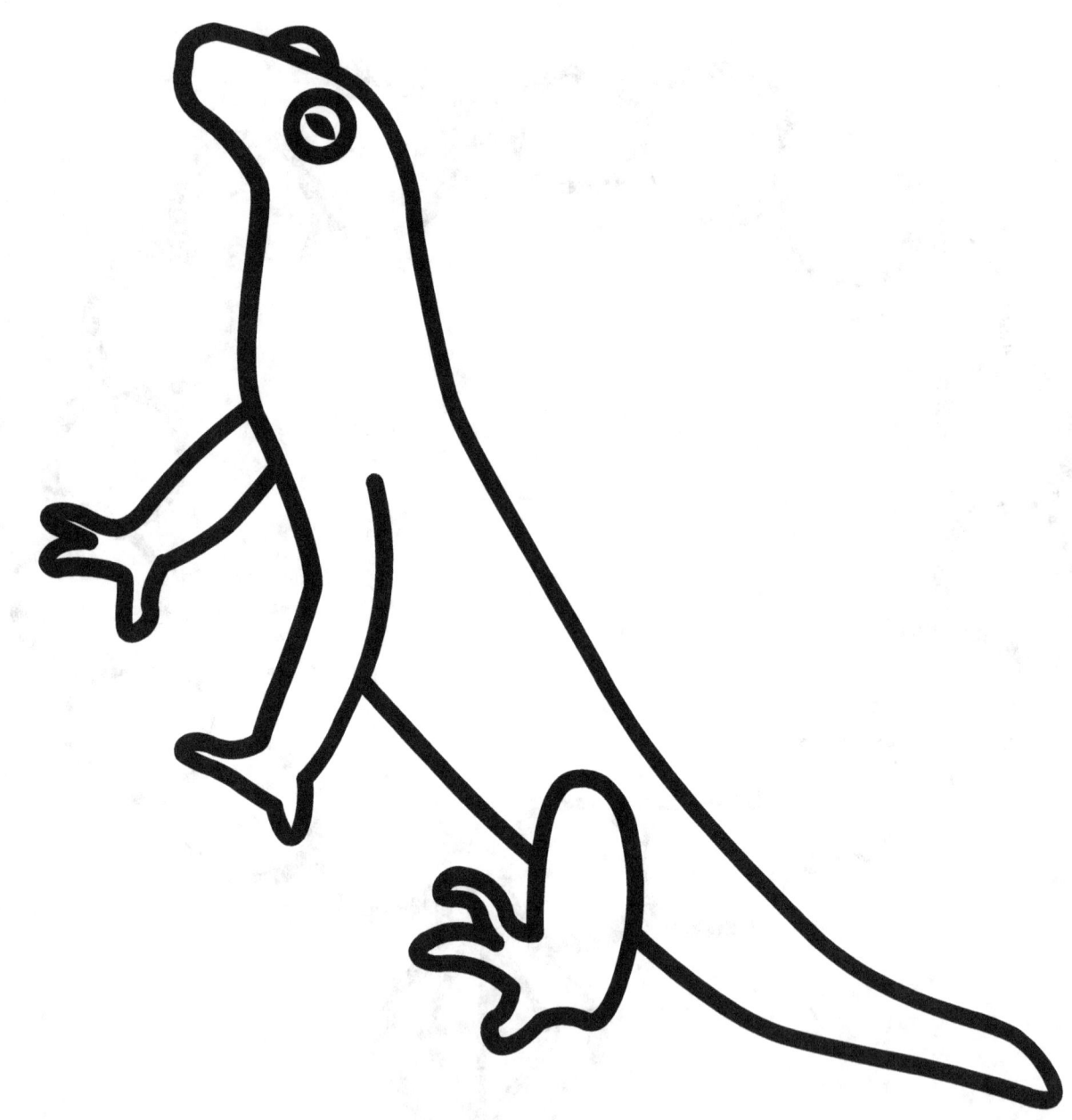

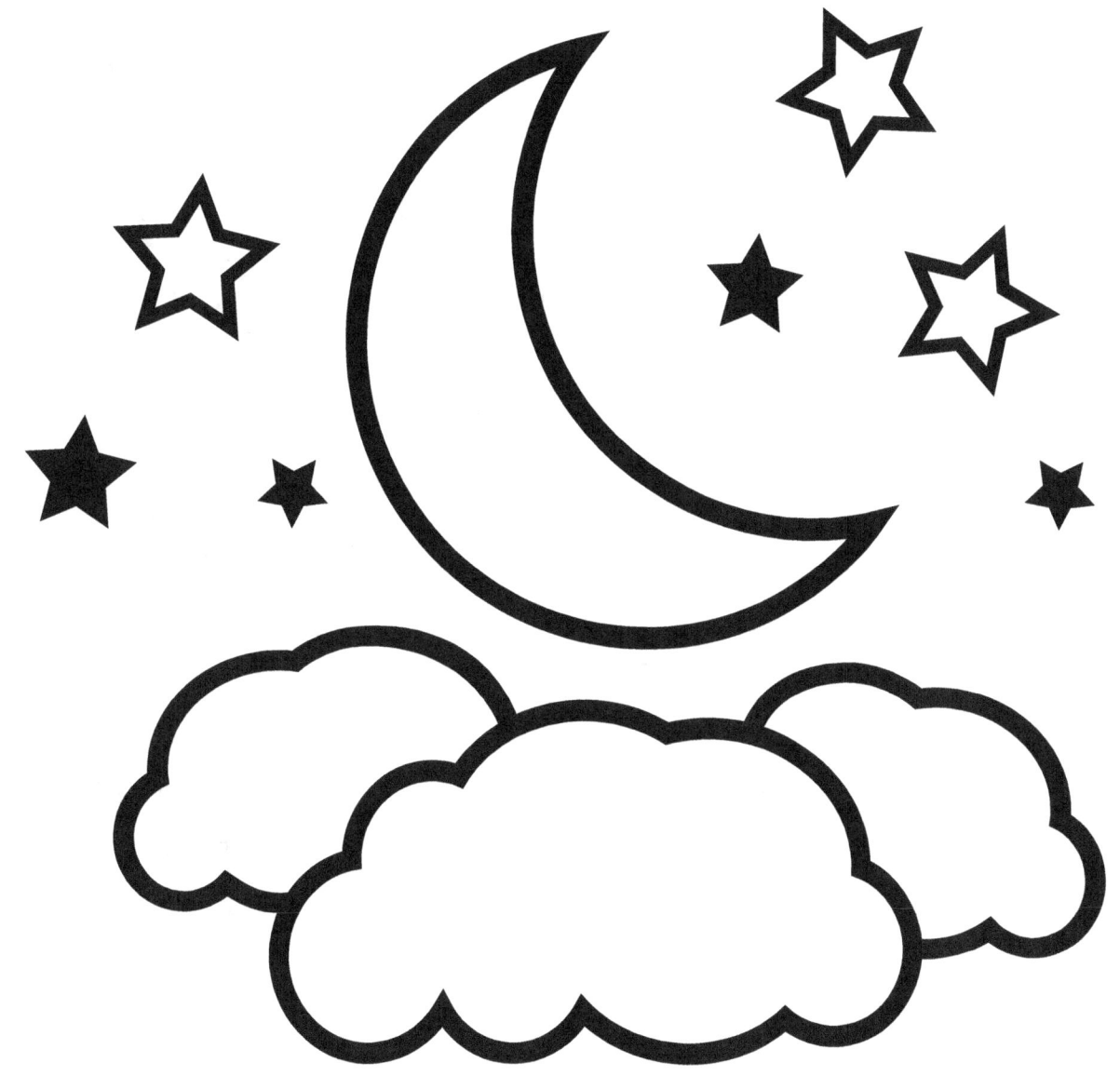

night

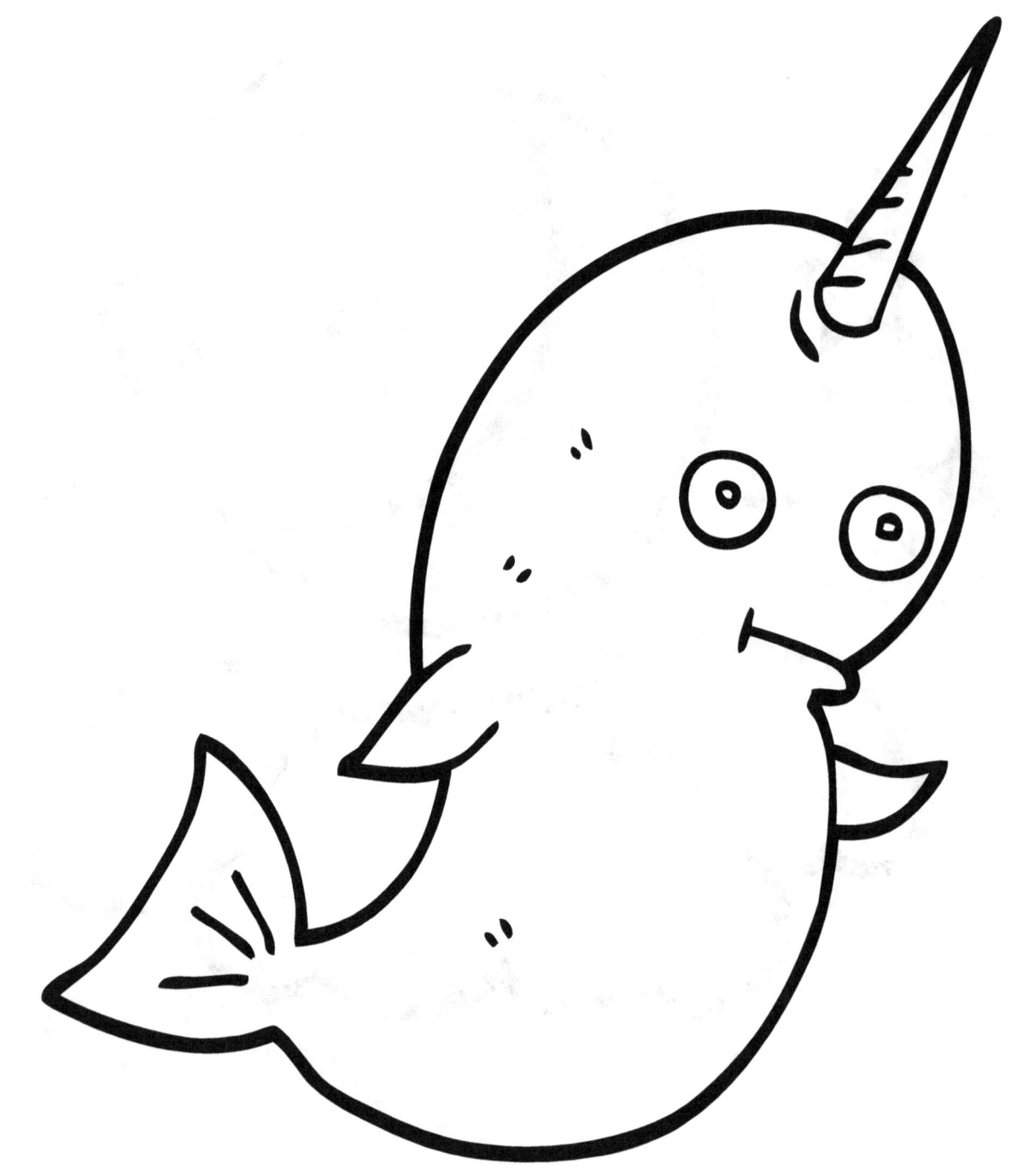

narwal

Name:

Nn Nn Nn Nn

Nn Nn Nn Nn

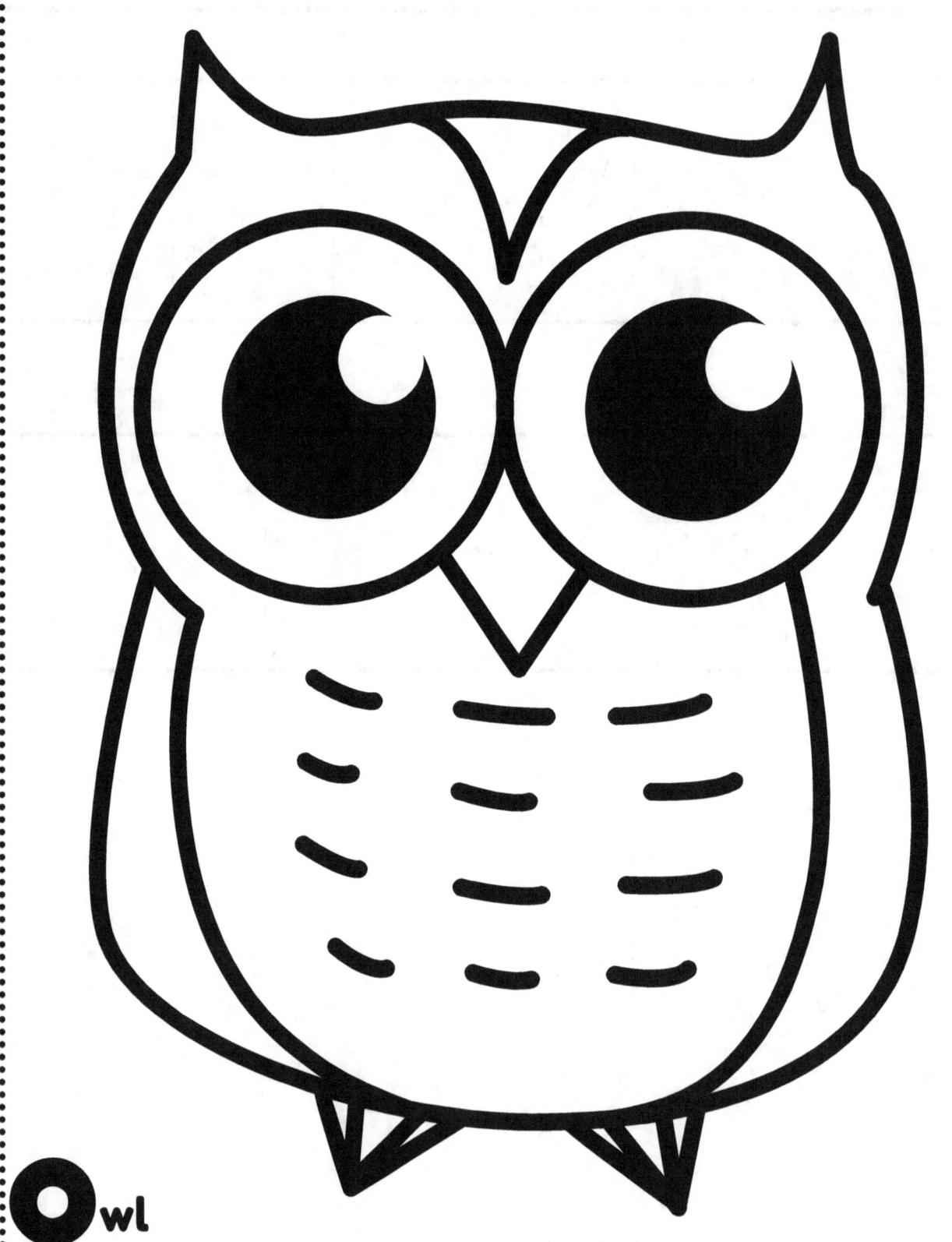

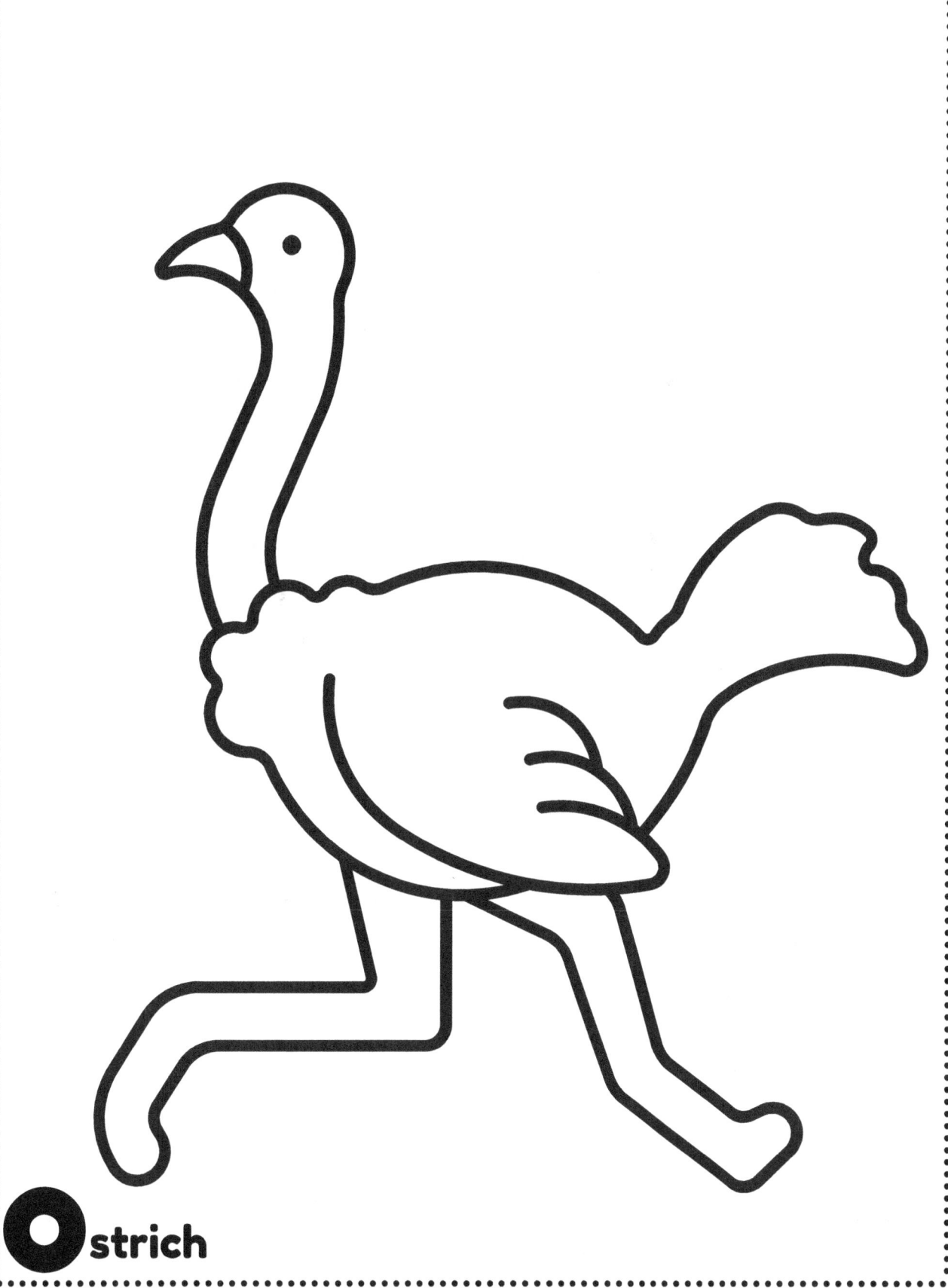

Ostrich

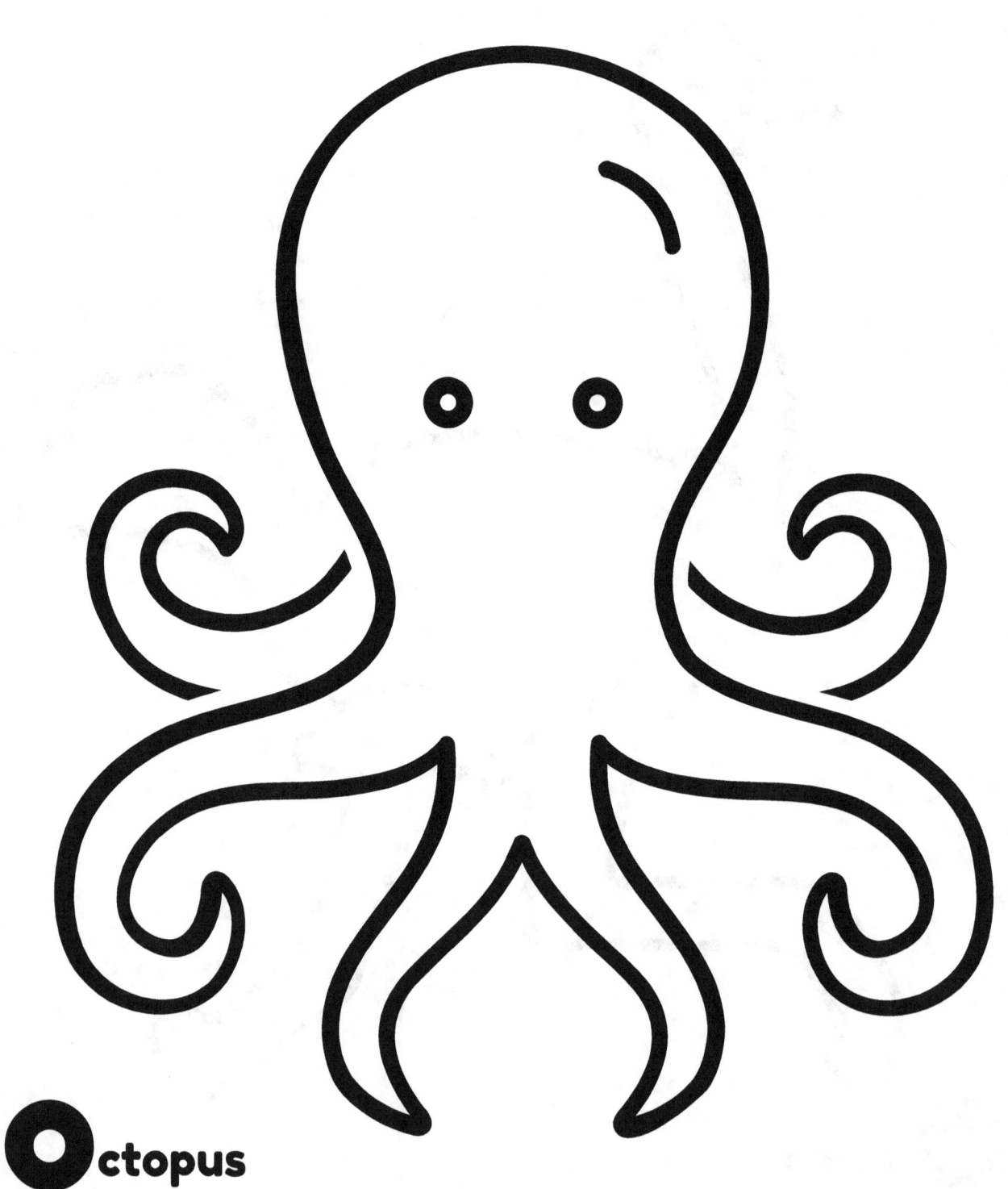

Octopus

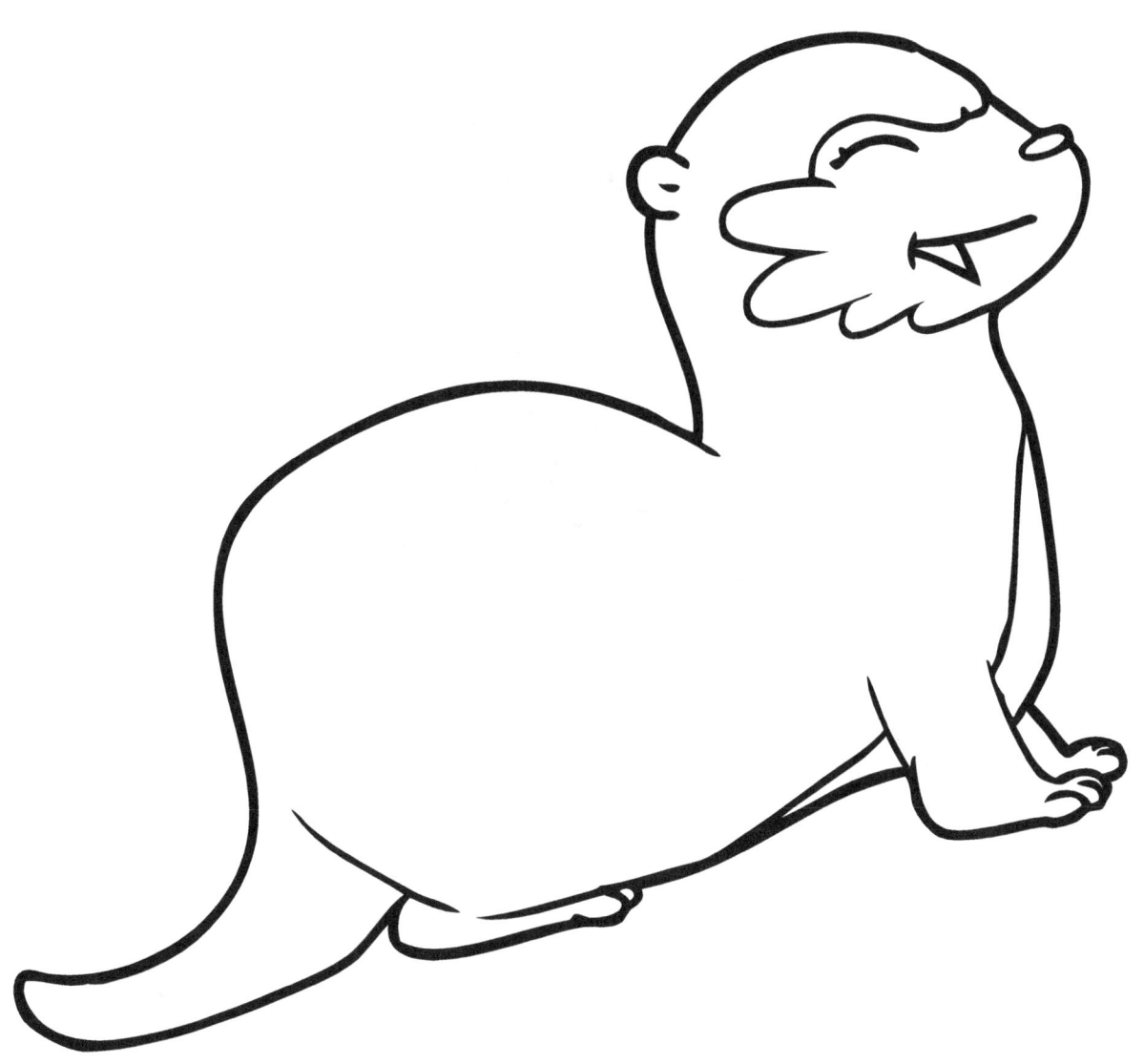

Otter

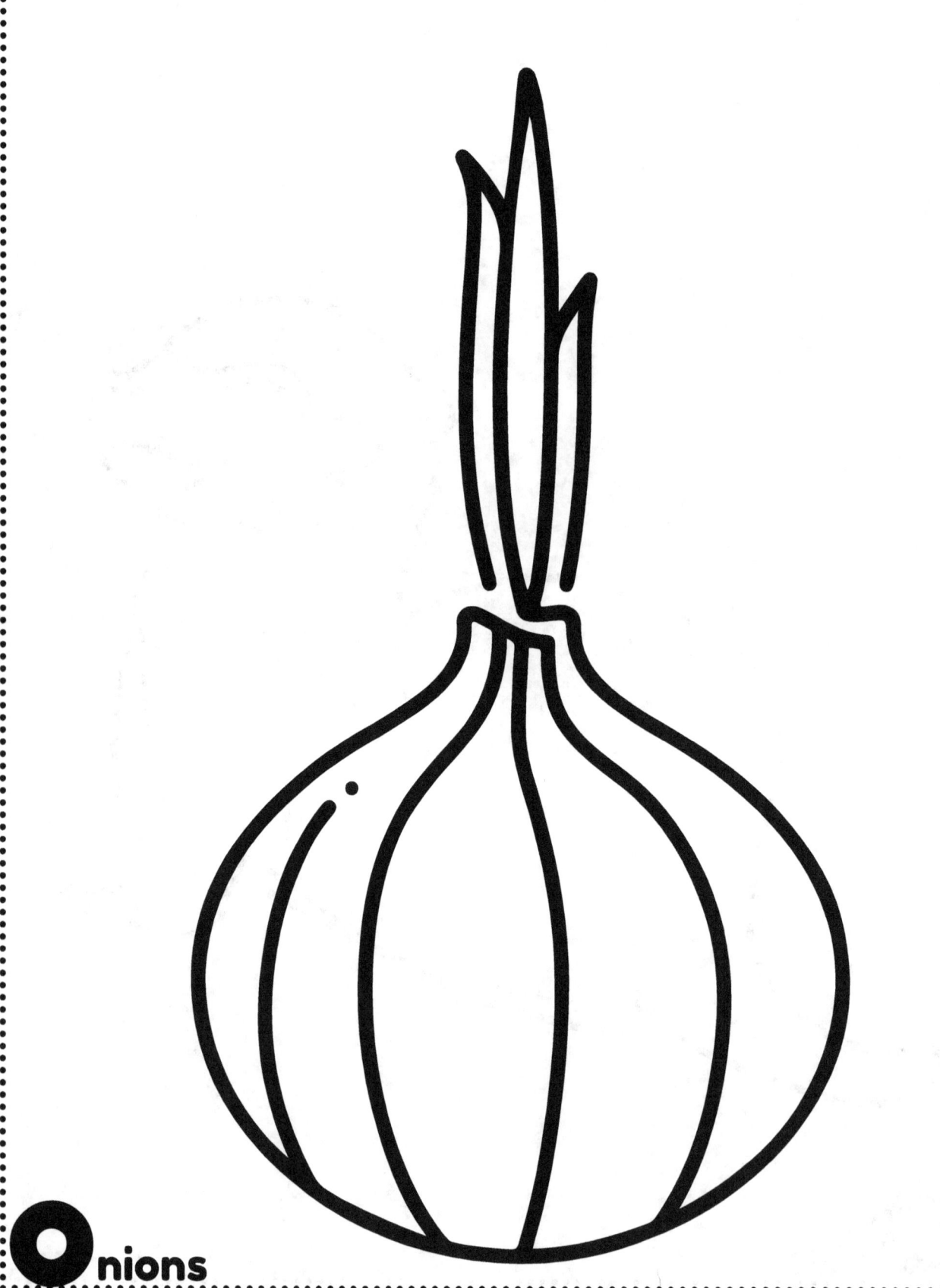

Onions

Name:

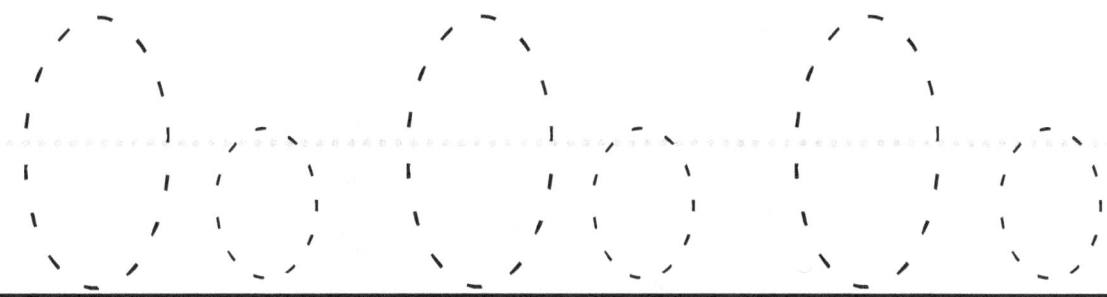

penguin

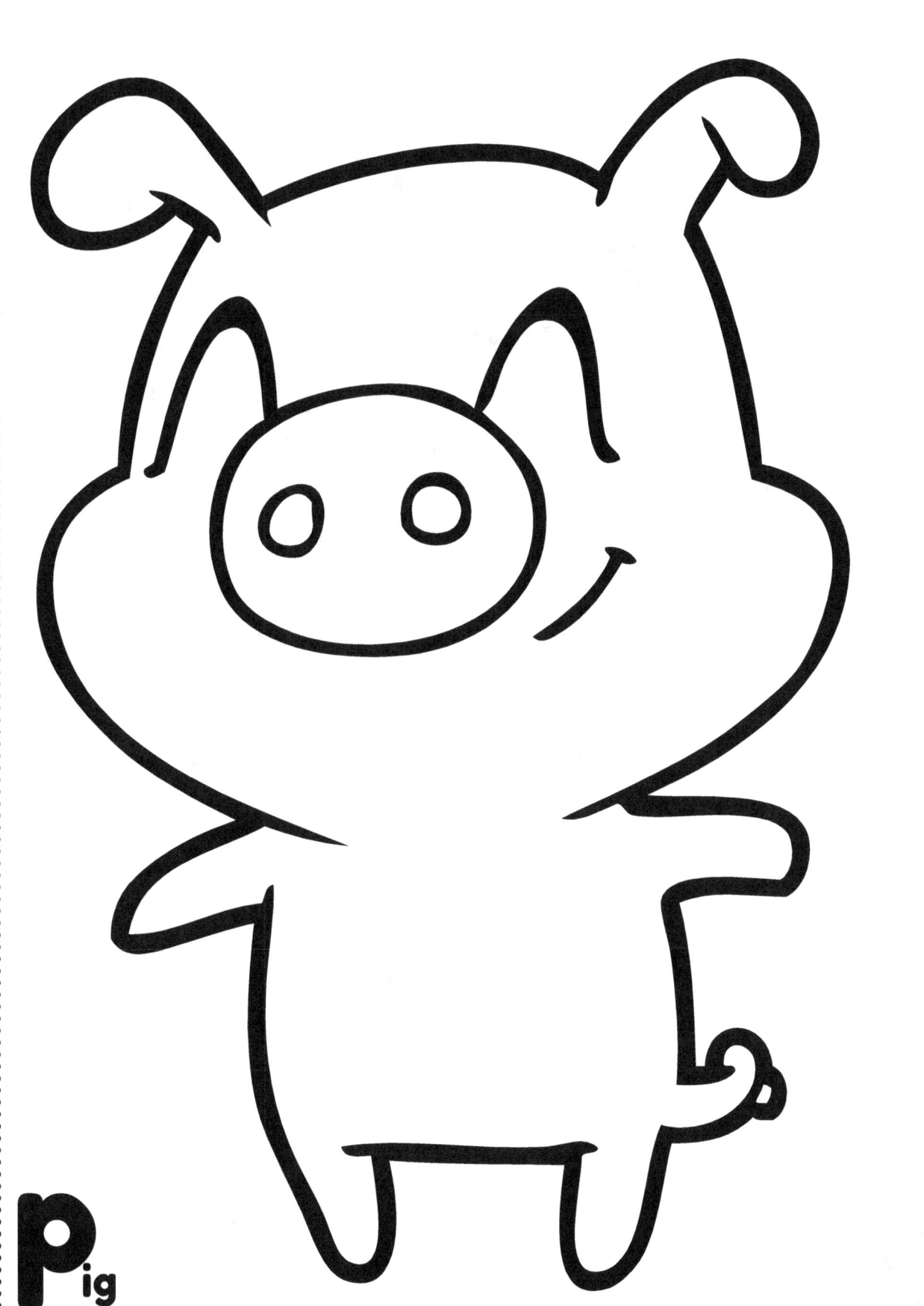

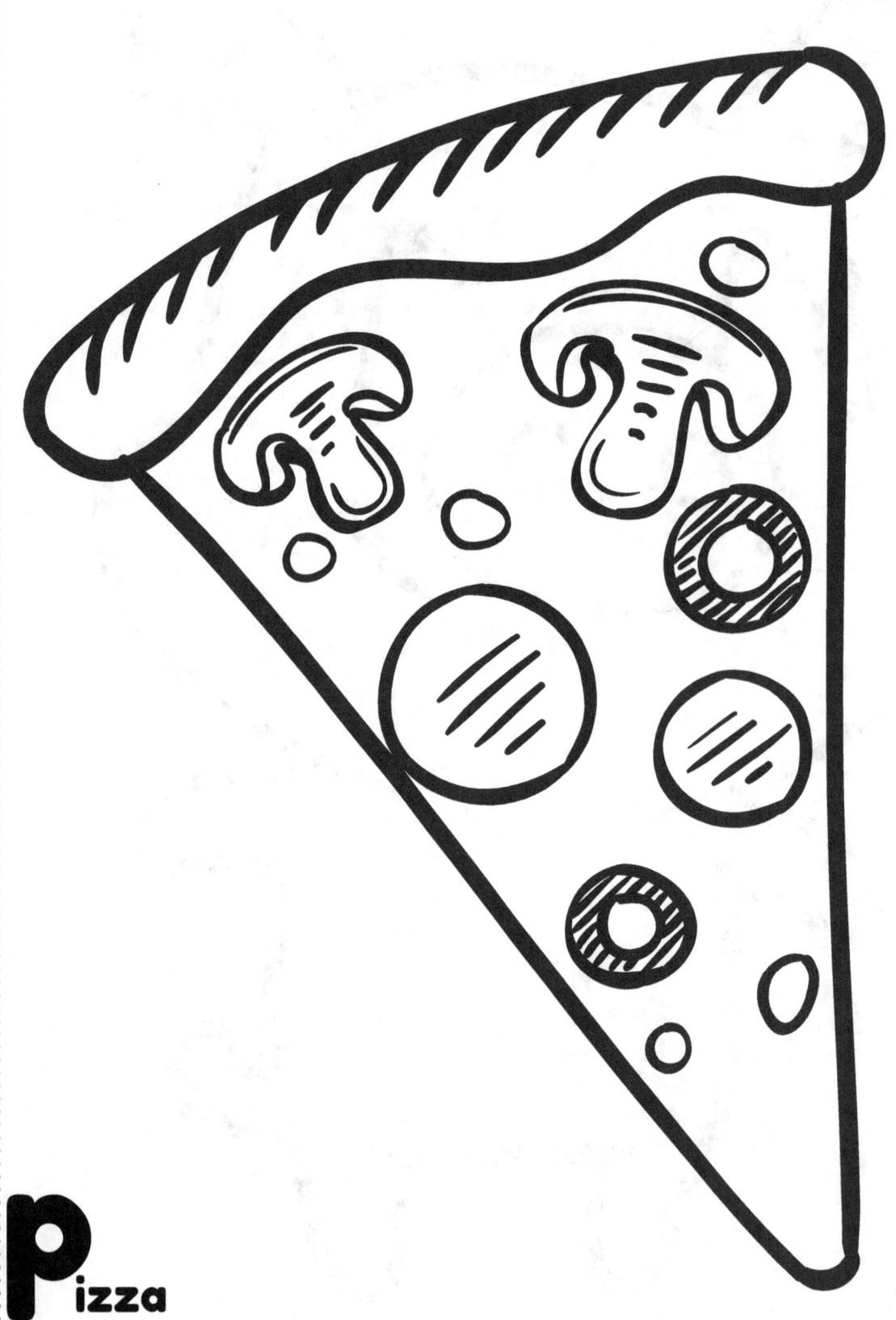

Pizza

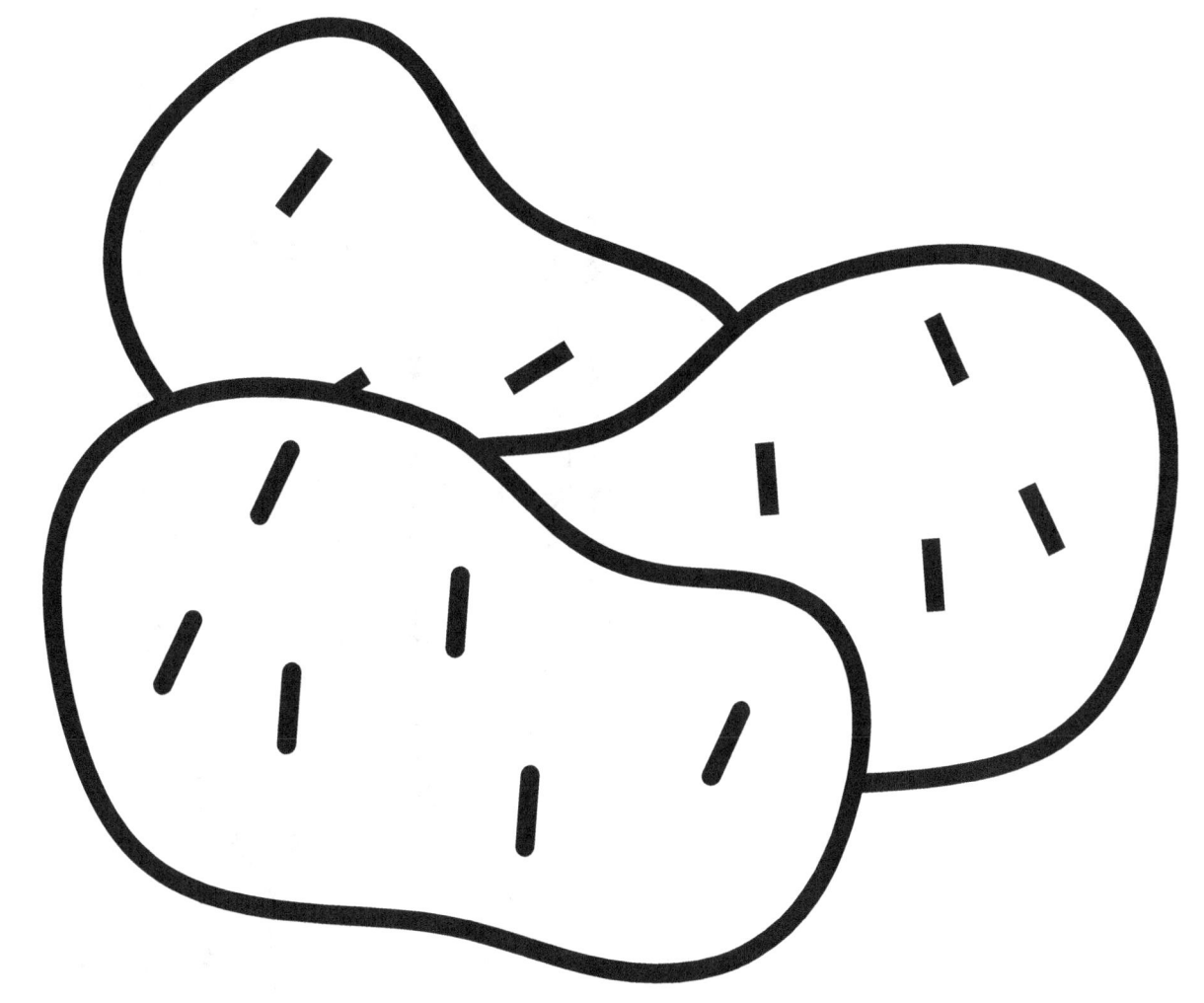

Potatoes

police car

Name:

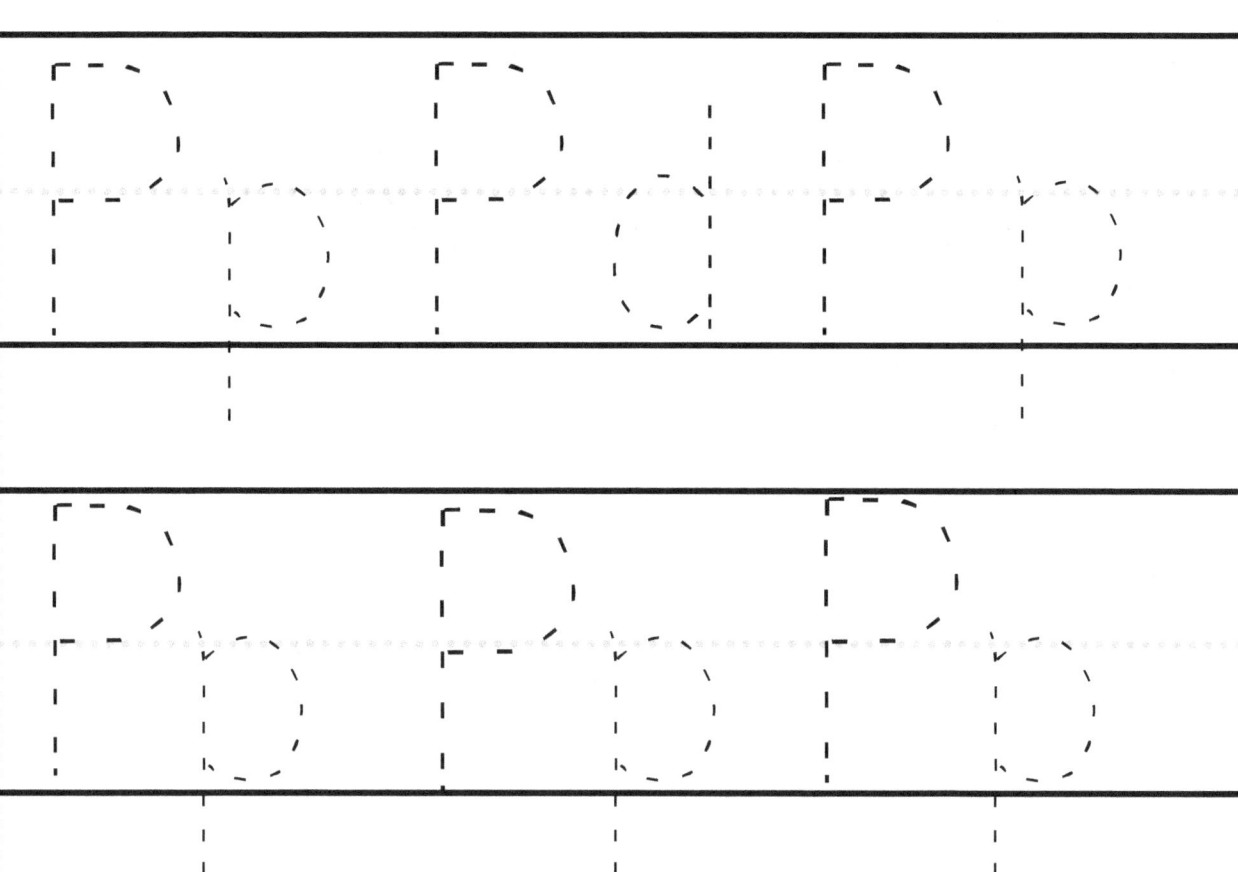

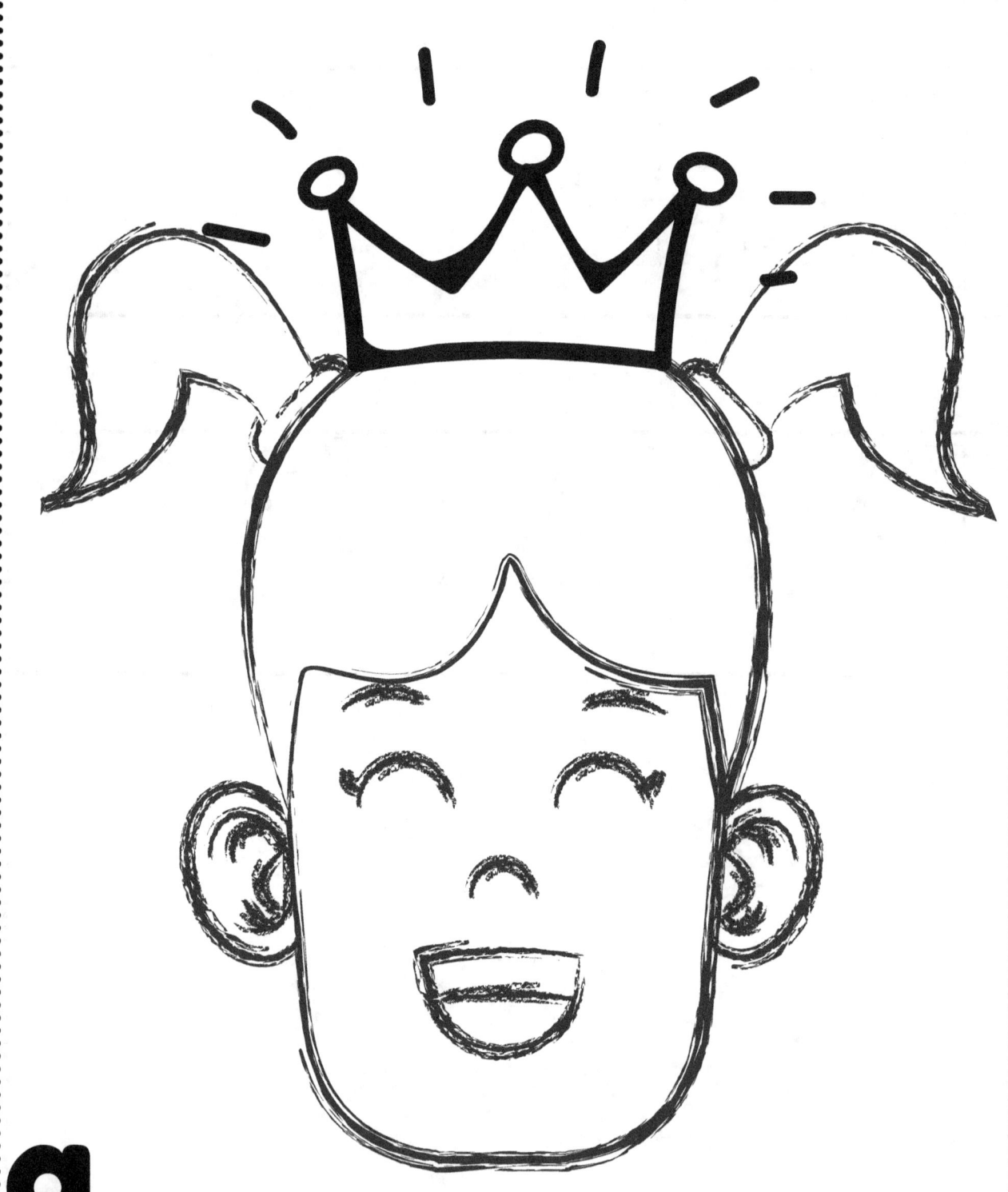

queen

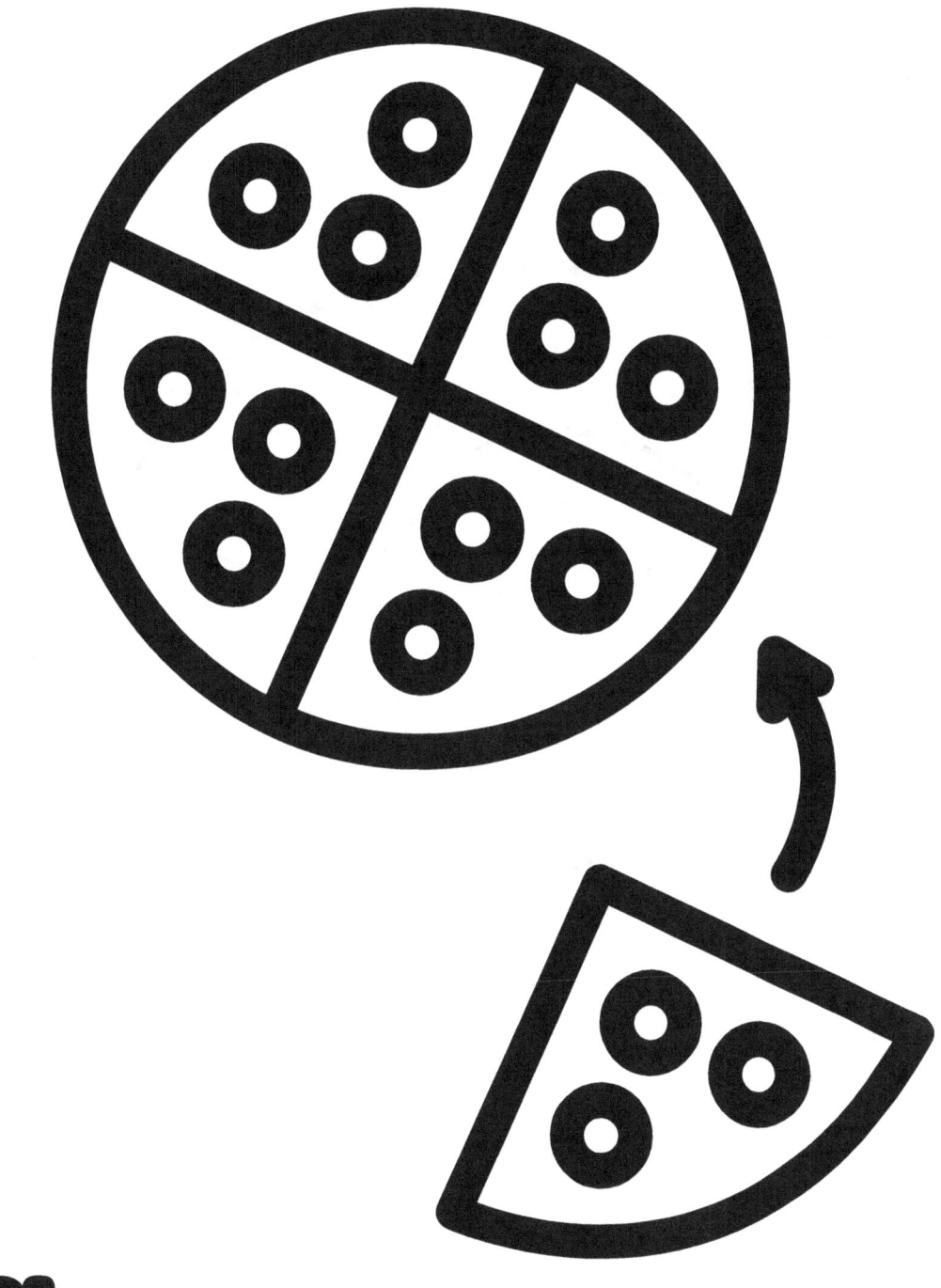

quarter

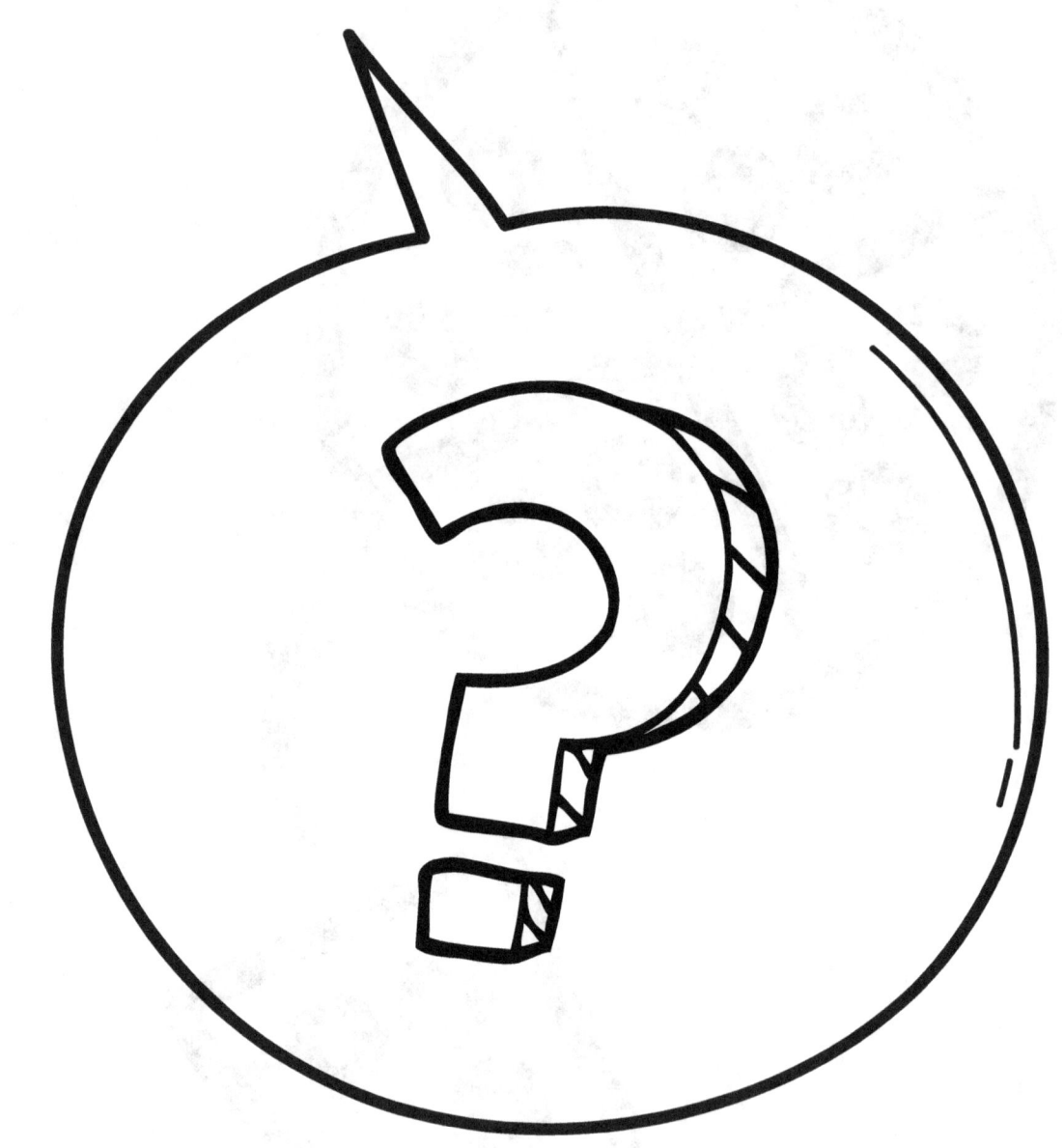

question

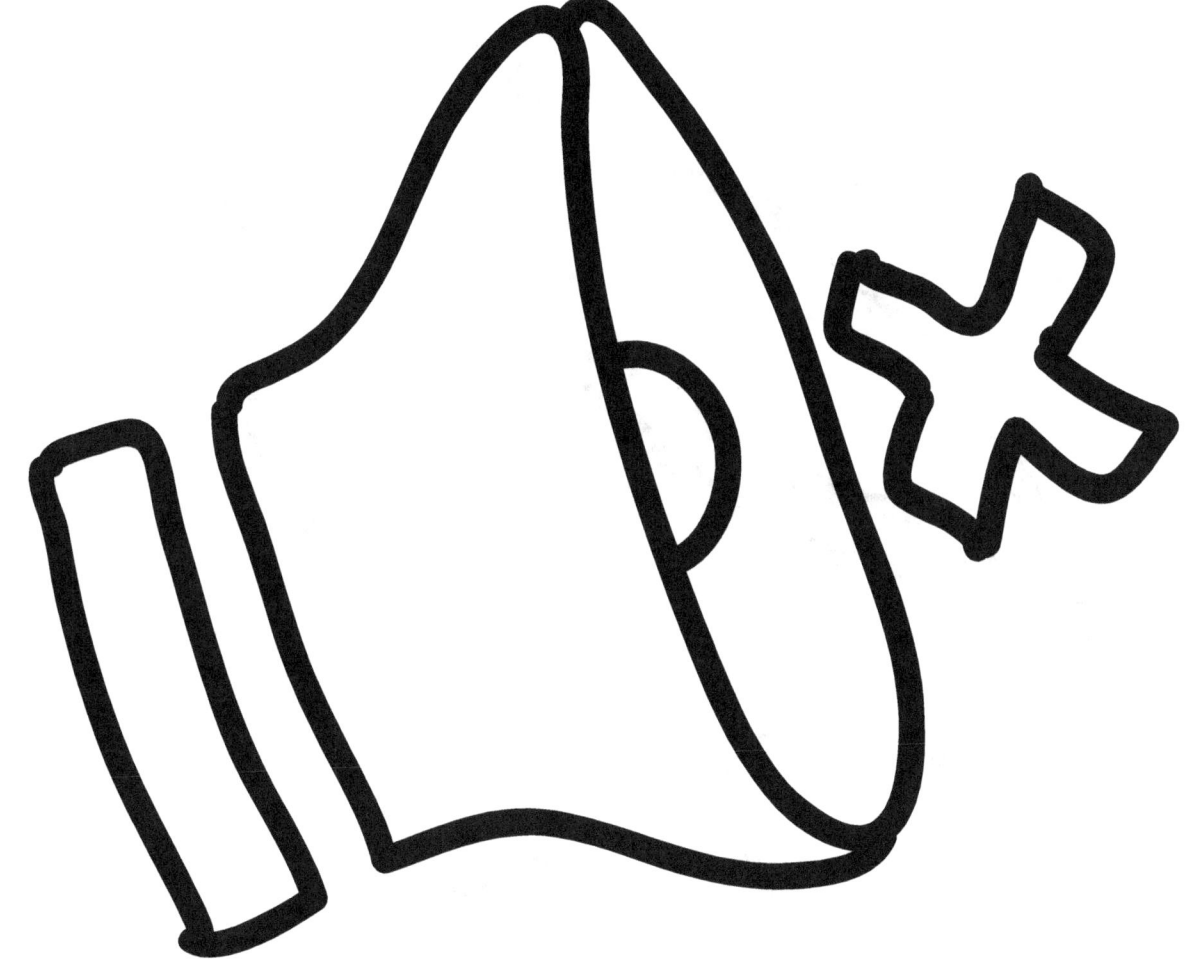

quiet

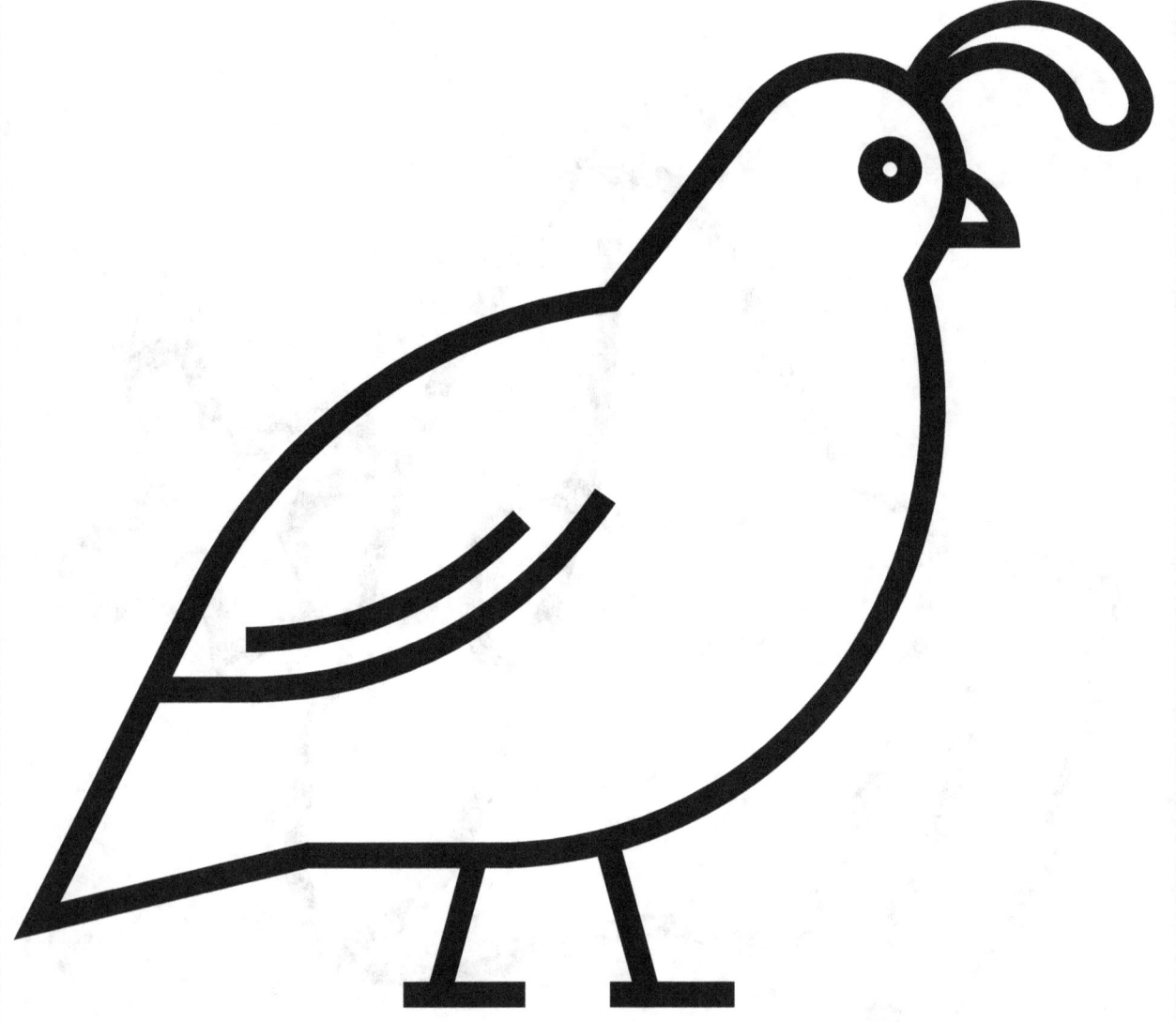

quail

Name: _____

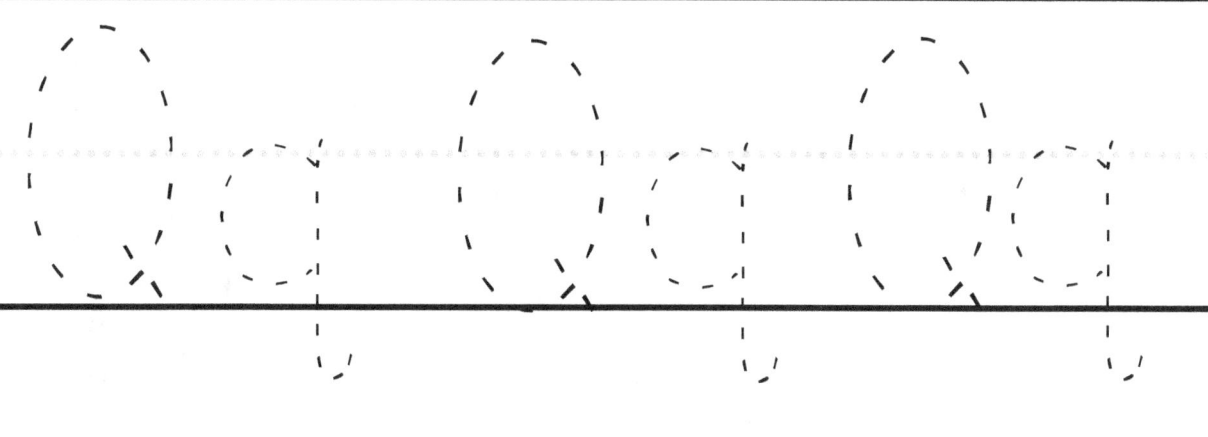

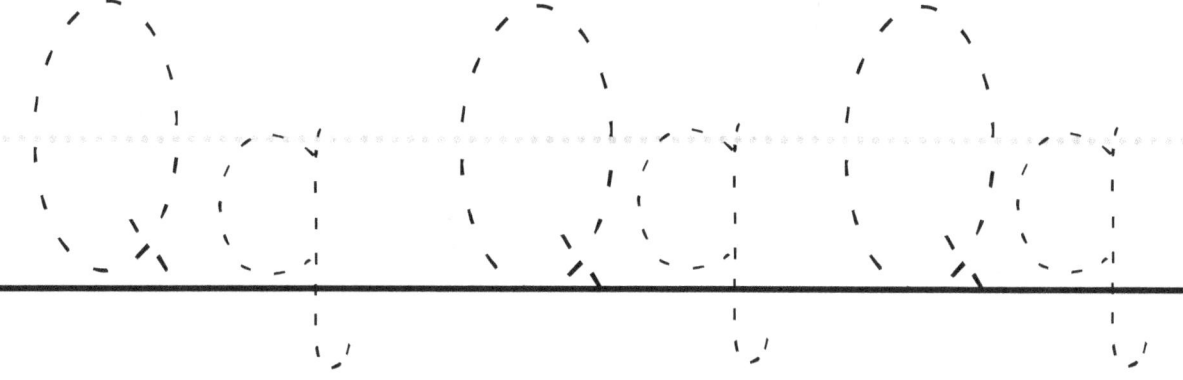

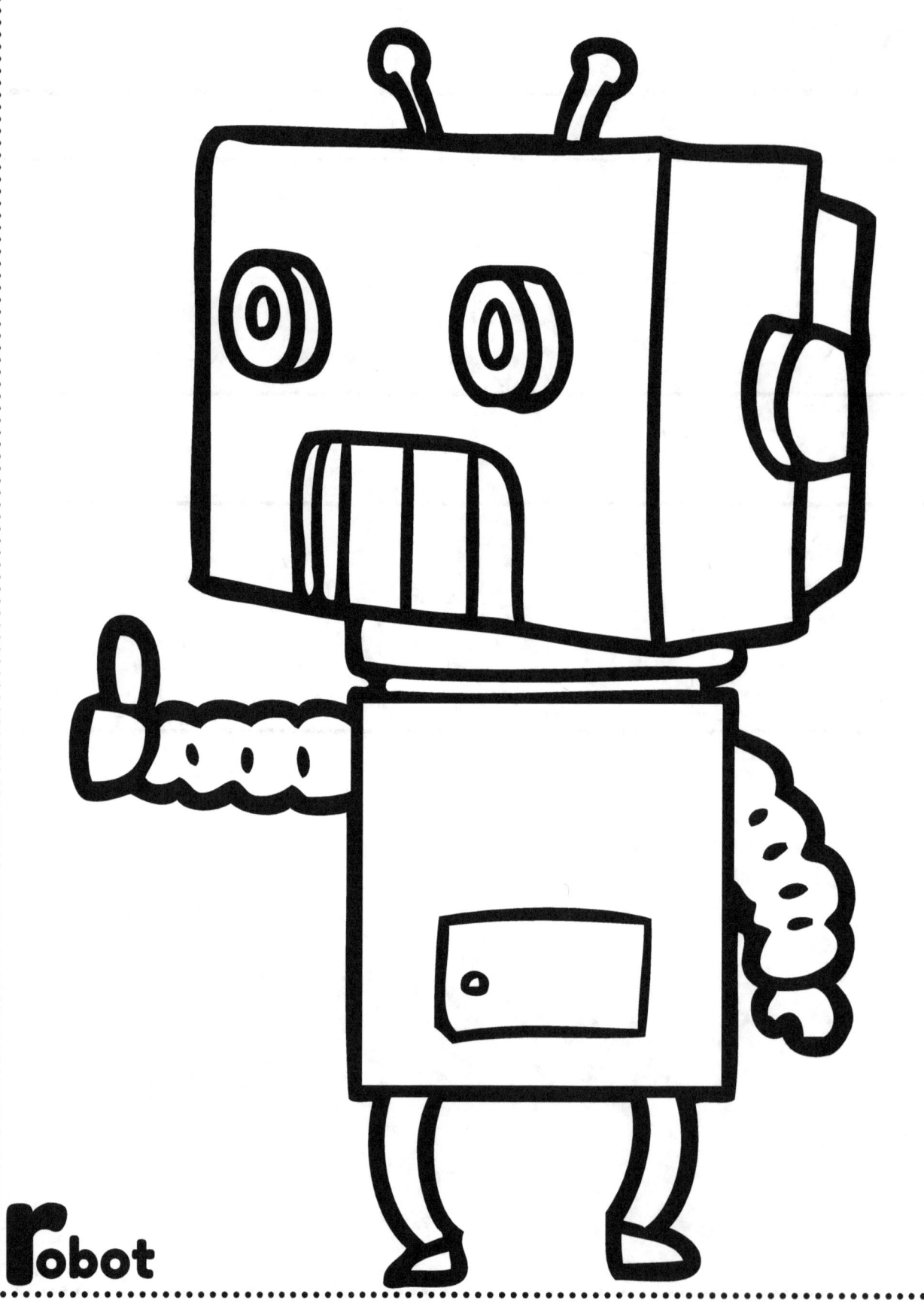
robot

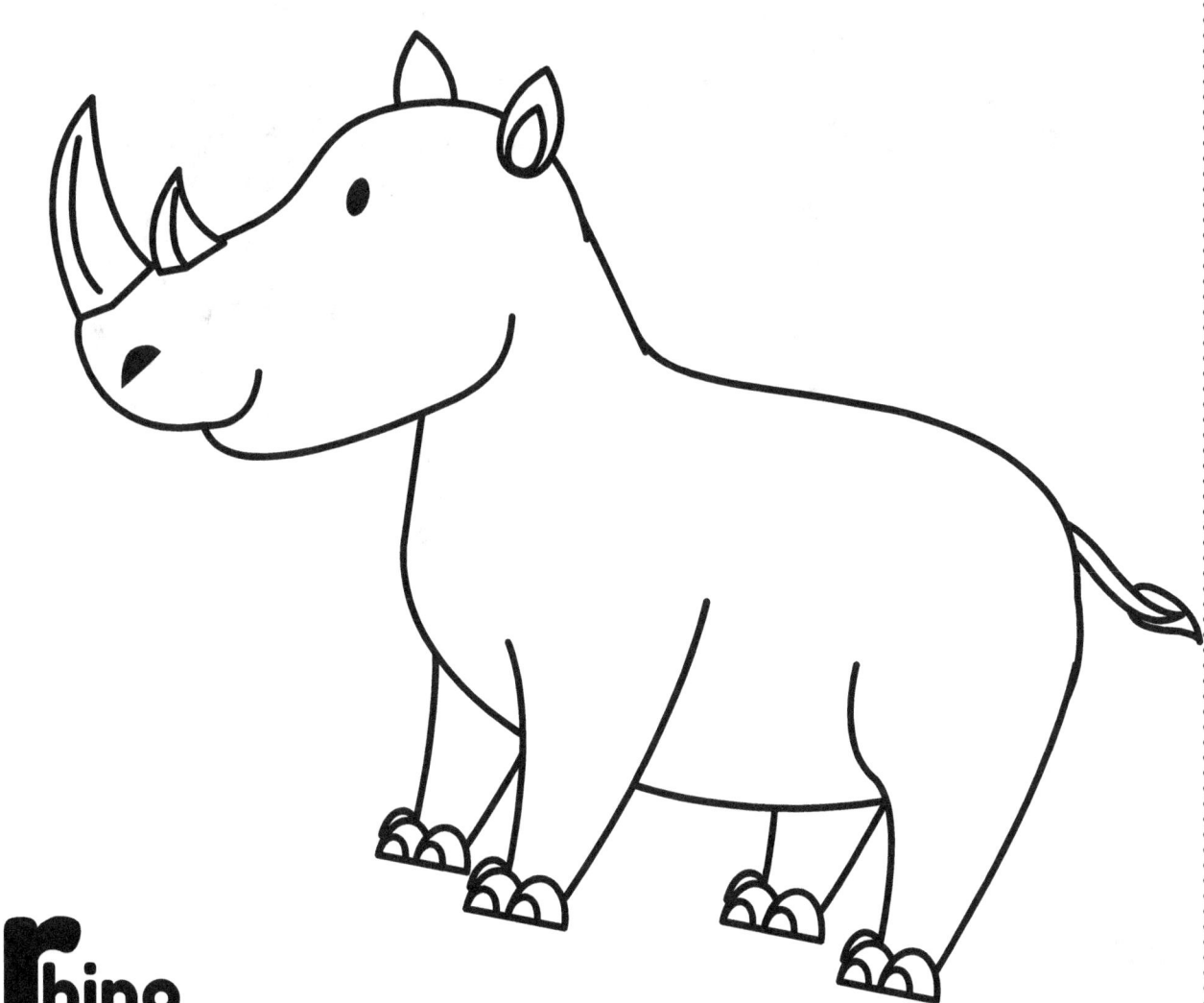

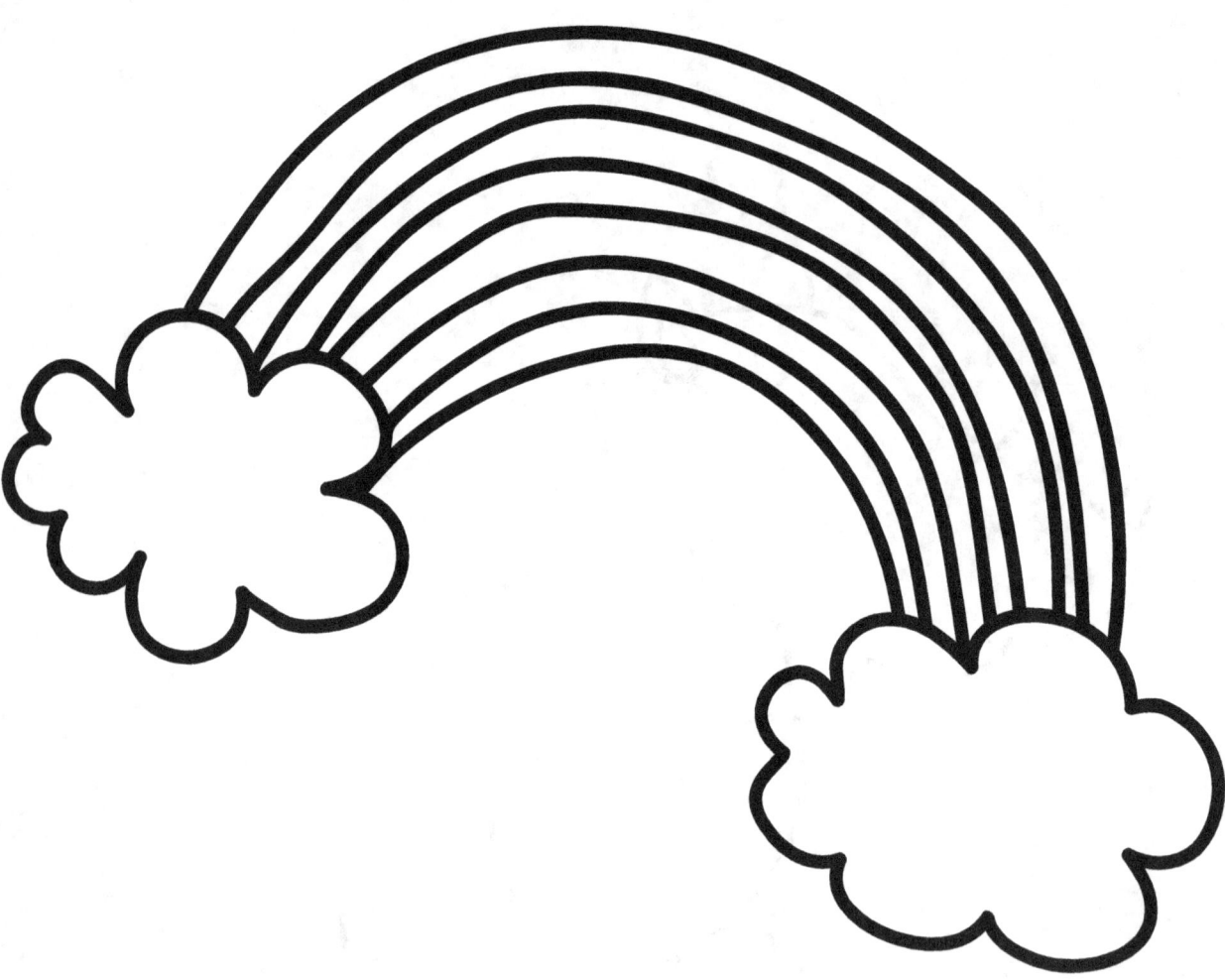

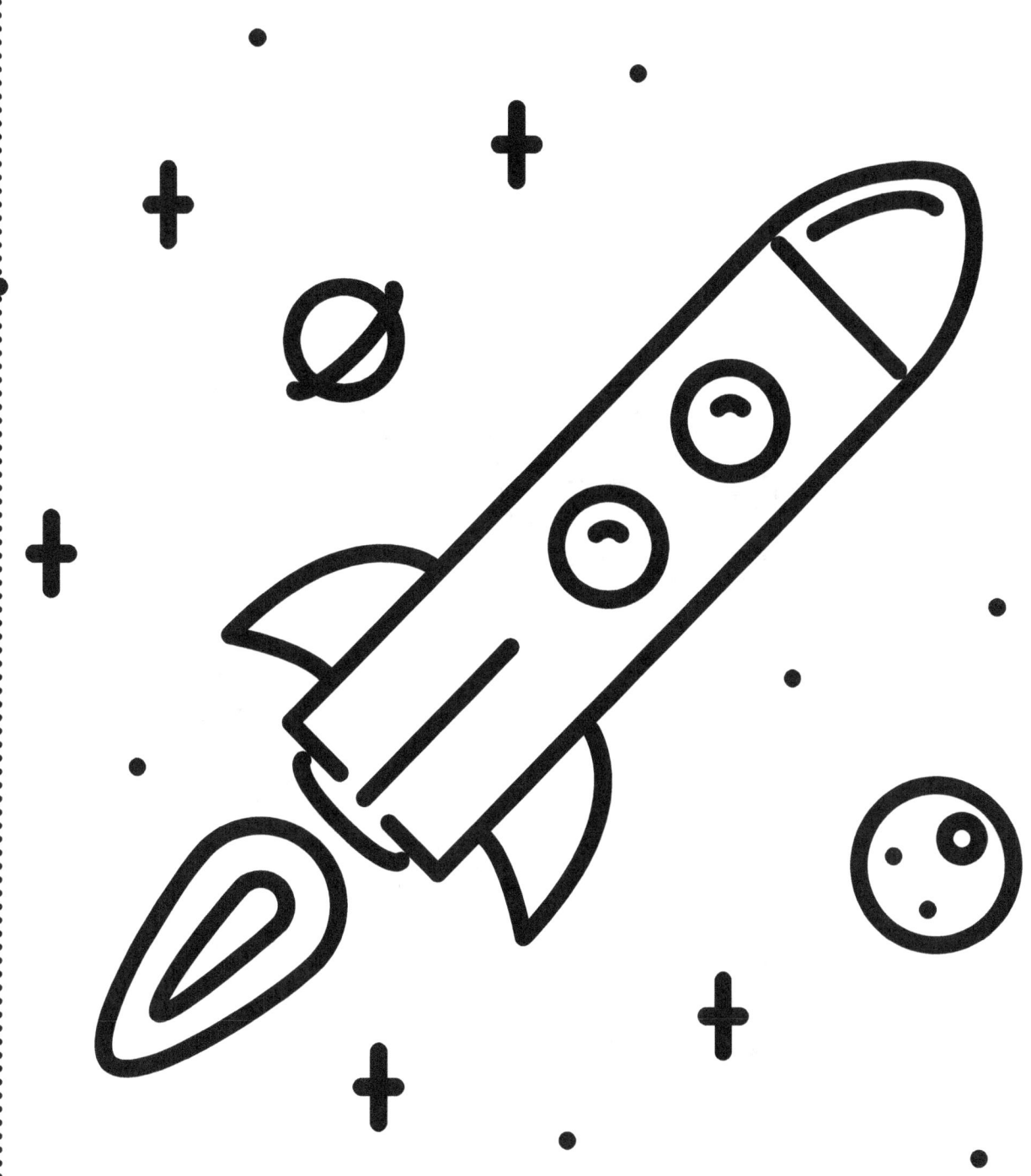

rocket

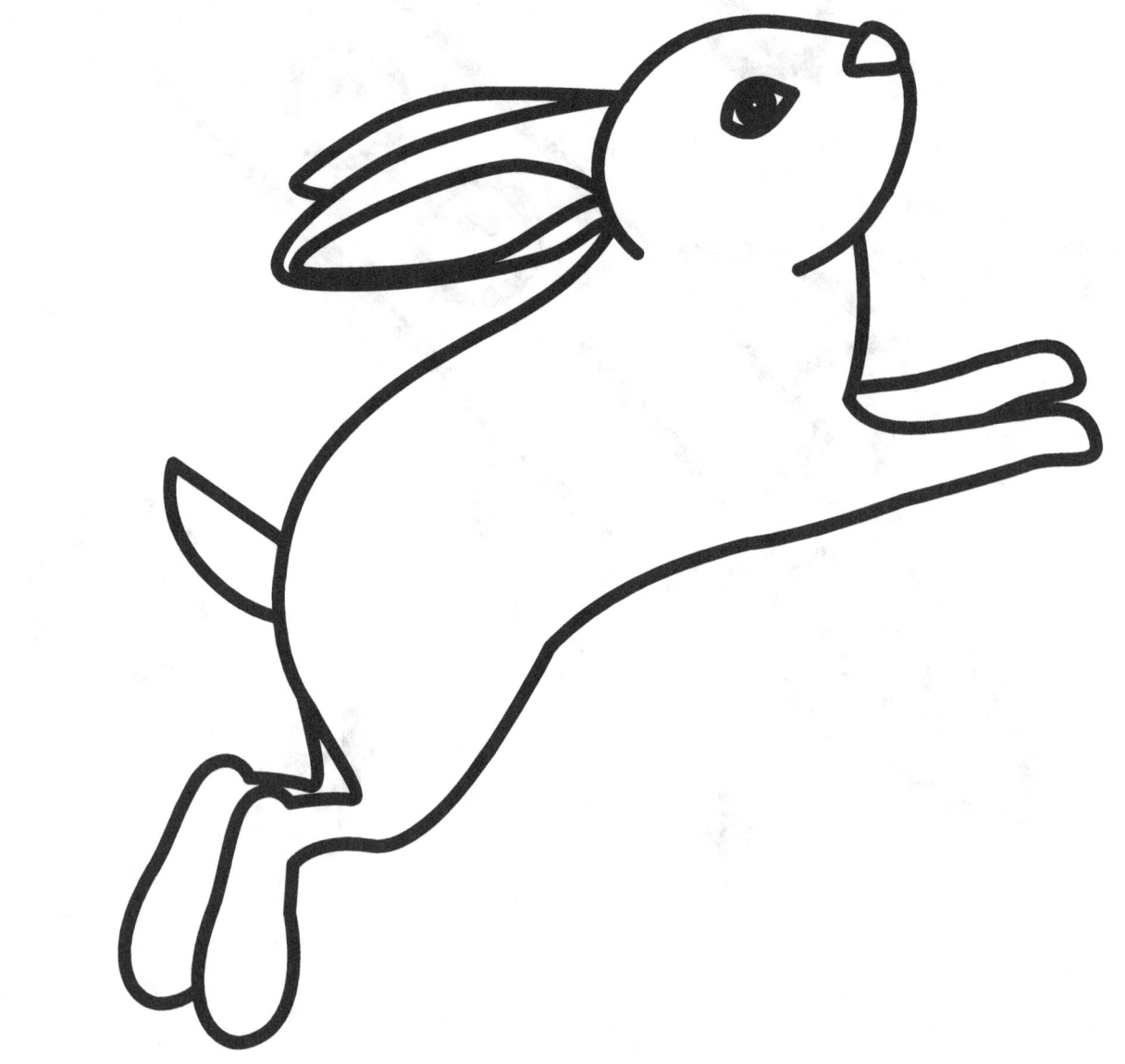

rabbit

Name:

Rr Rr Rr

Rr Rr Rr

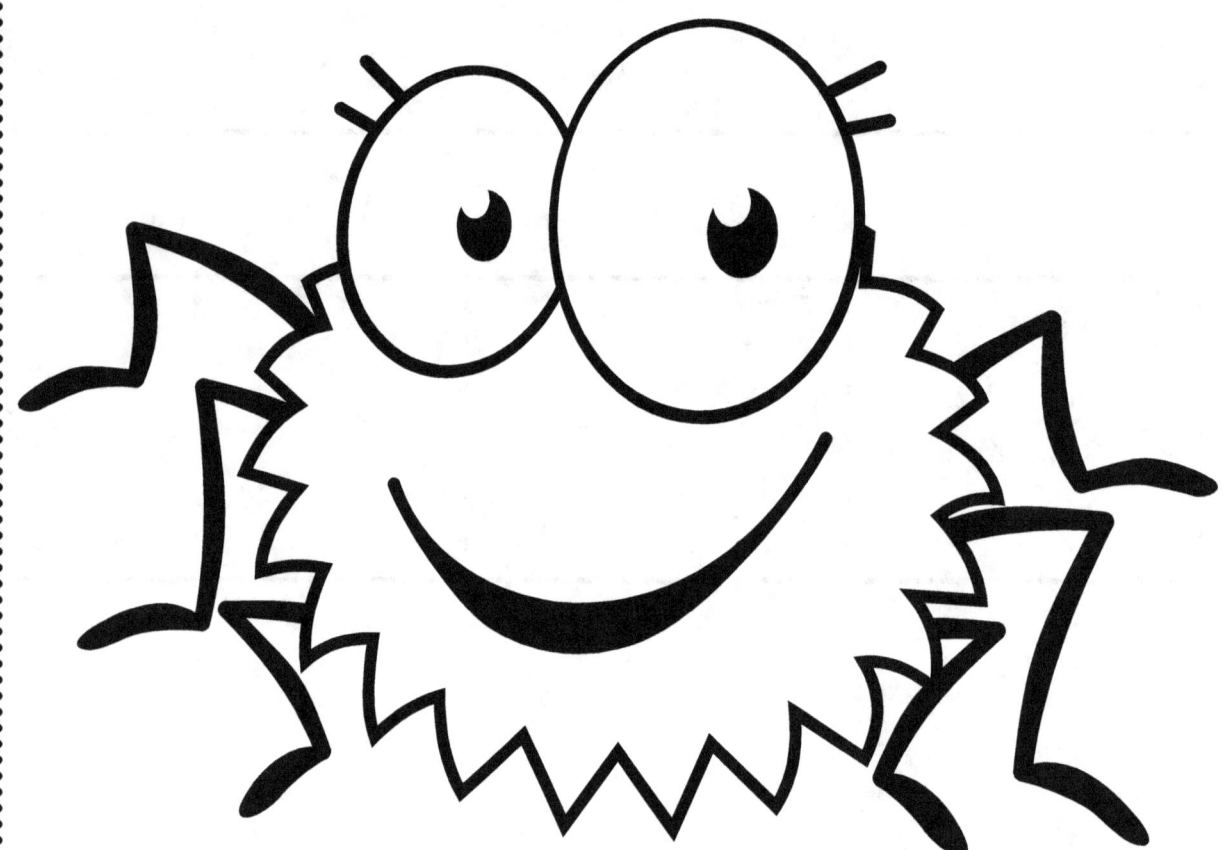

Spider

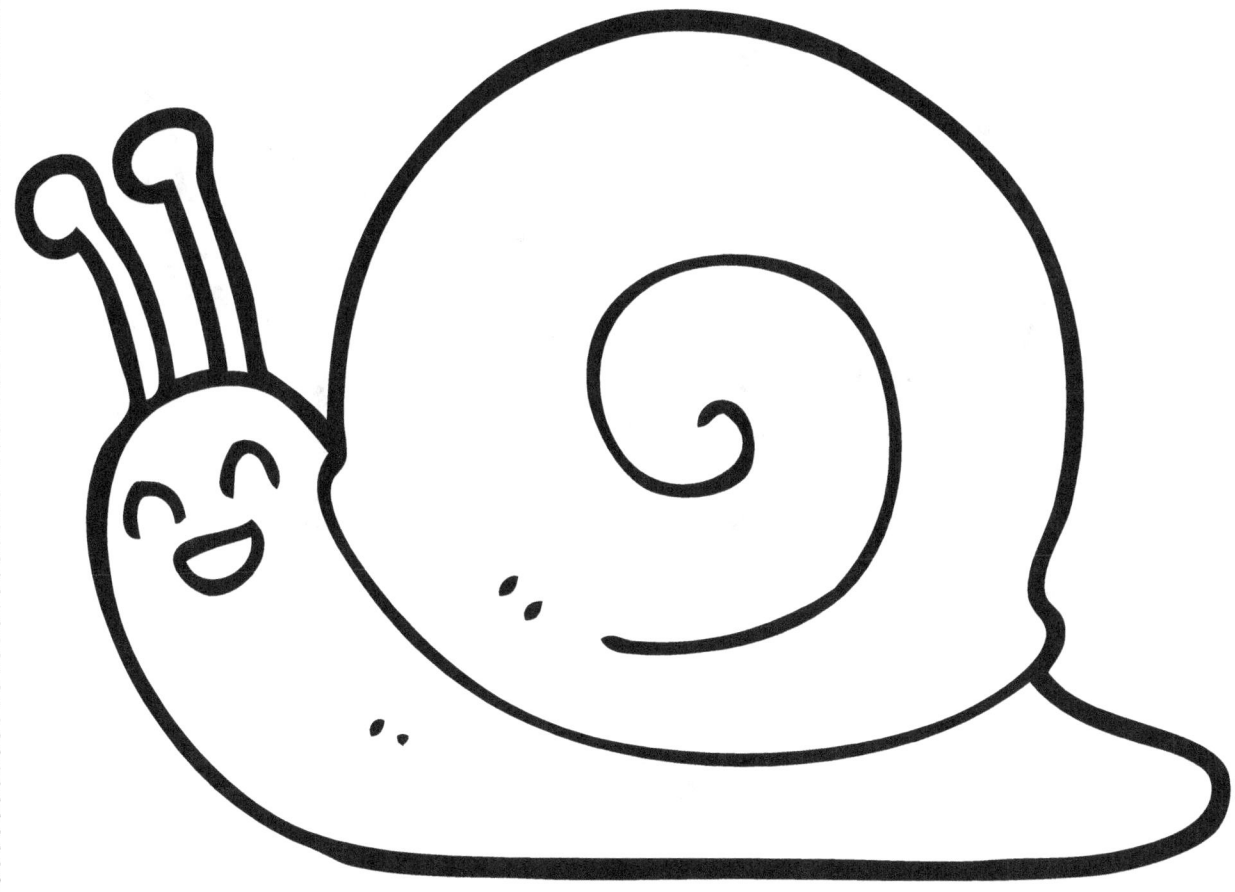

Snail

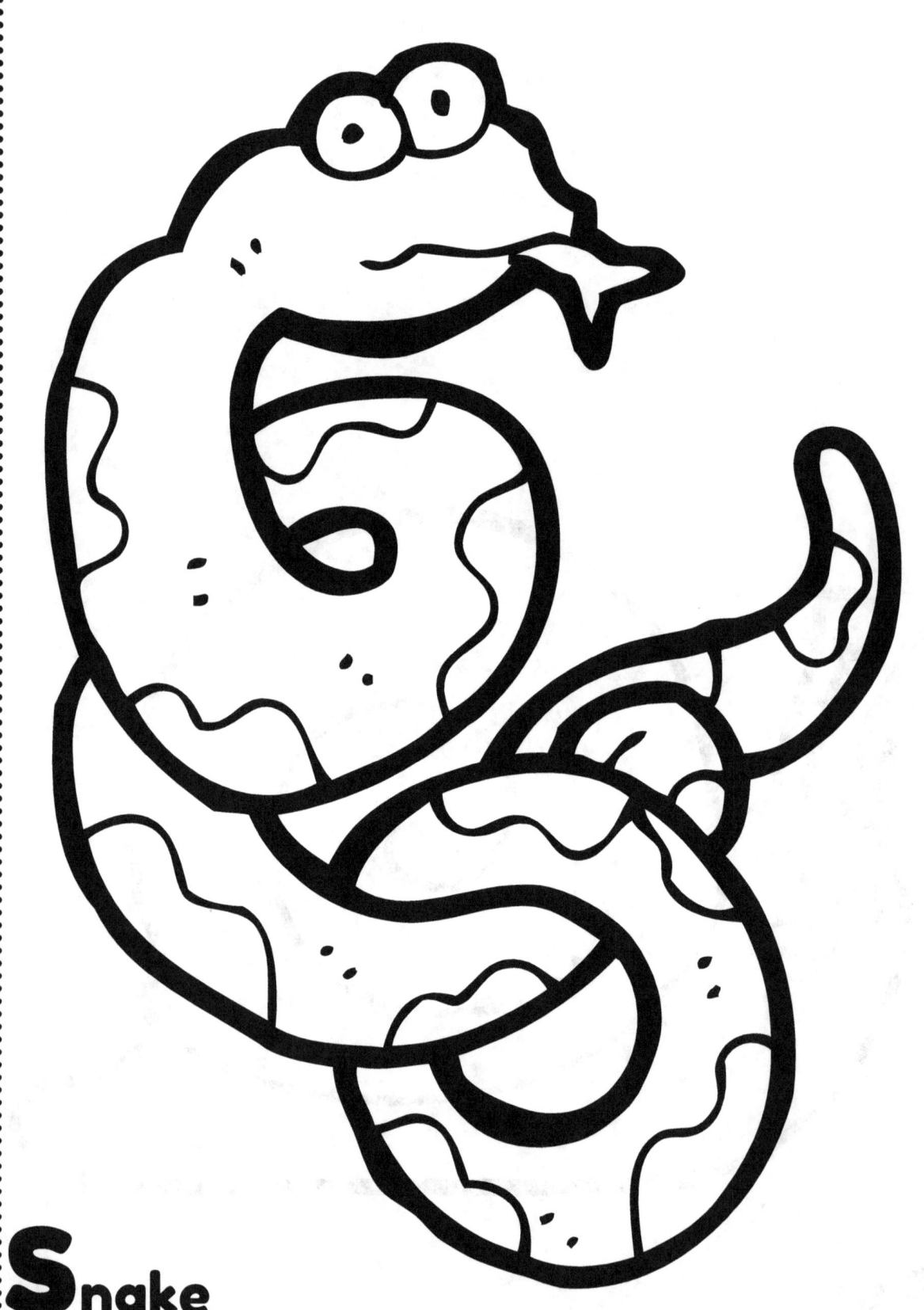

Snake

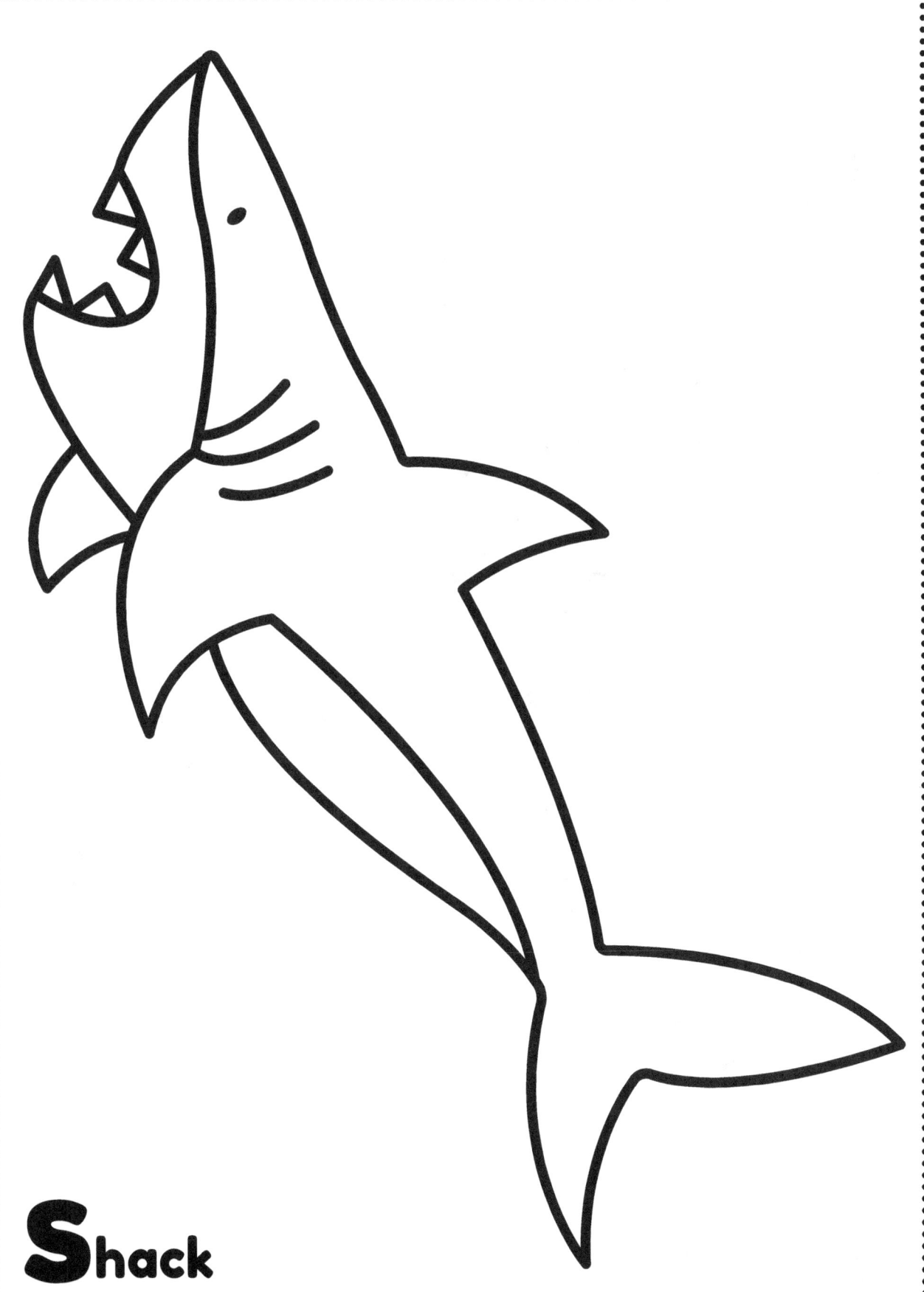

Shack

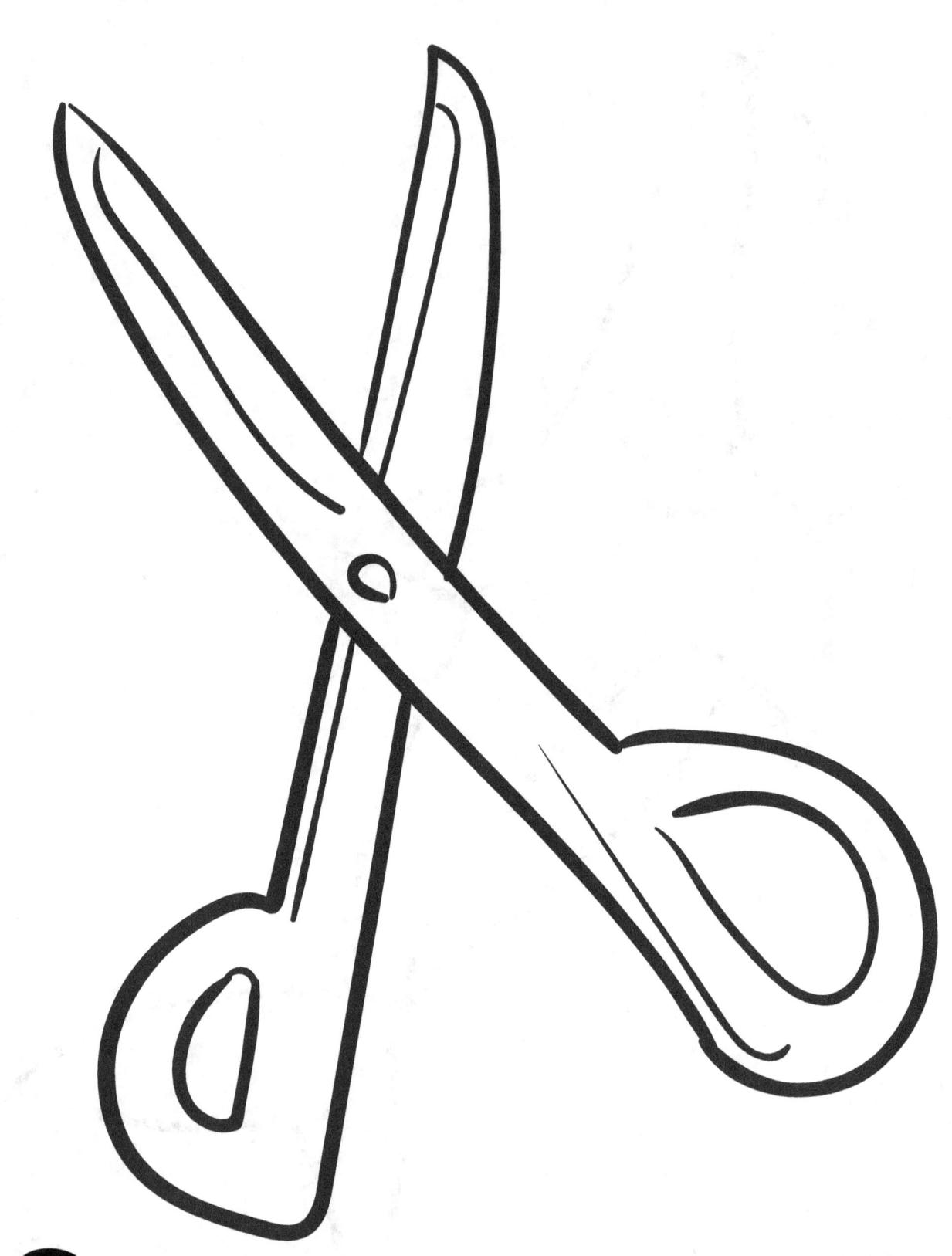

Scissors

Name:

Ss Ss Ss

Ss Ss Ss

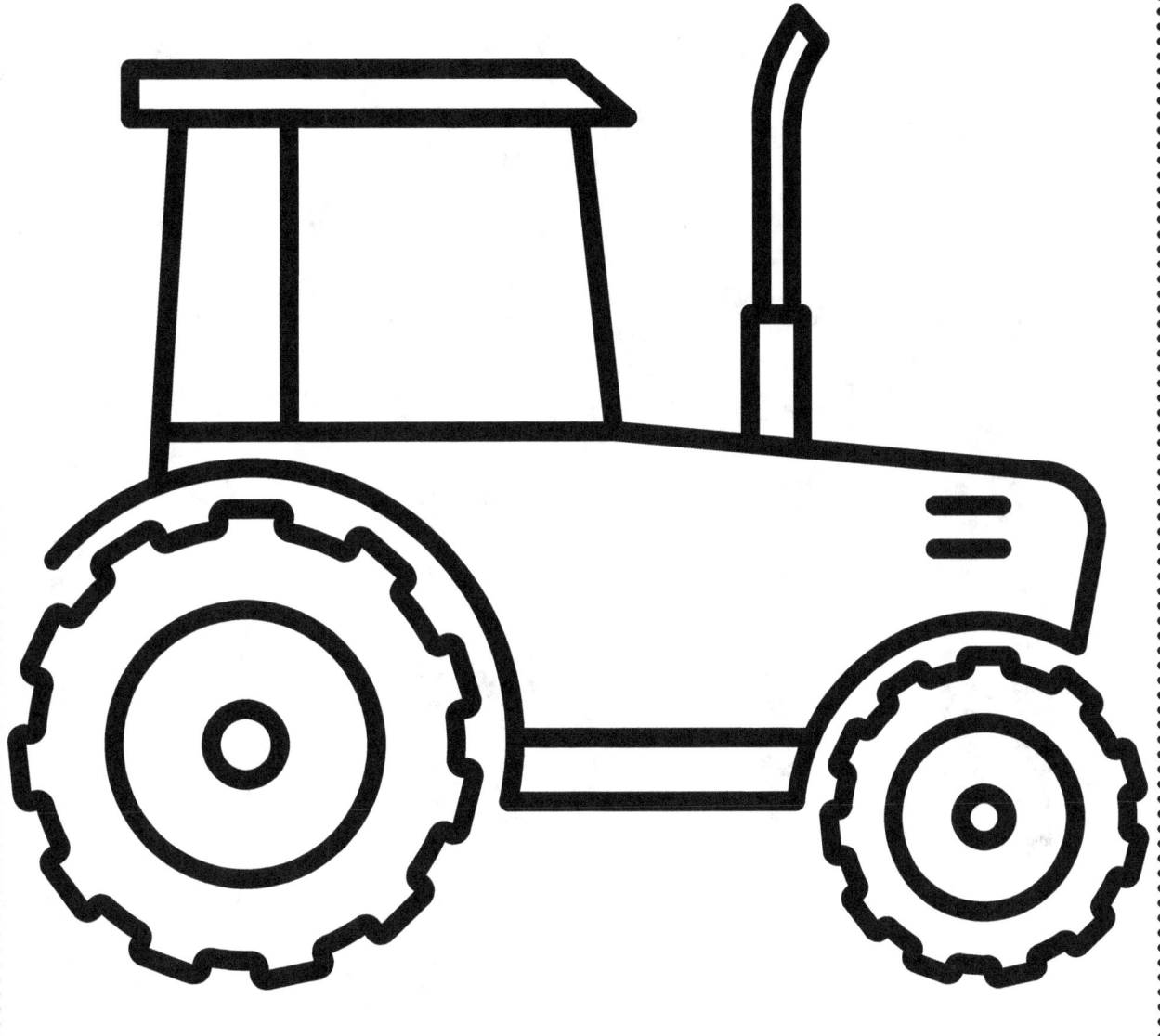

tractor

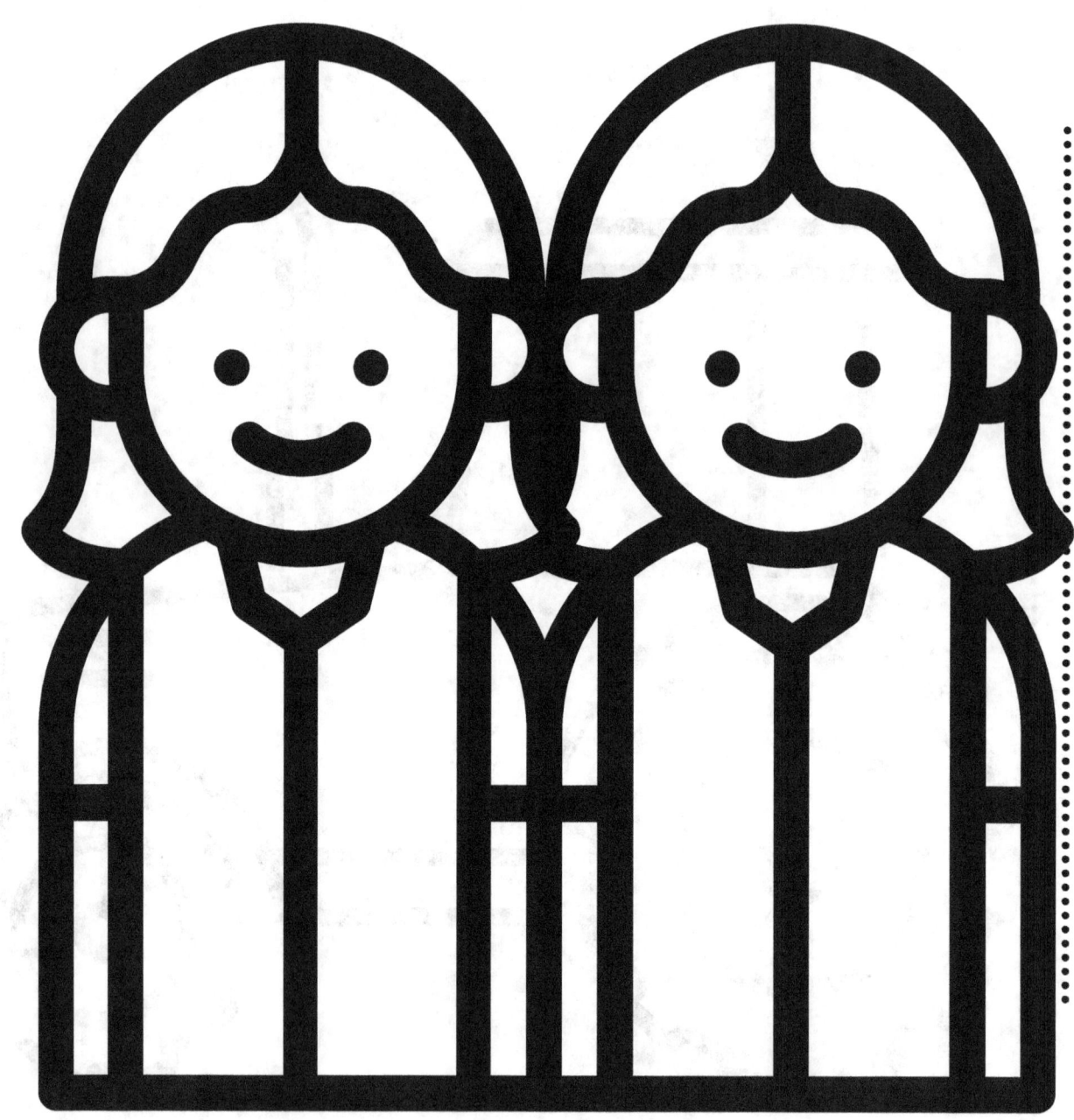

twins

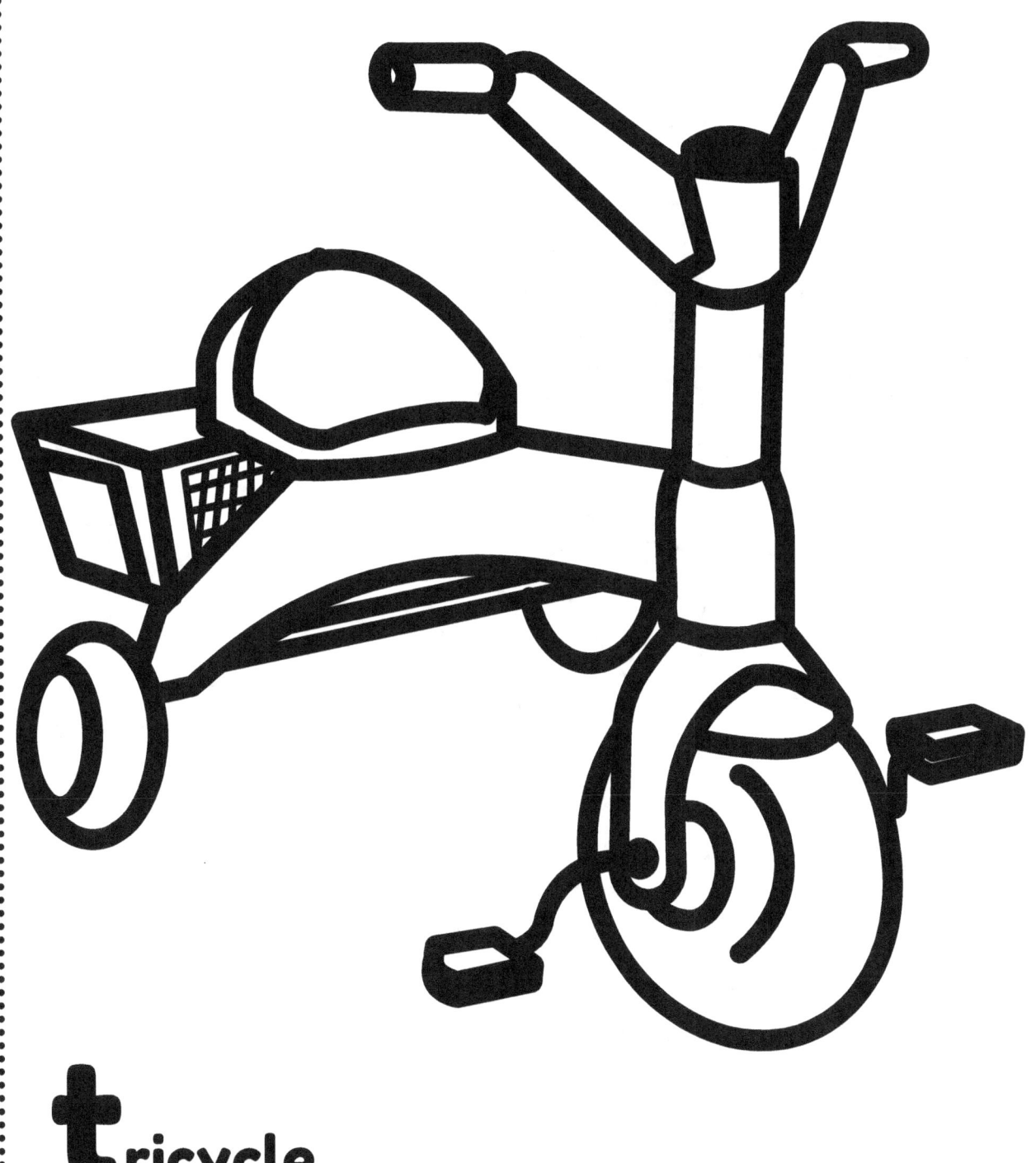

tricycle

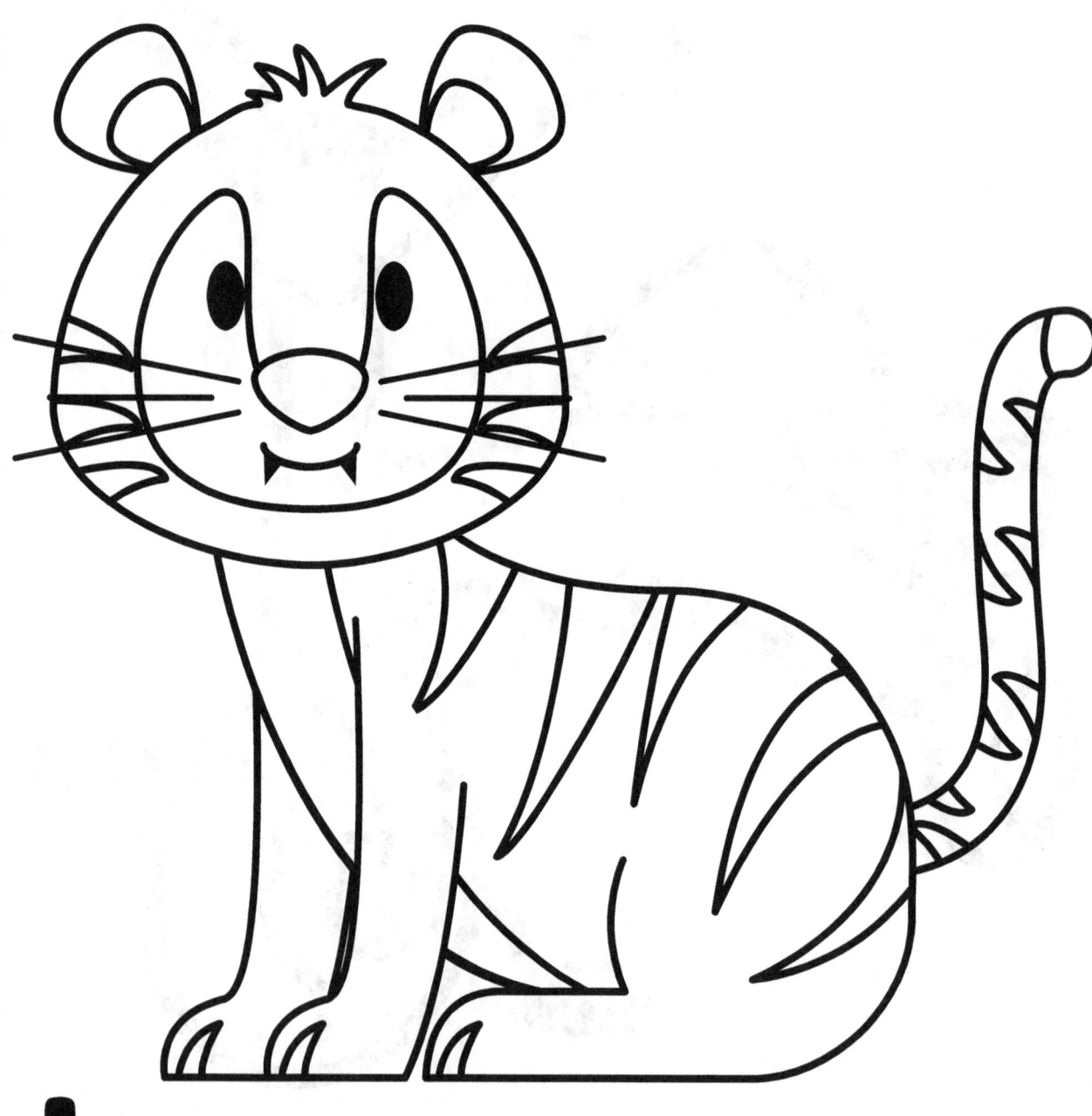

Name:

T T T T

T T T T

u tensils

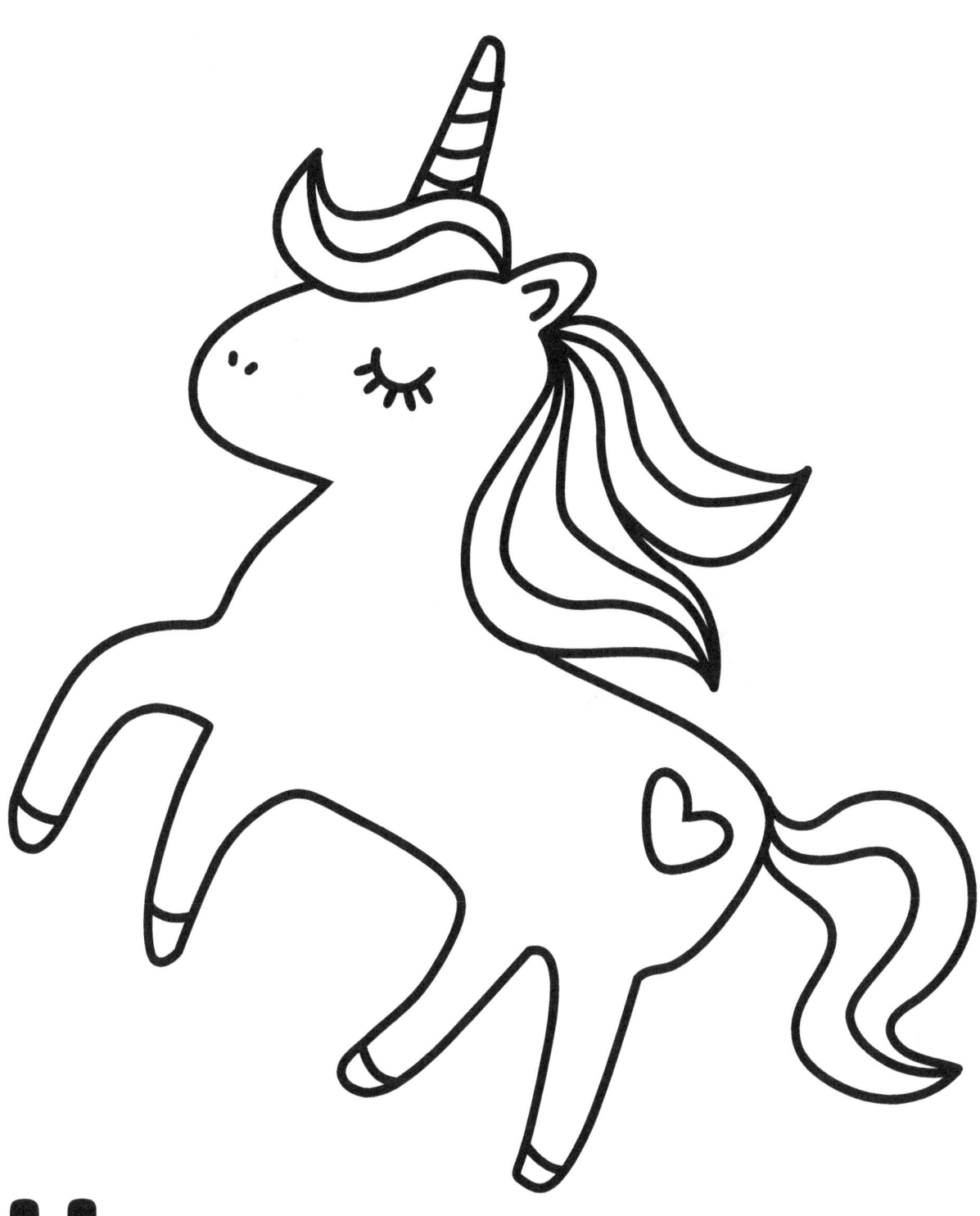

unicorn

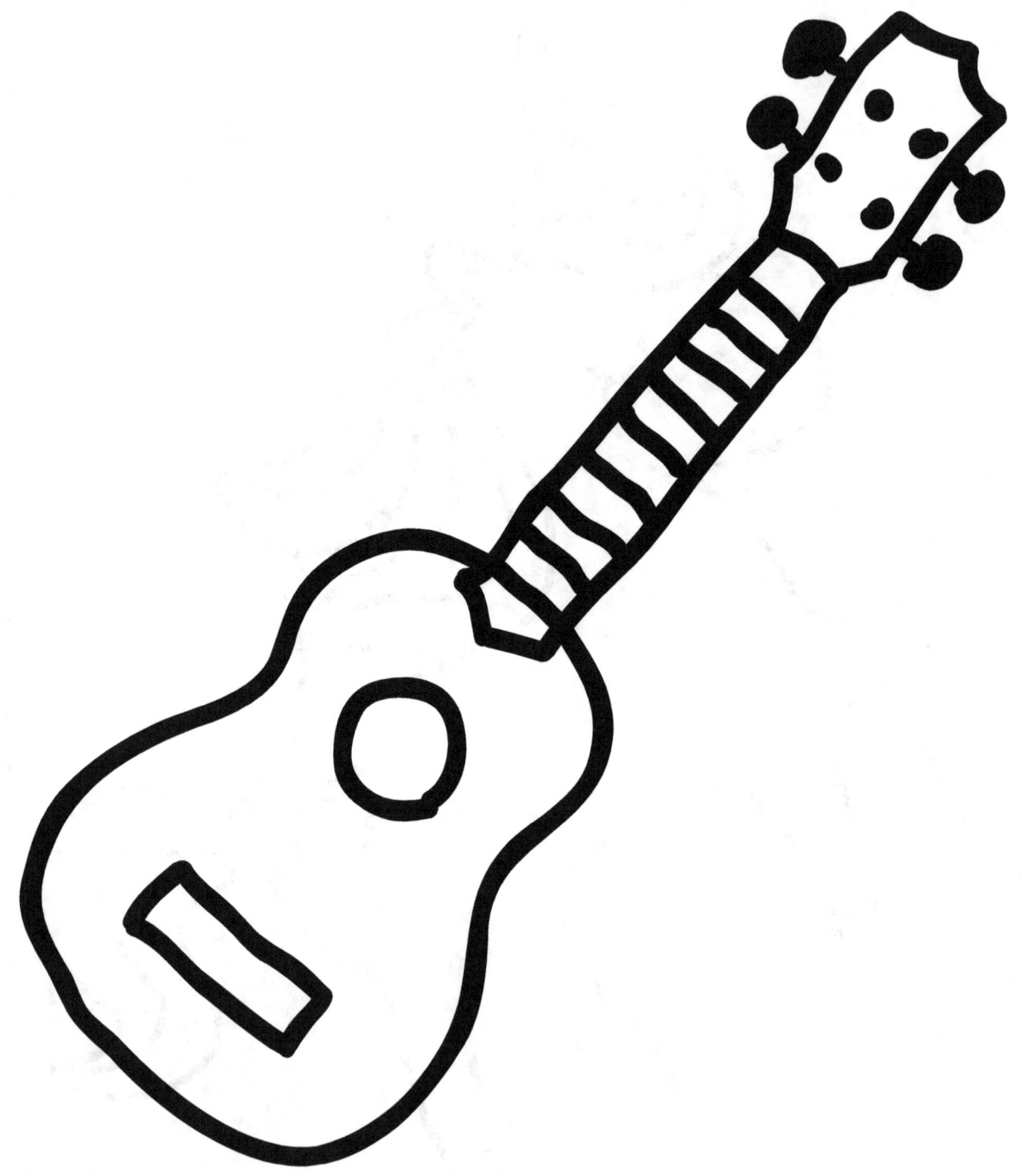

Ukelele

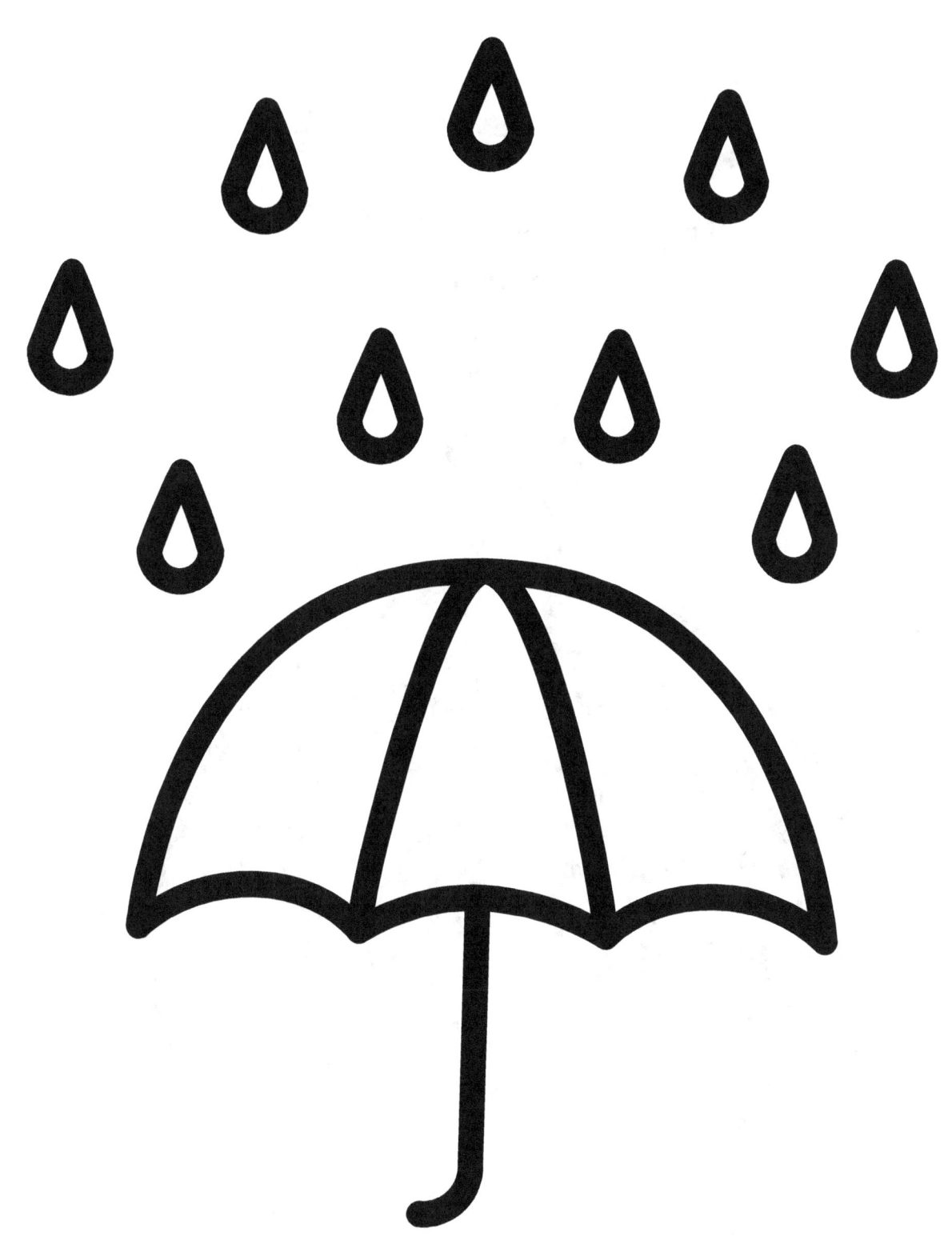

Umbrella

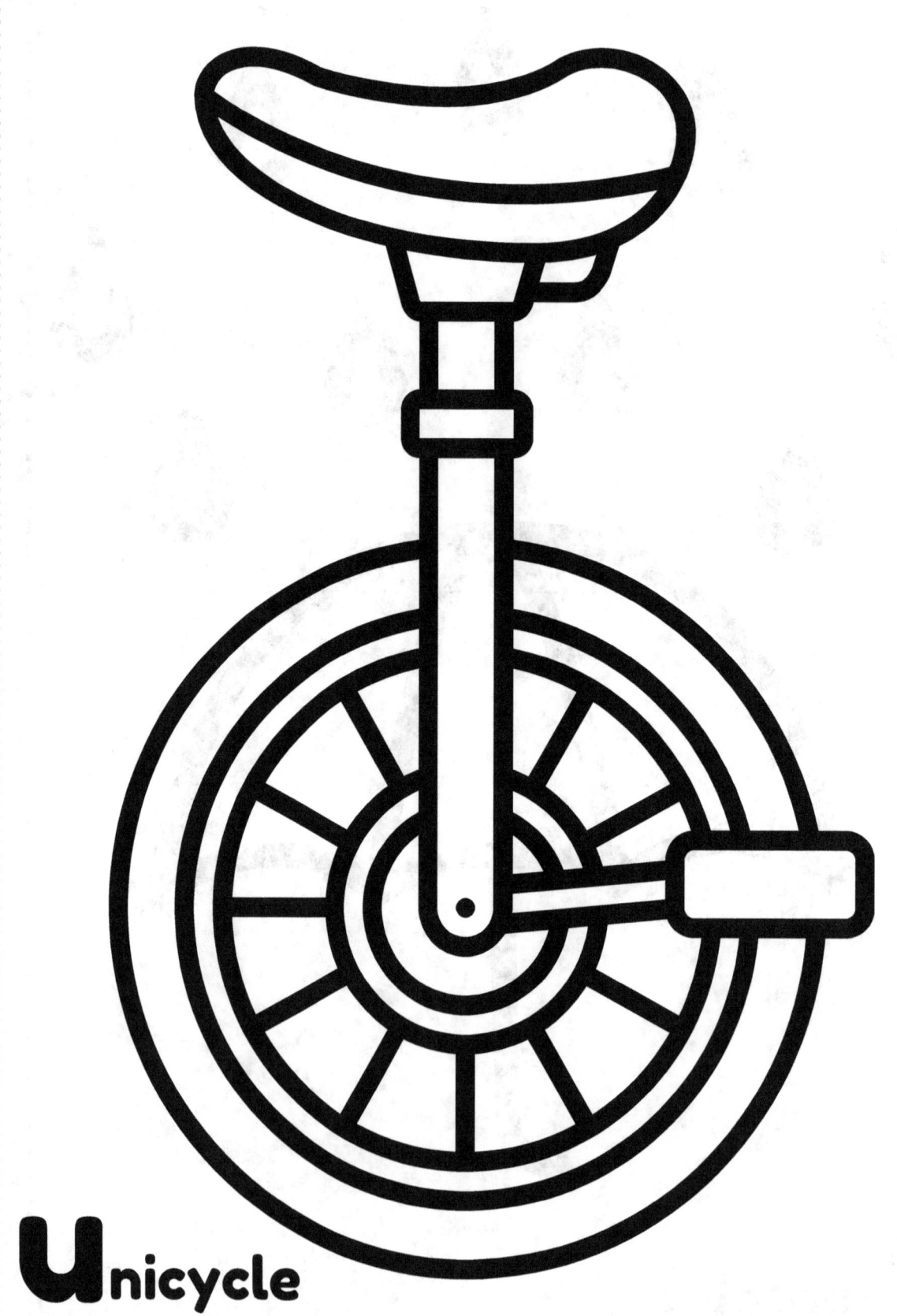

Name:

Uu Uu Uu Uu Uu Uu

Uu Uu Uu Uu Uu Uu

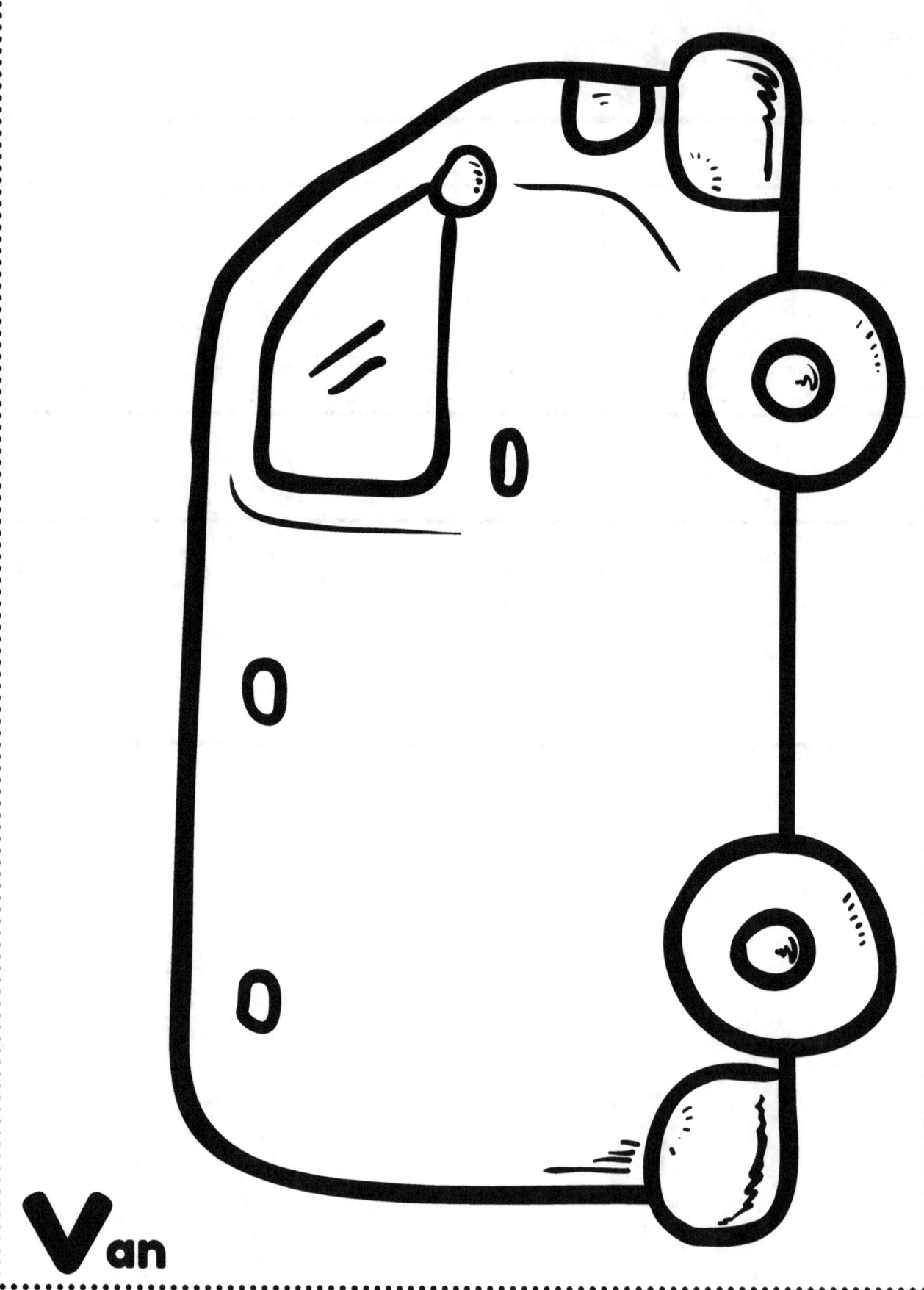

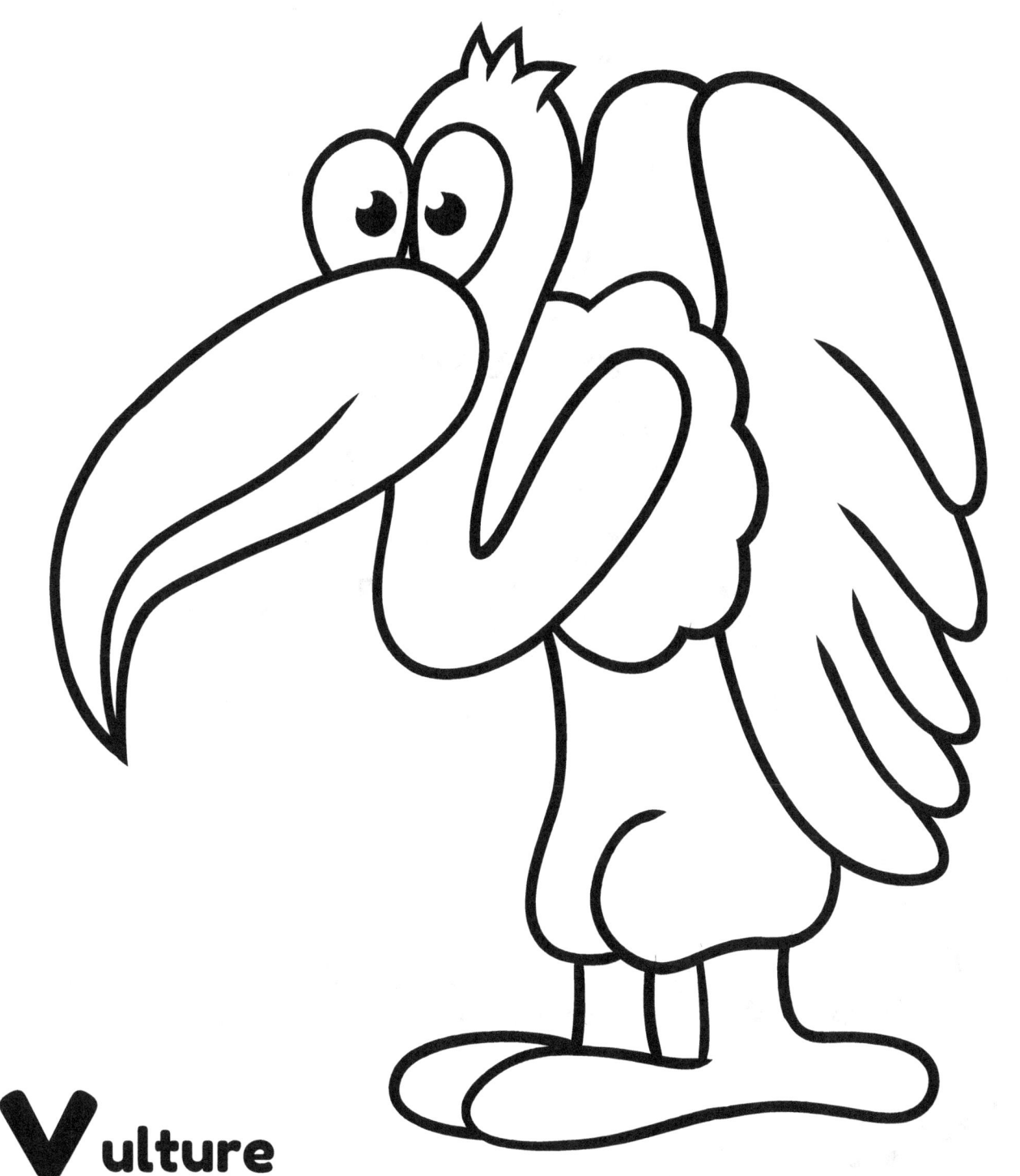

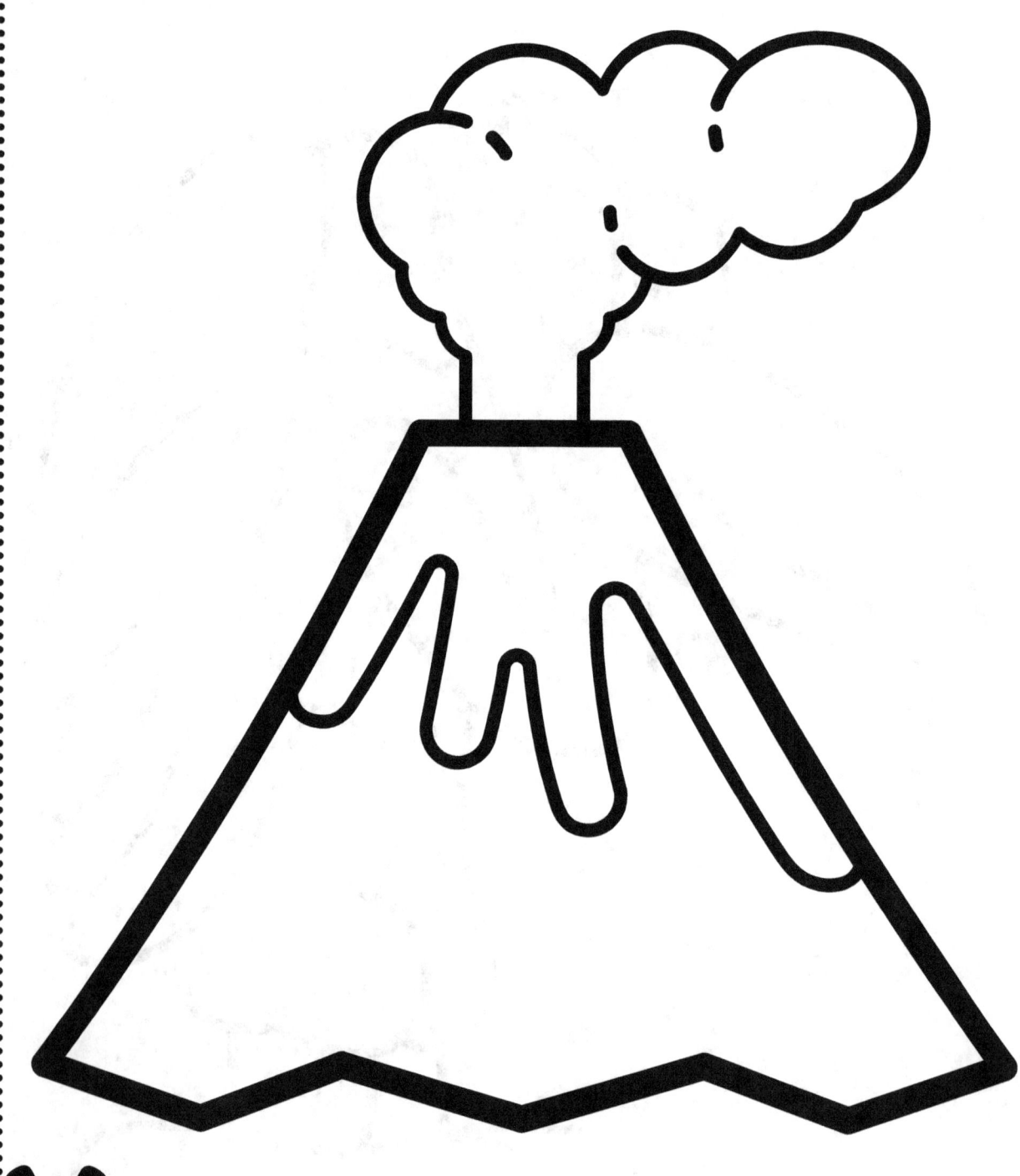

Volcano

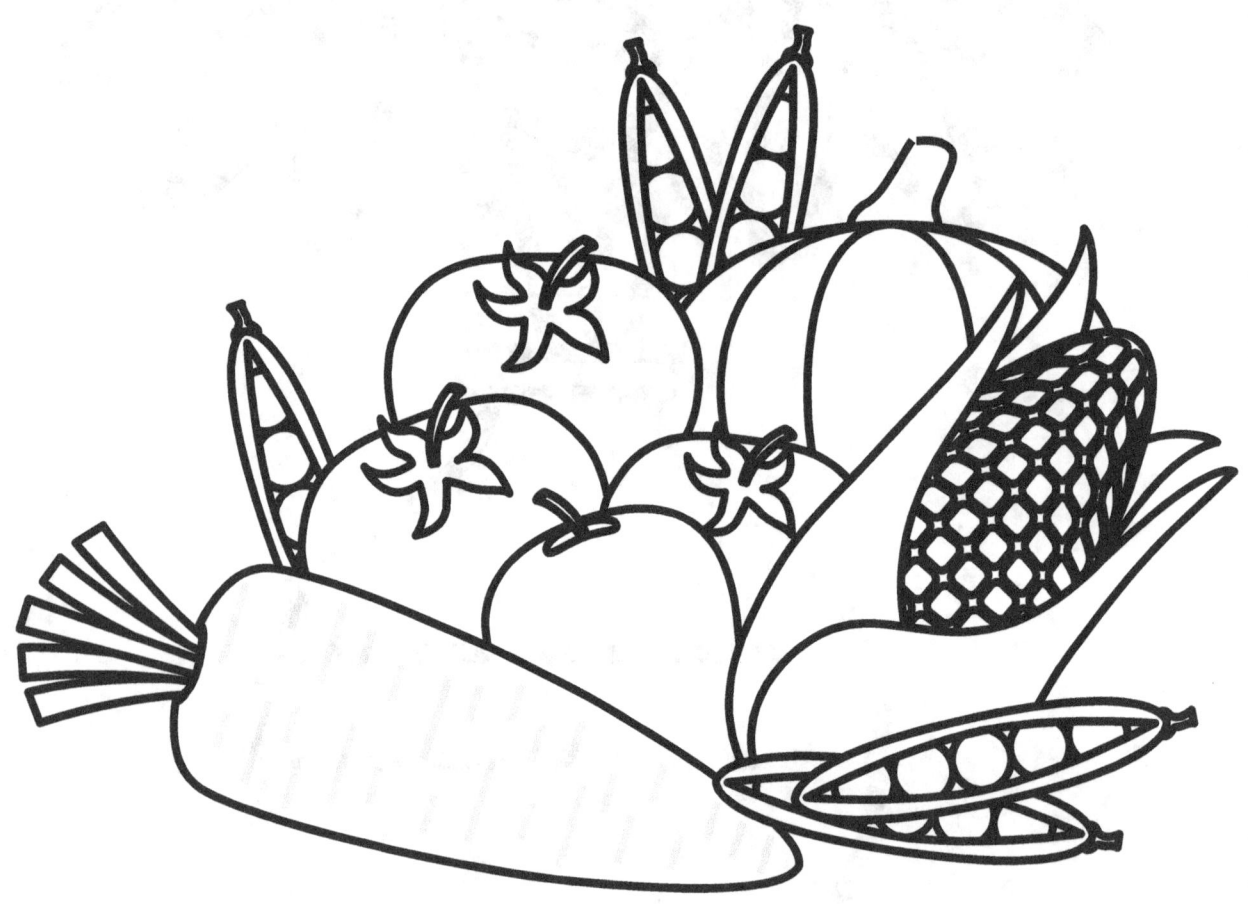

Vegetables

Name:

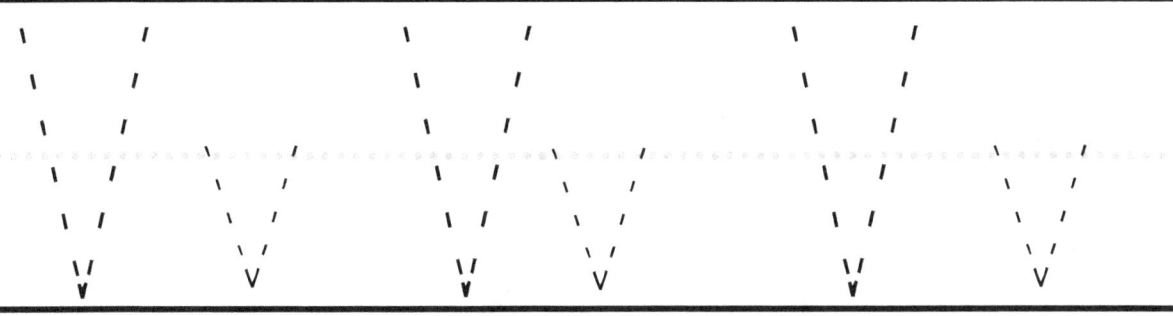

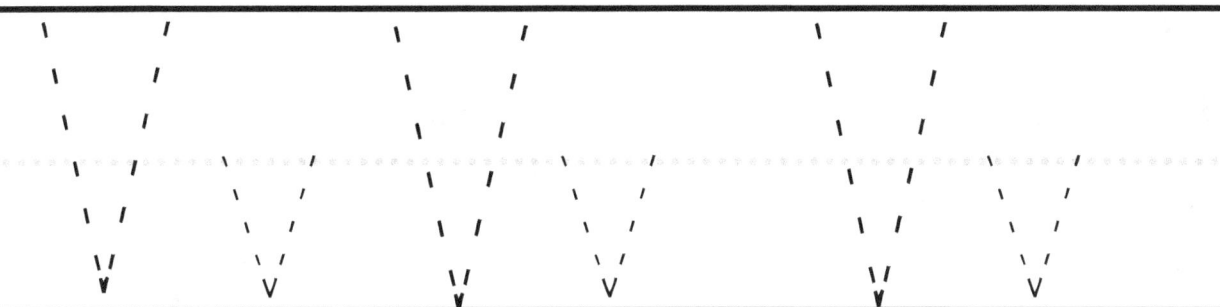

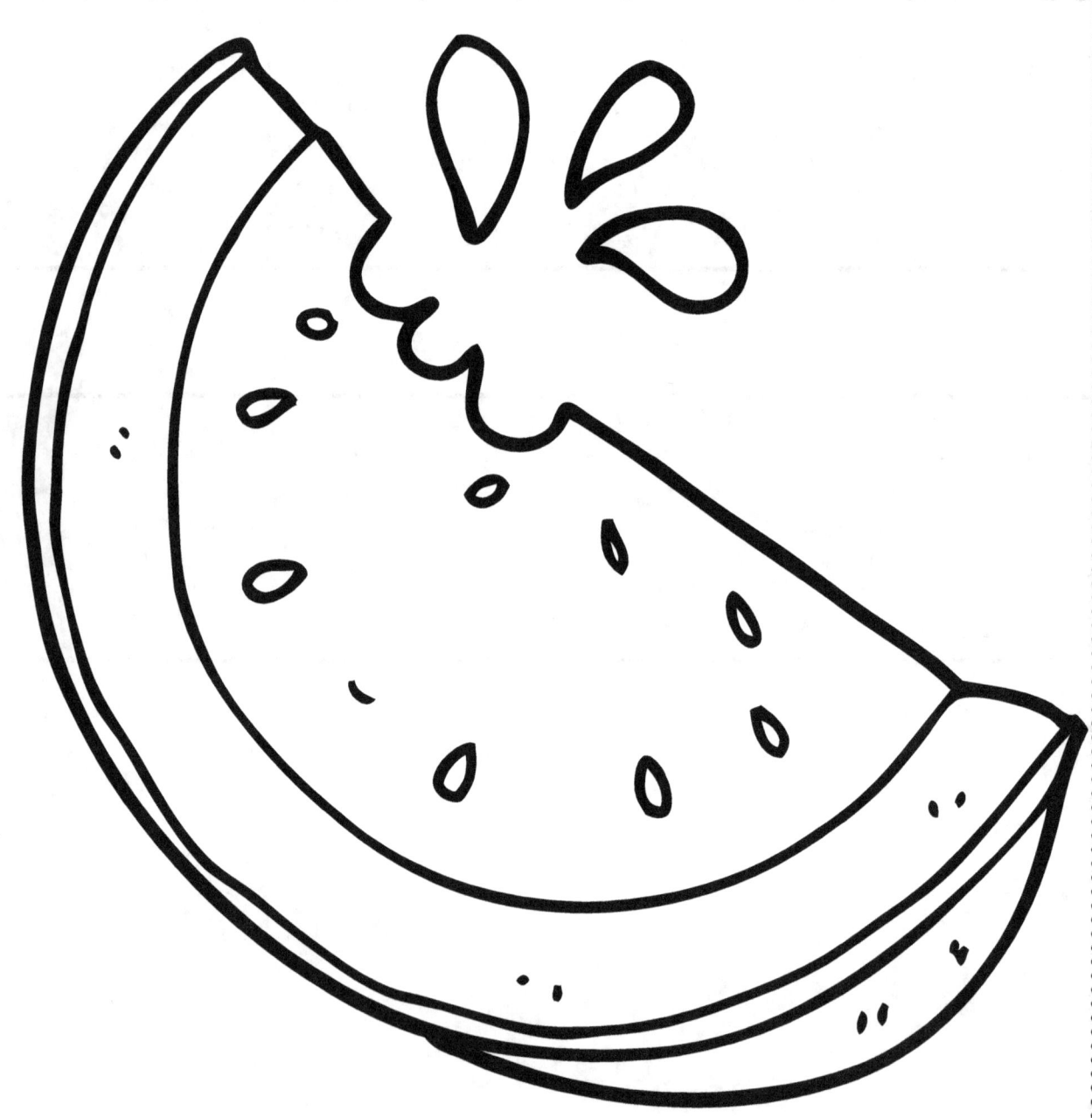

Watermelon

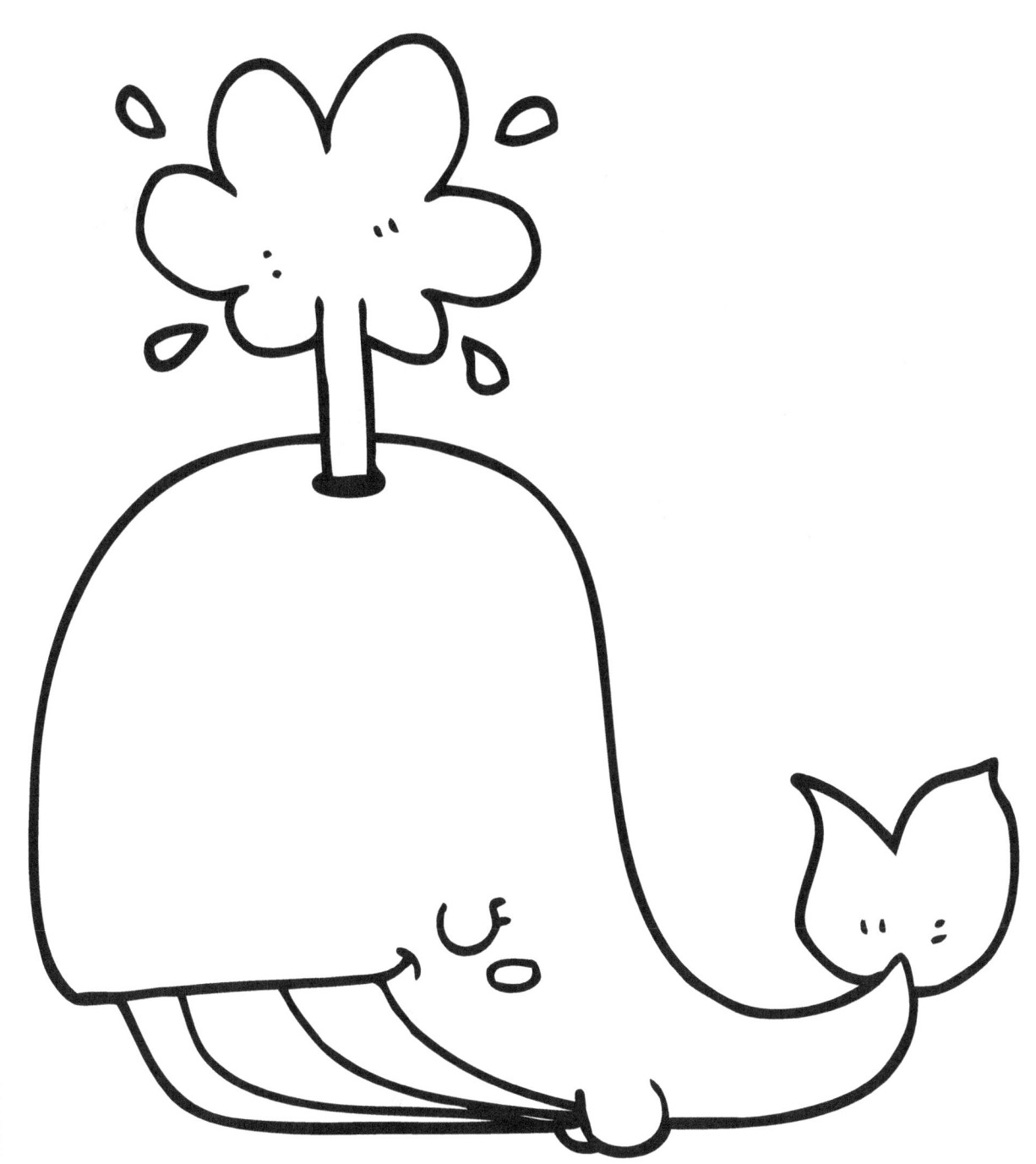

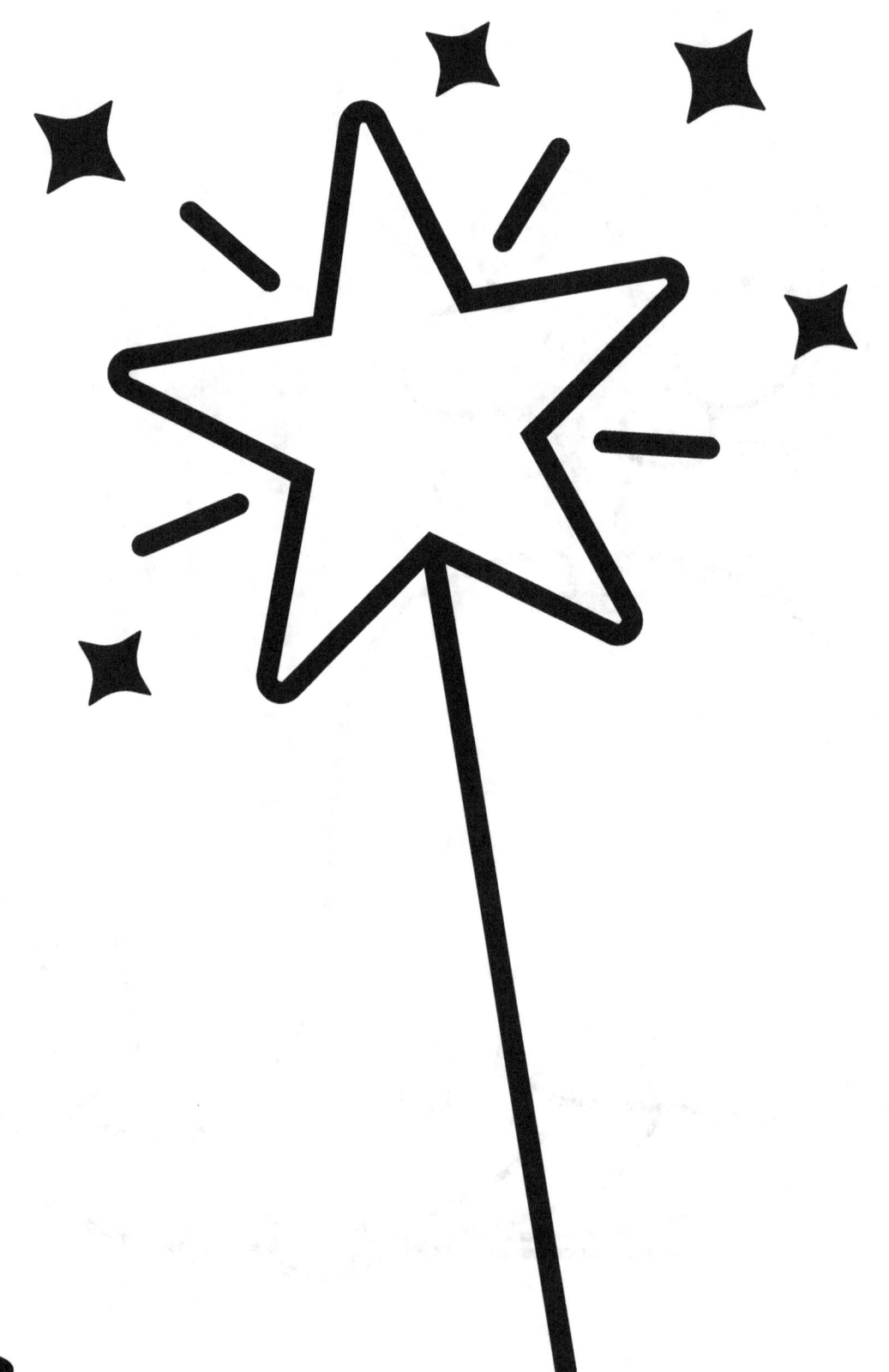

Wand

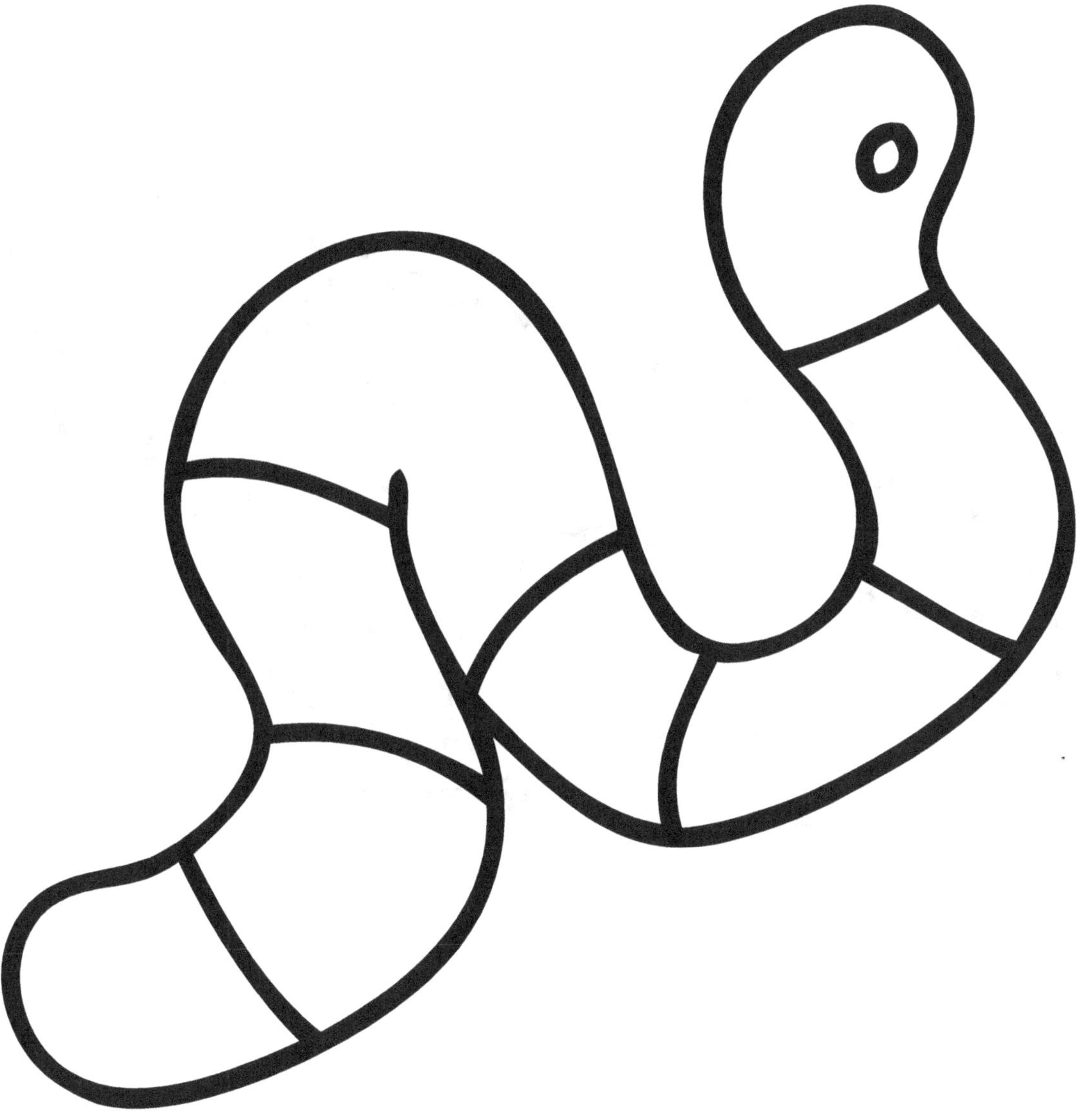

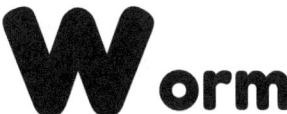

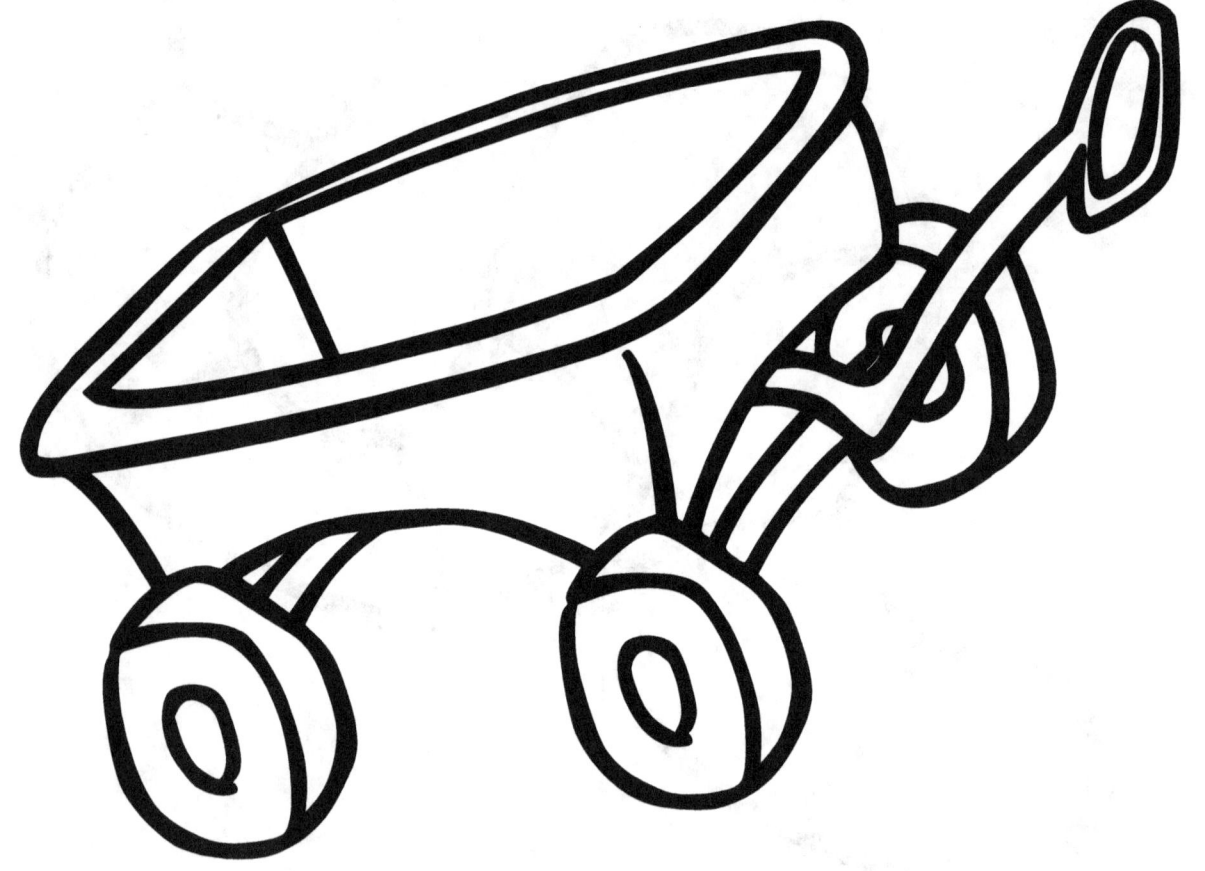

Wagon

Name:

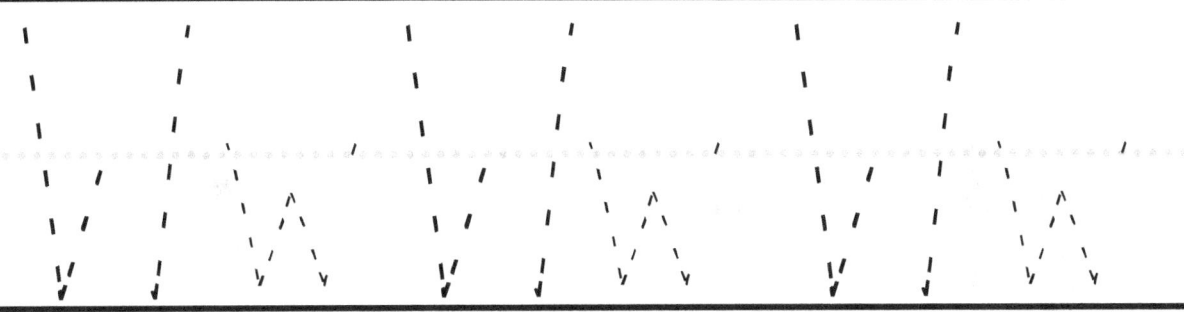

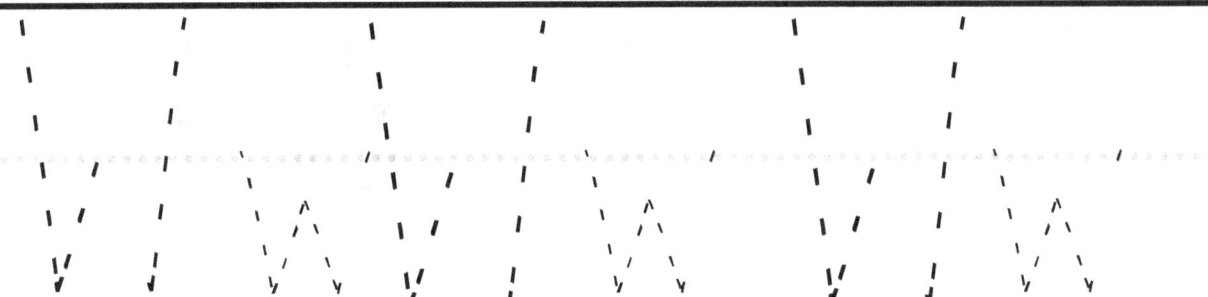

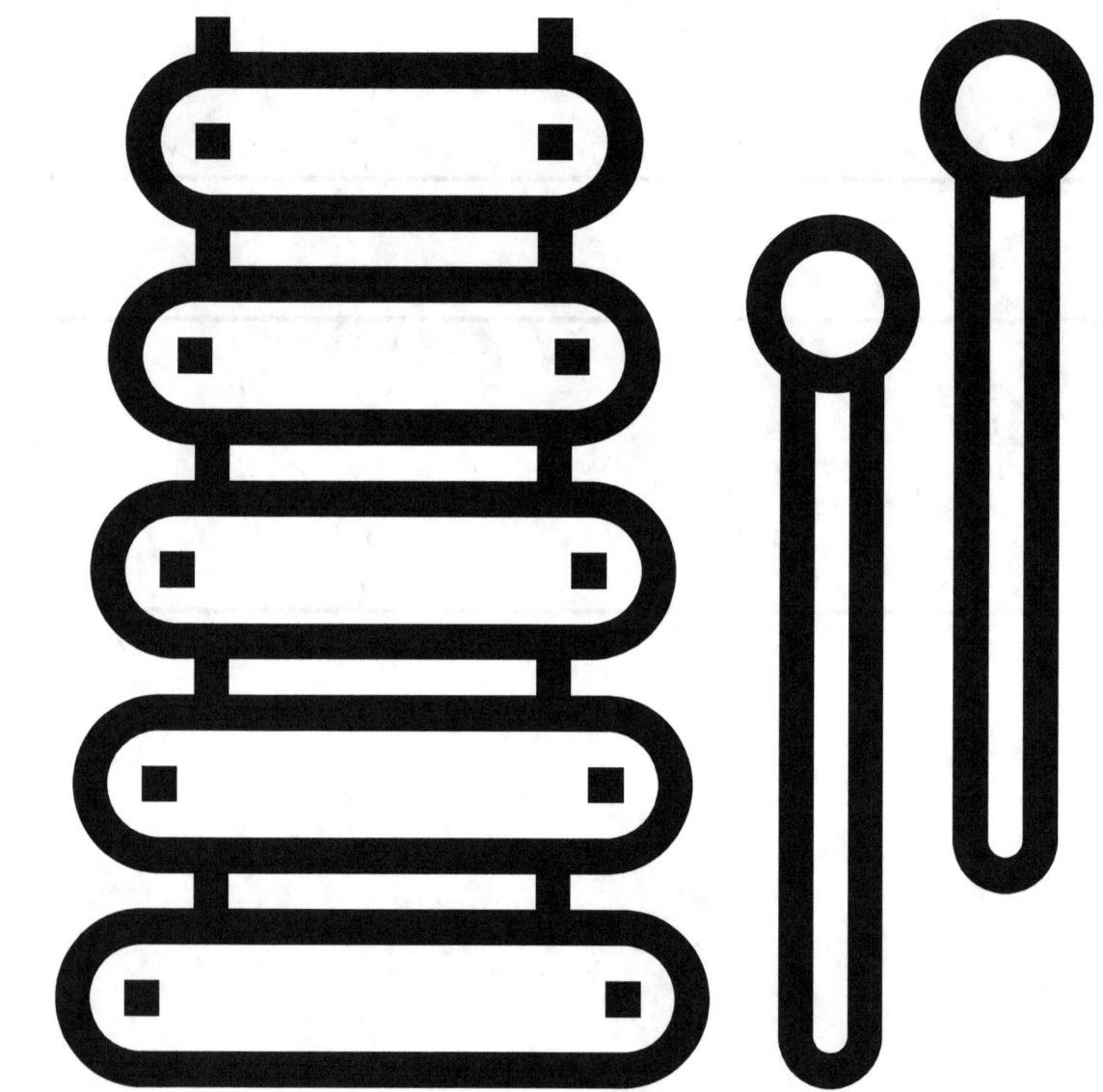

Xylophone

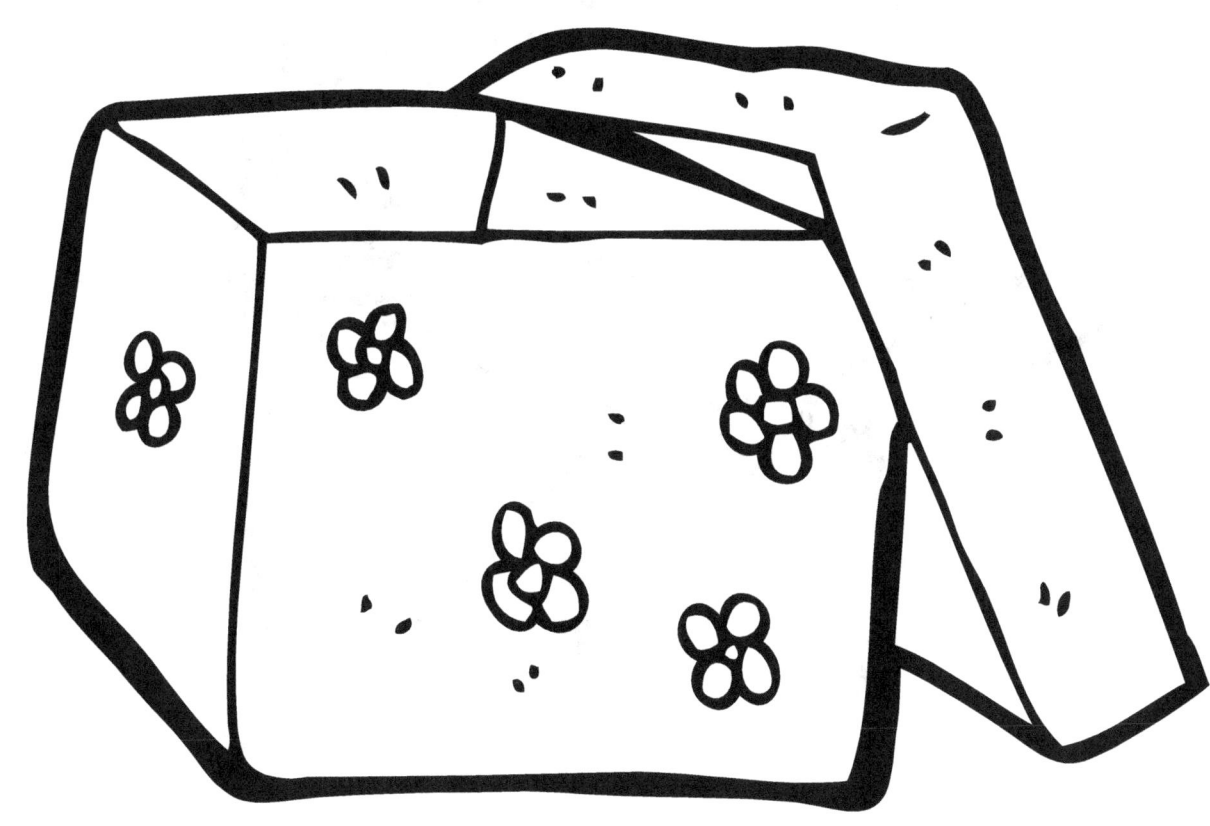

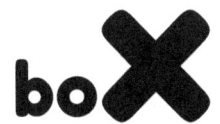

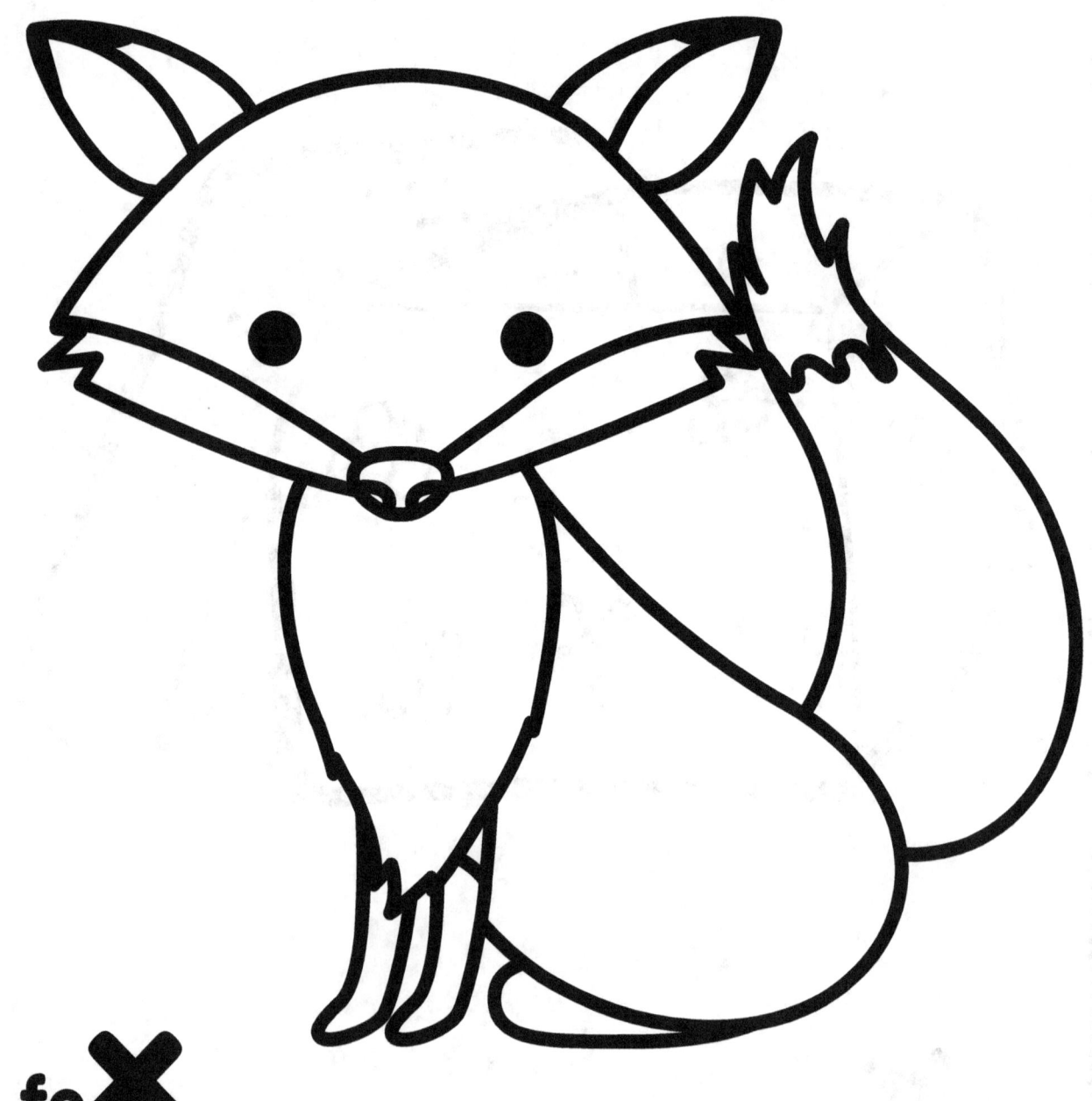

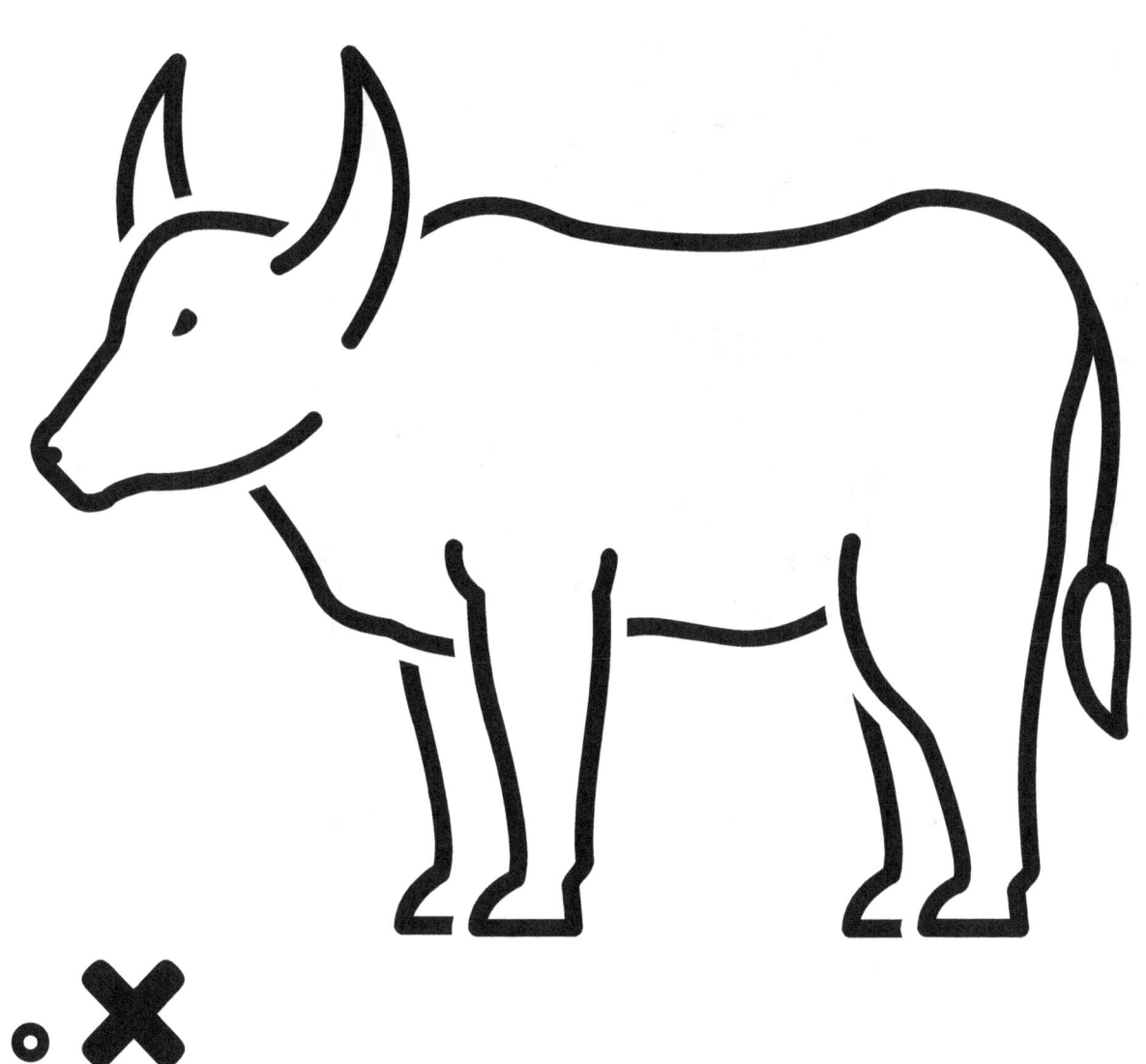

ox

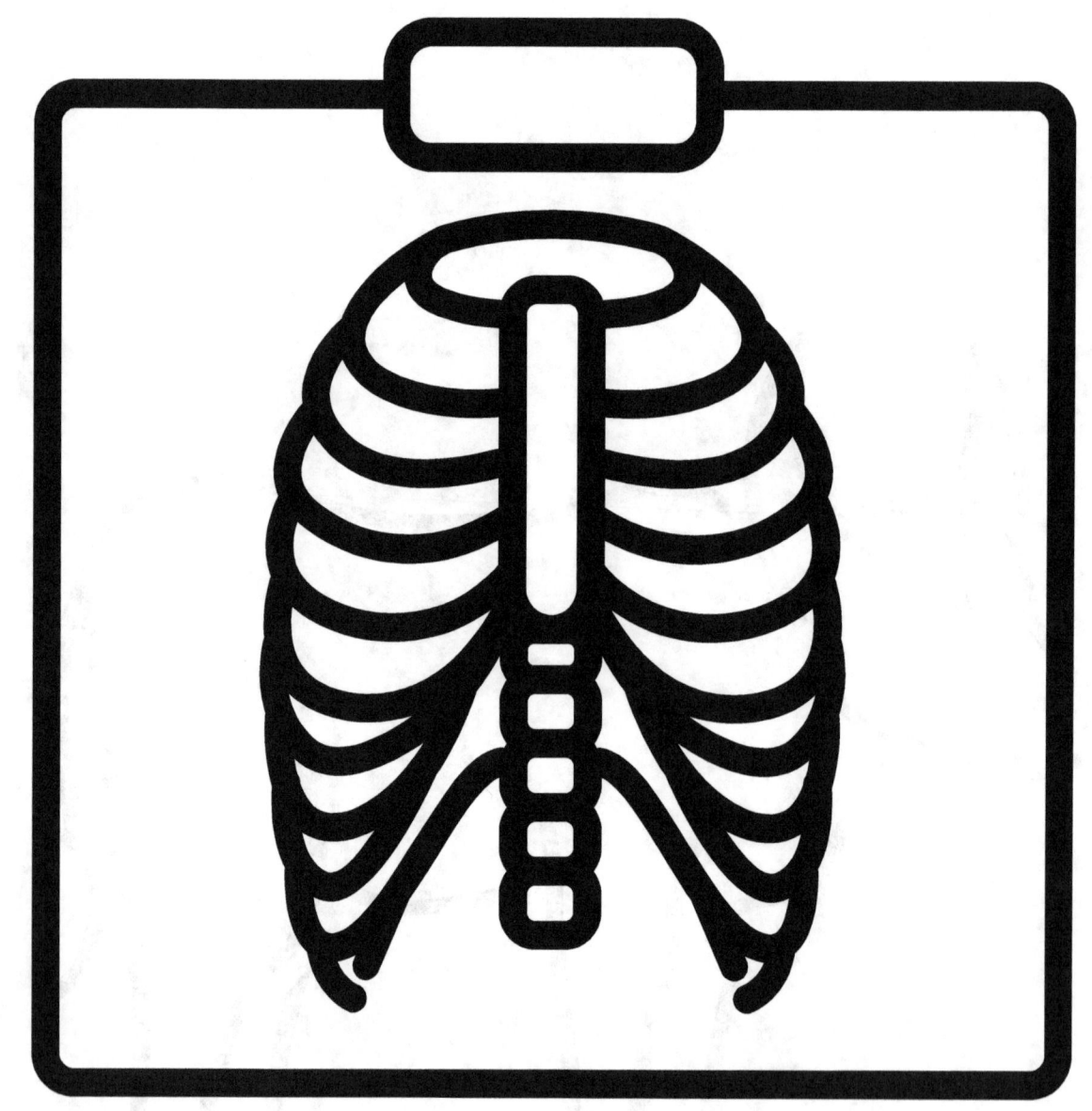

Xray

Name:

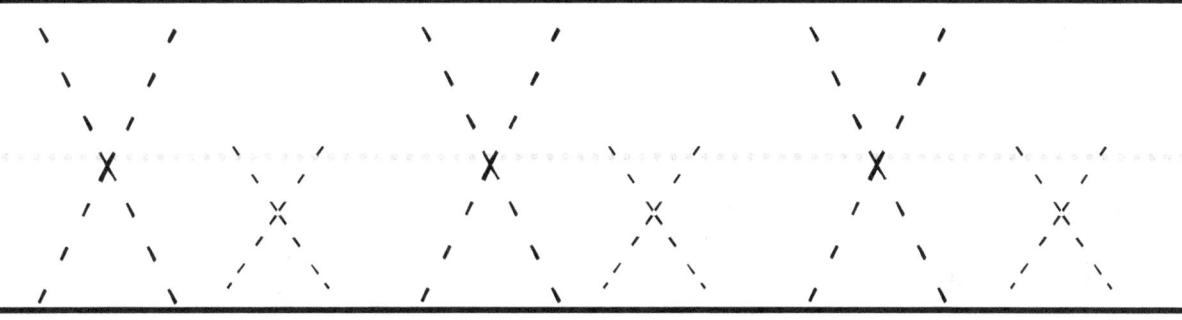

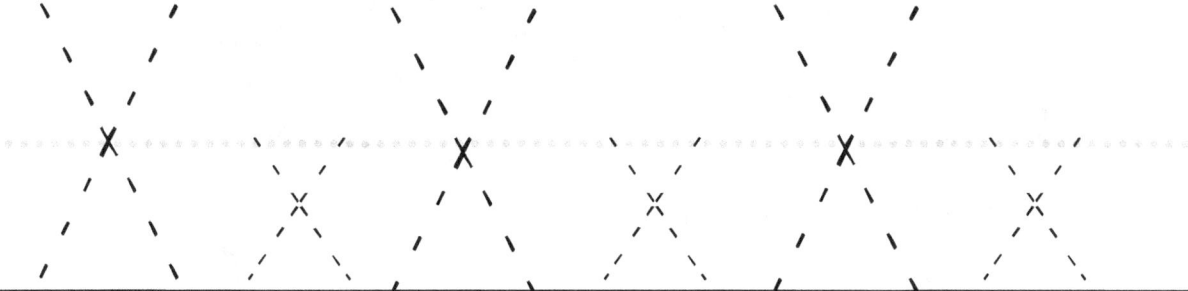

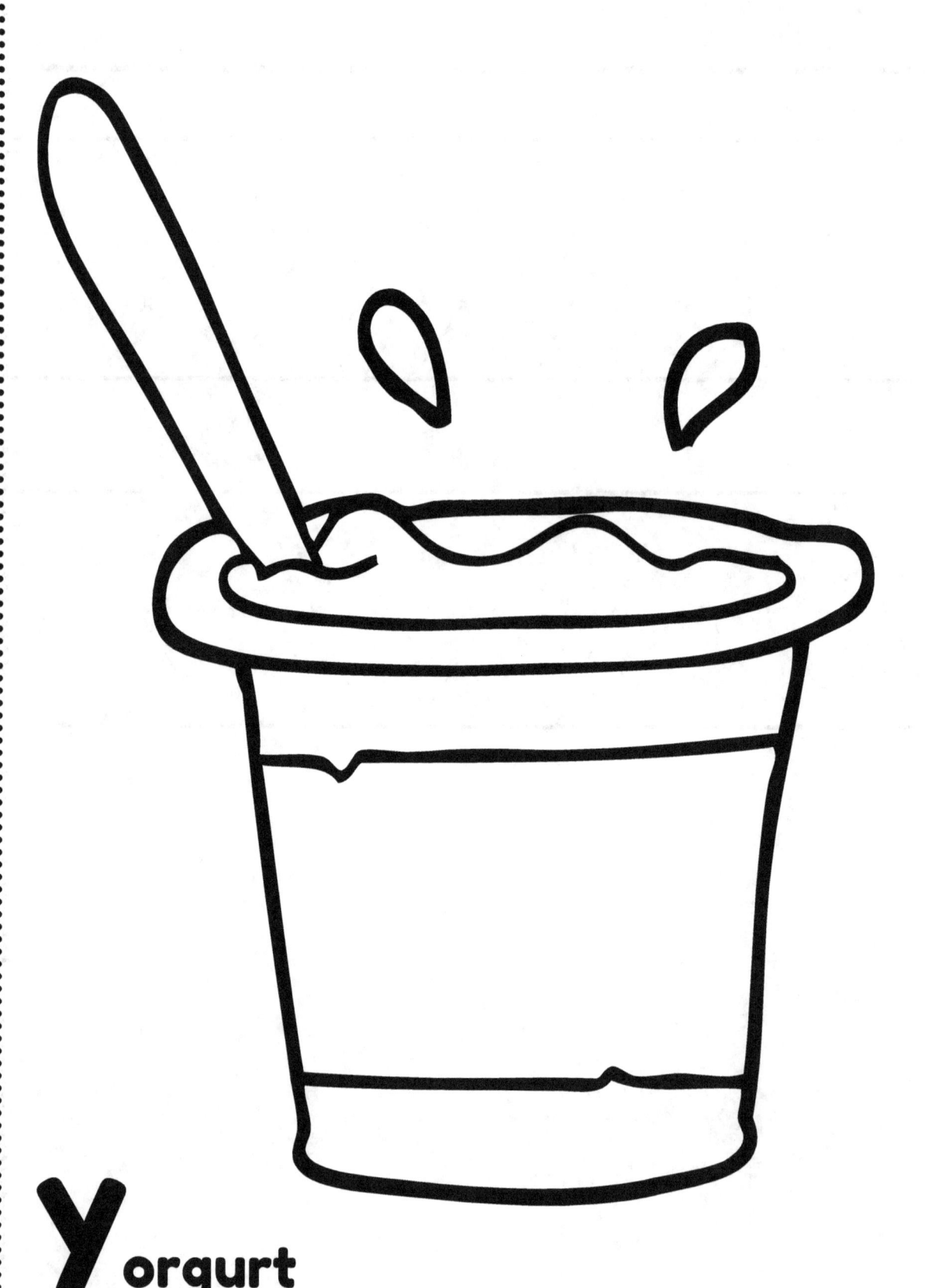

Y orgurt

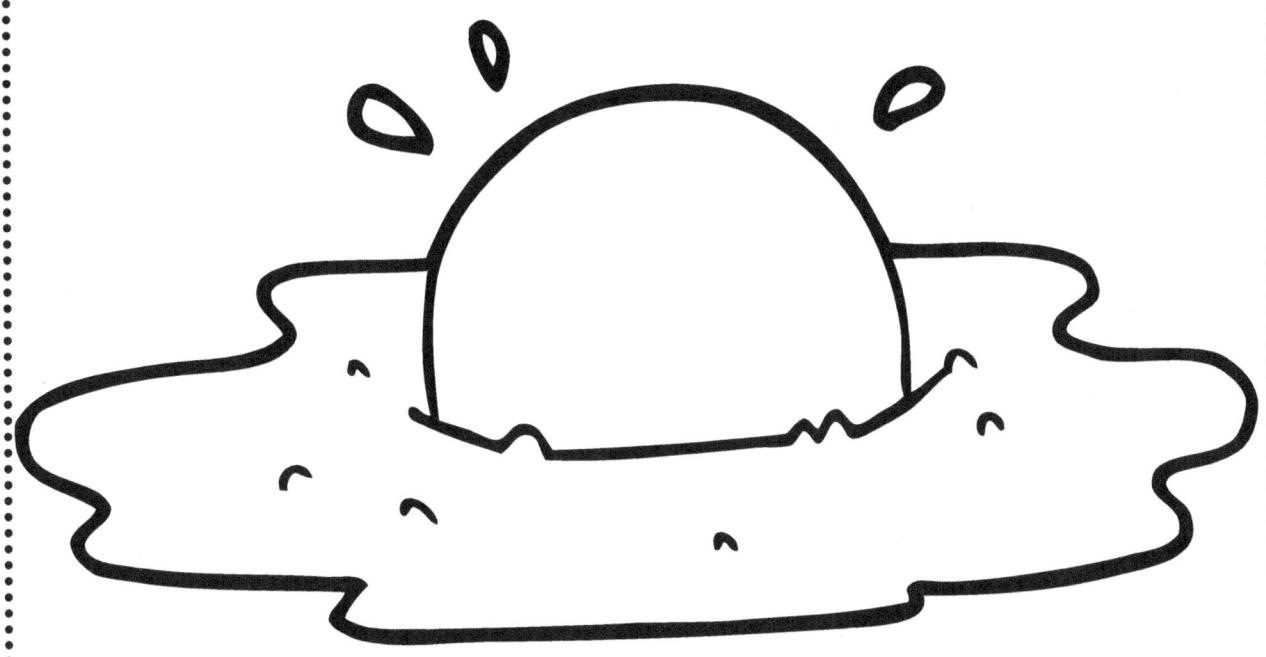

Yolk

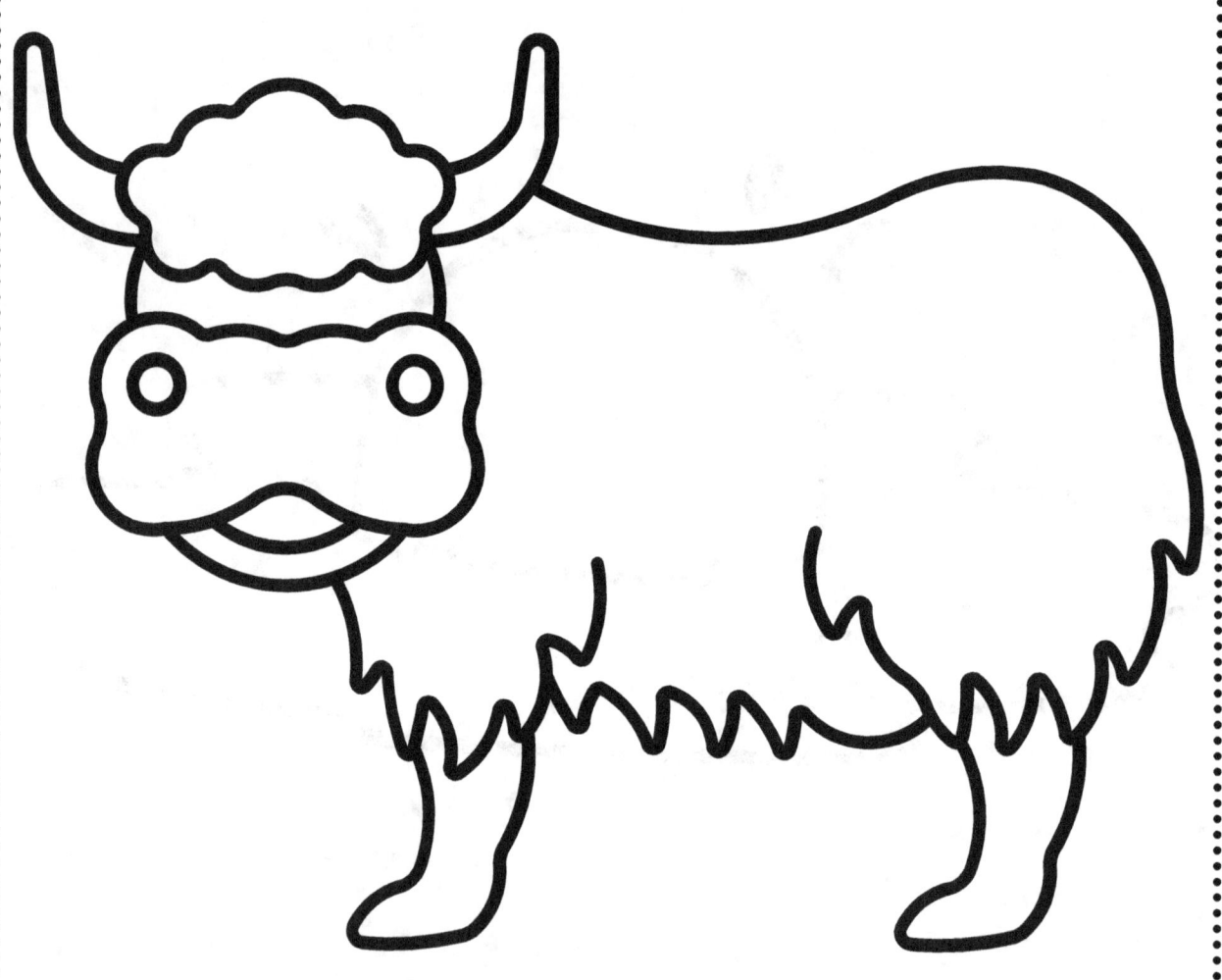

Yak

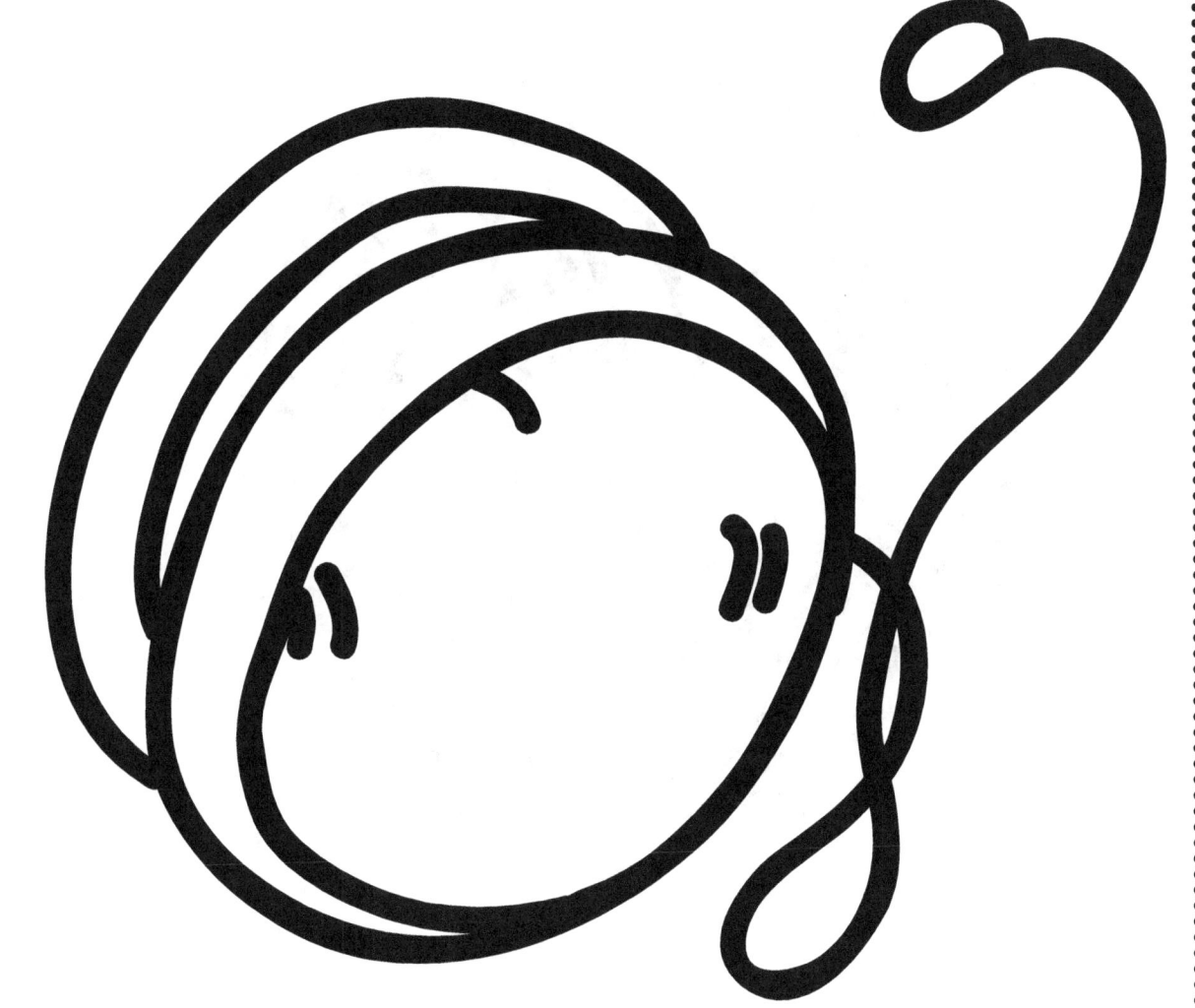

Yoyo

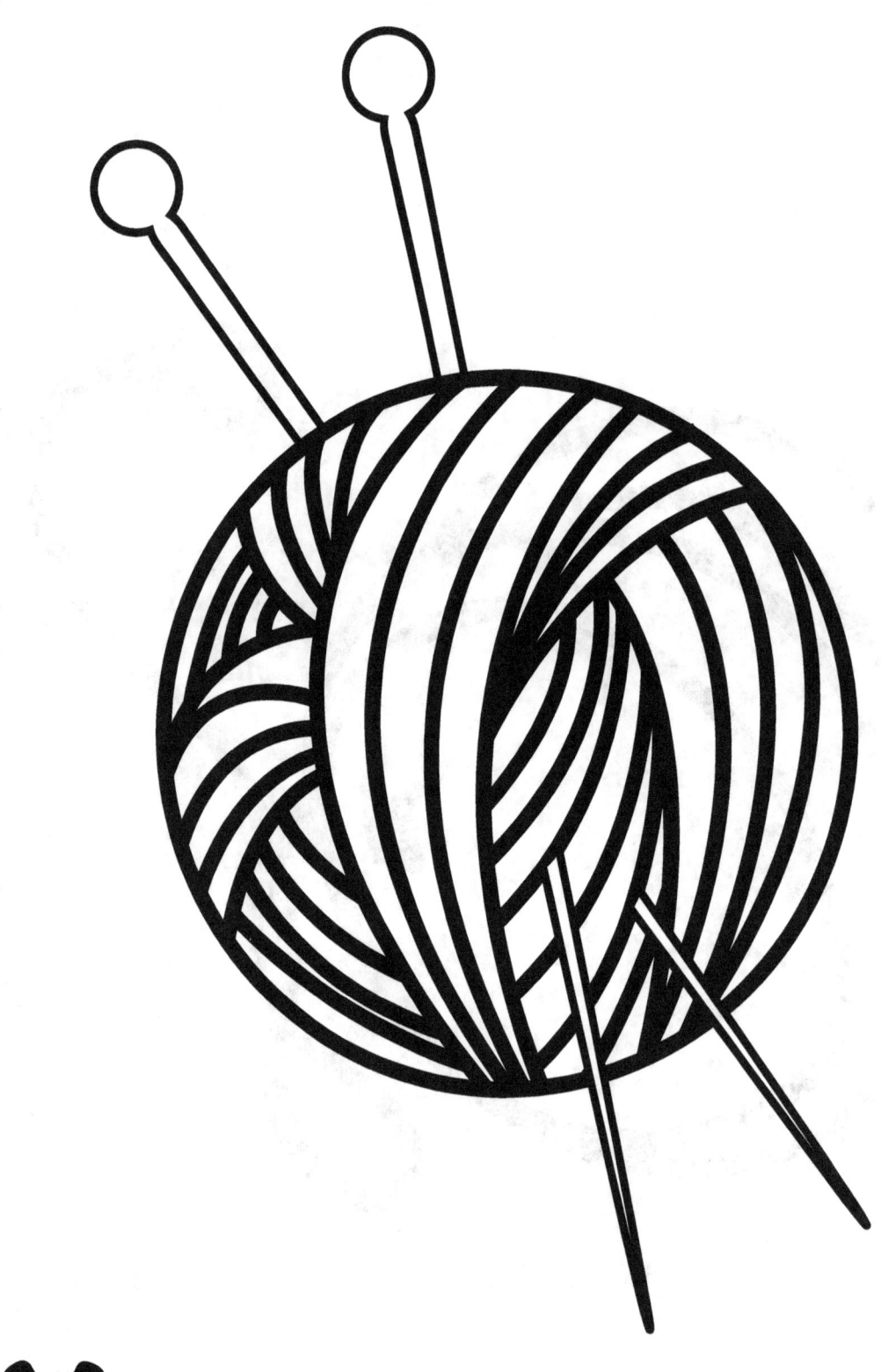

Yarn

Name:

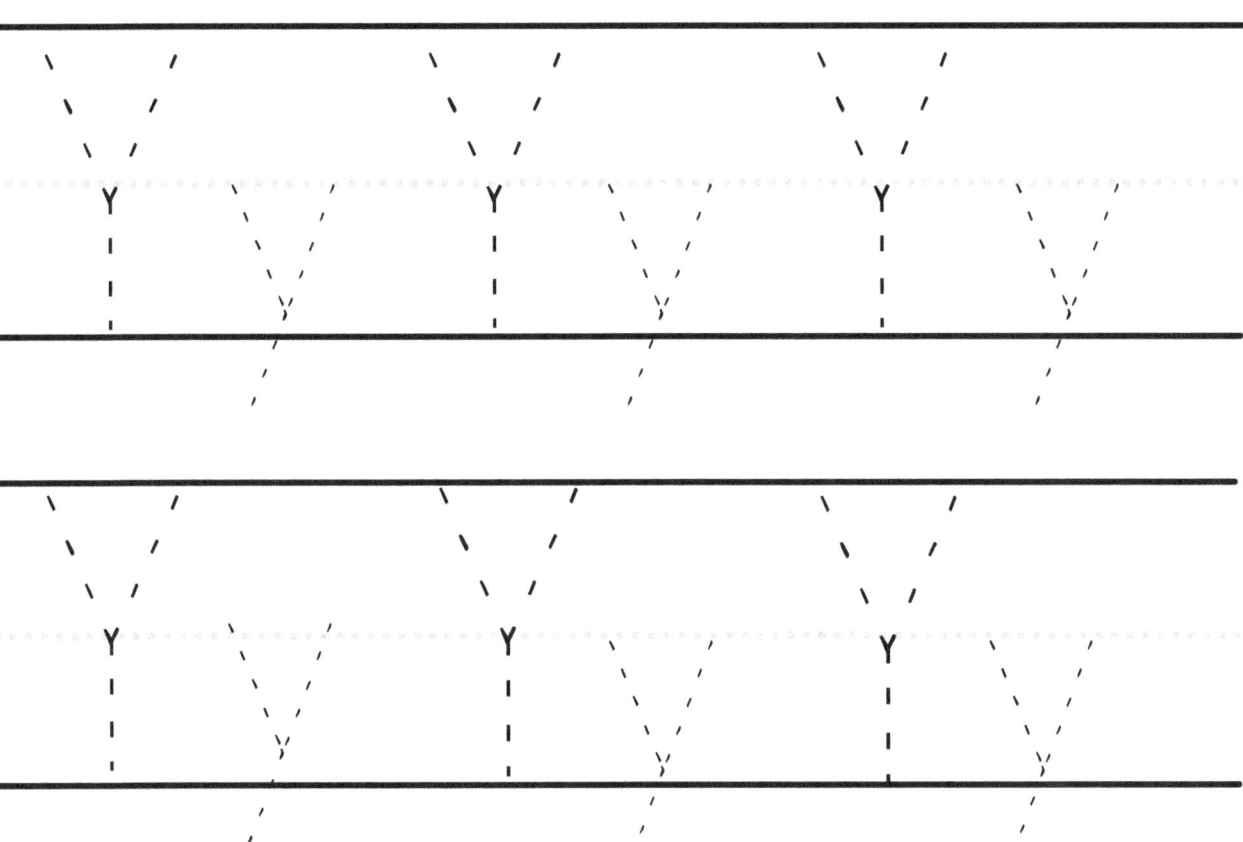

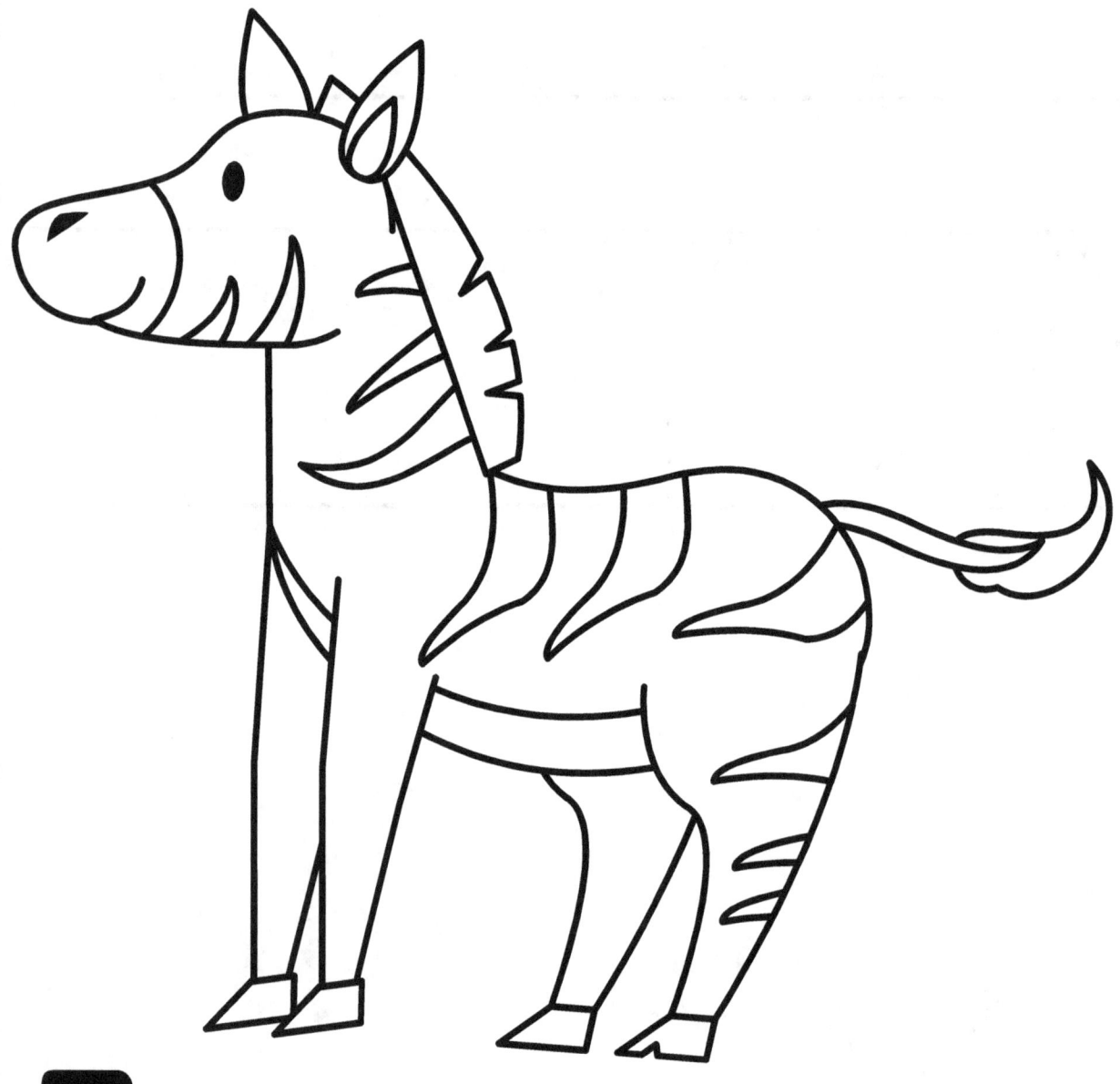

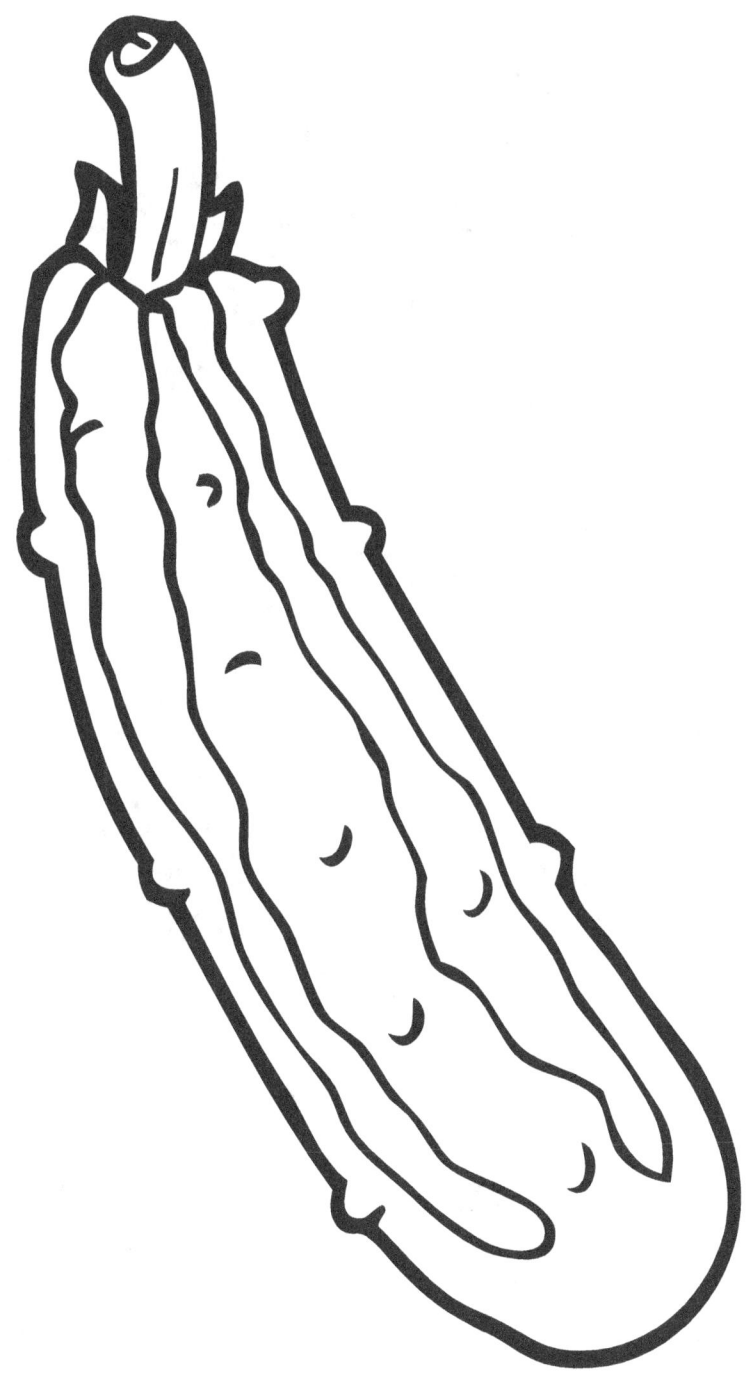

Zucchini

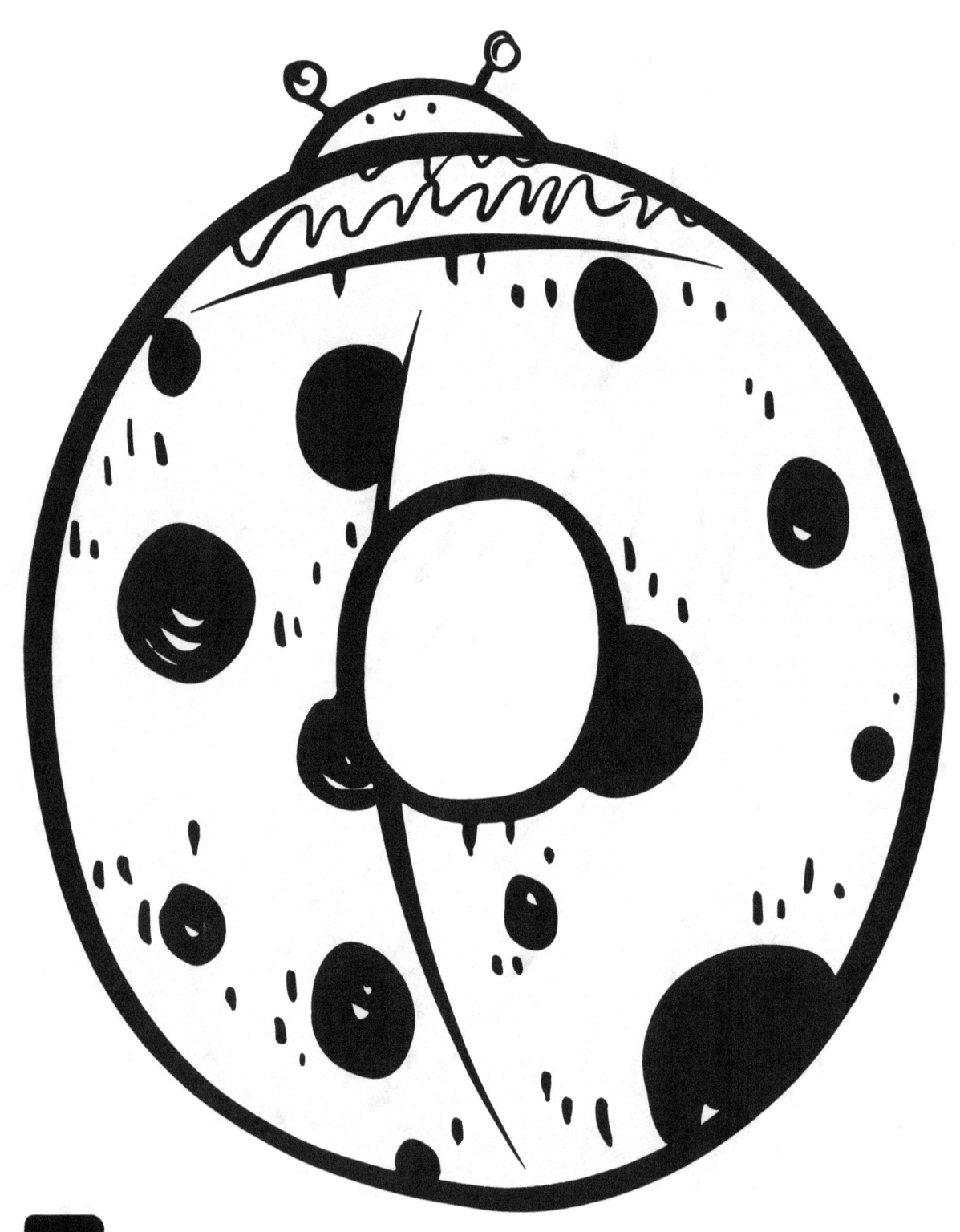

Zero

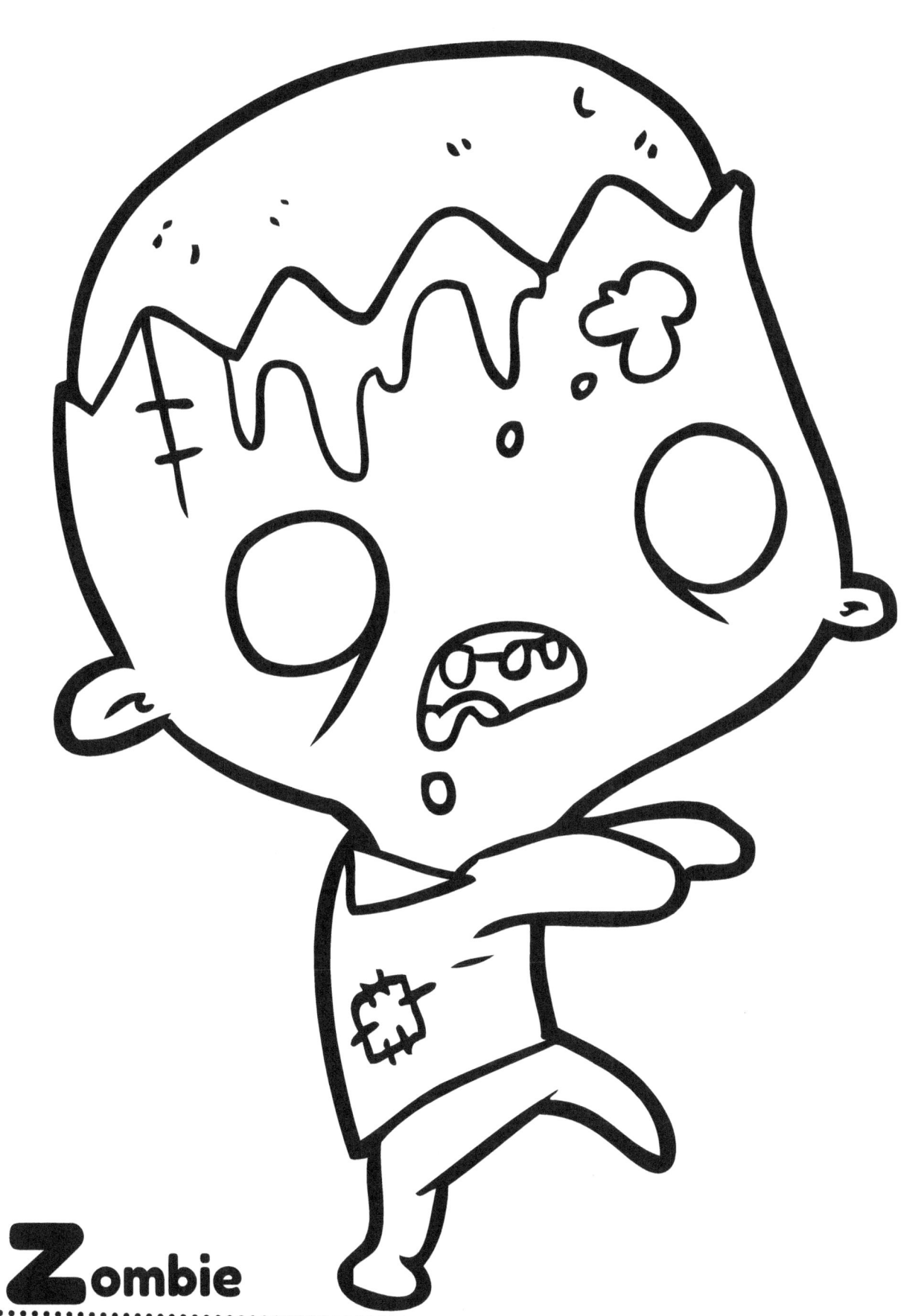
Zombie

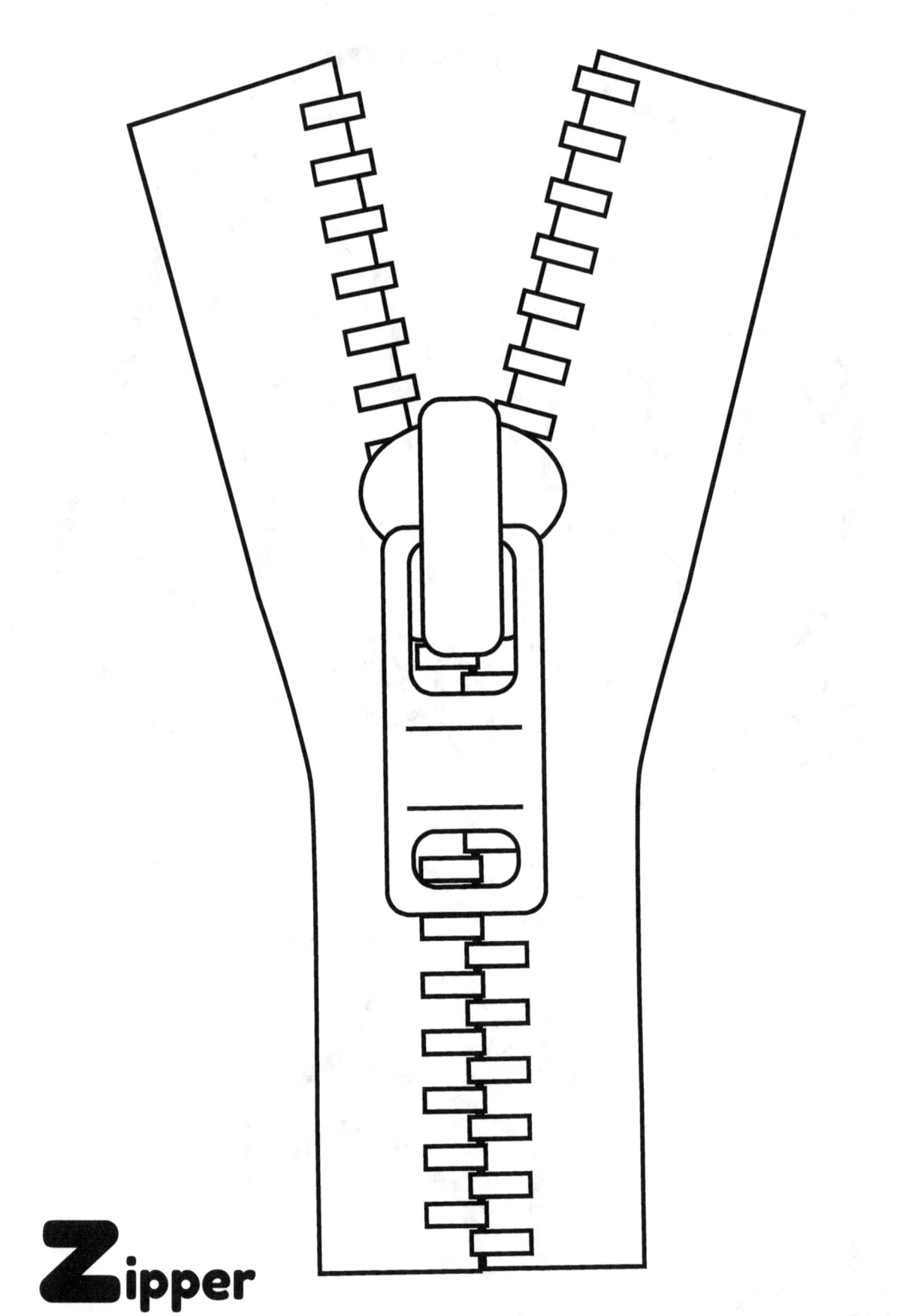

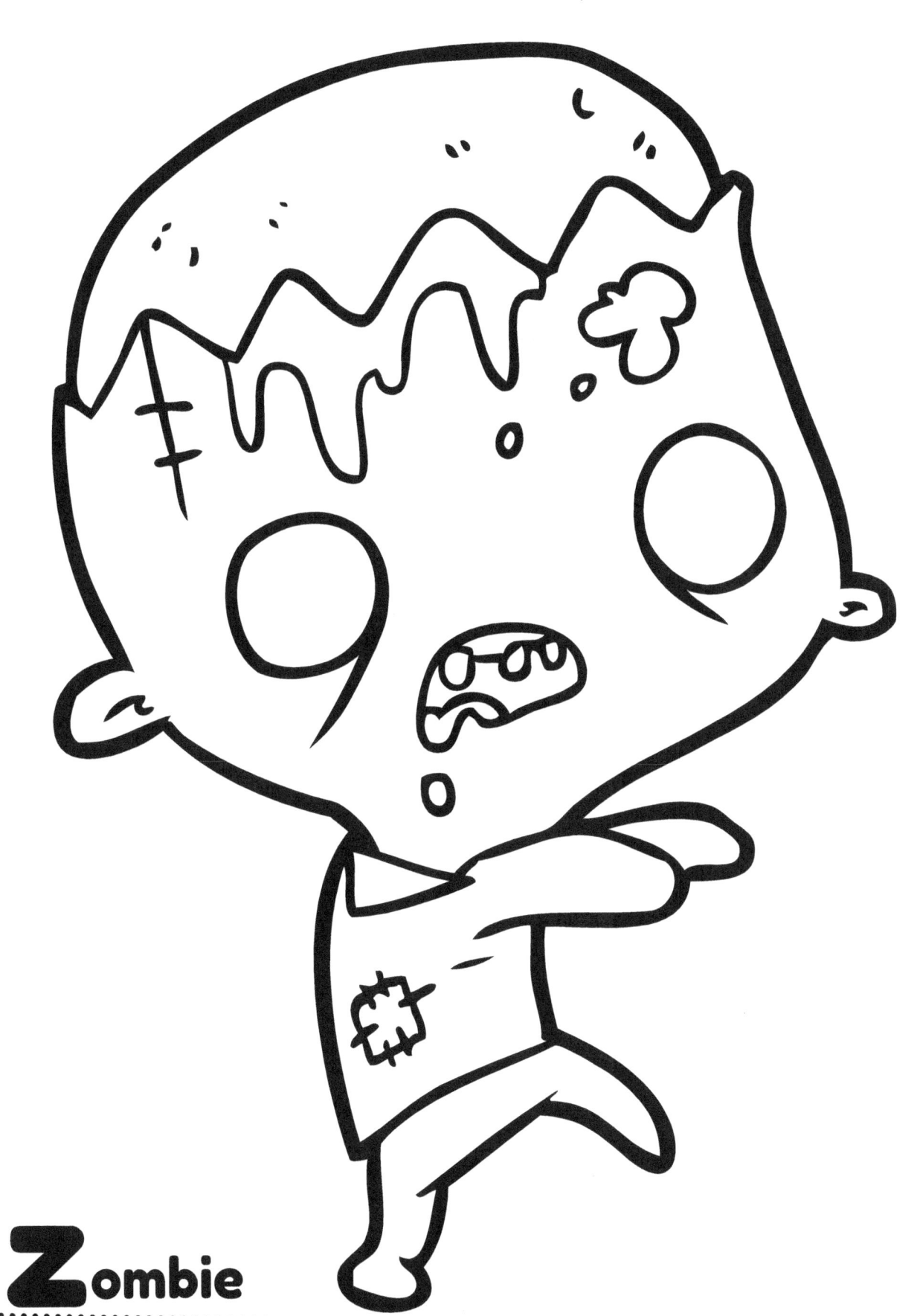

Zombie

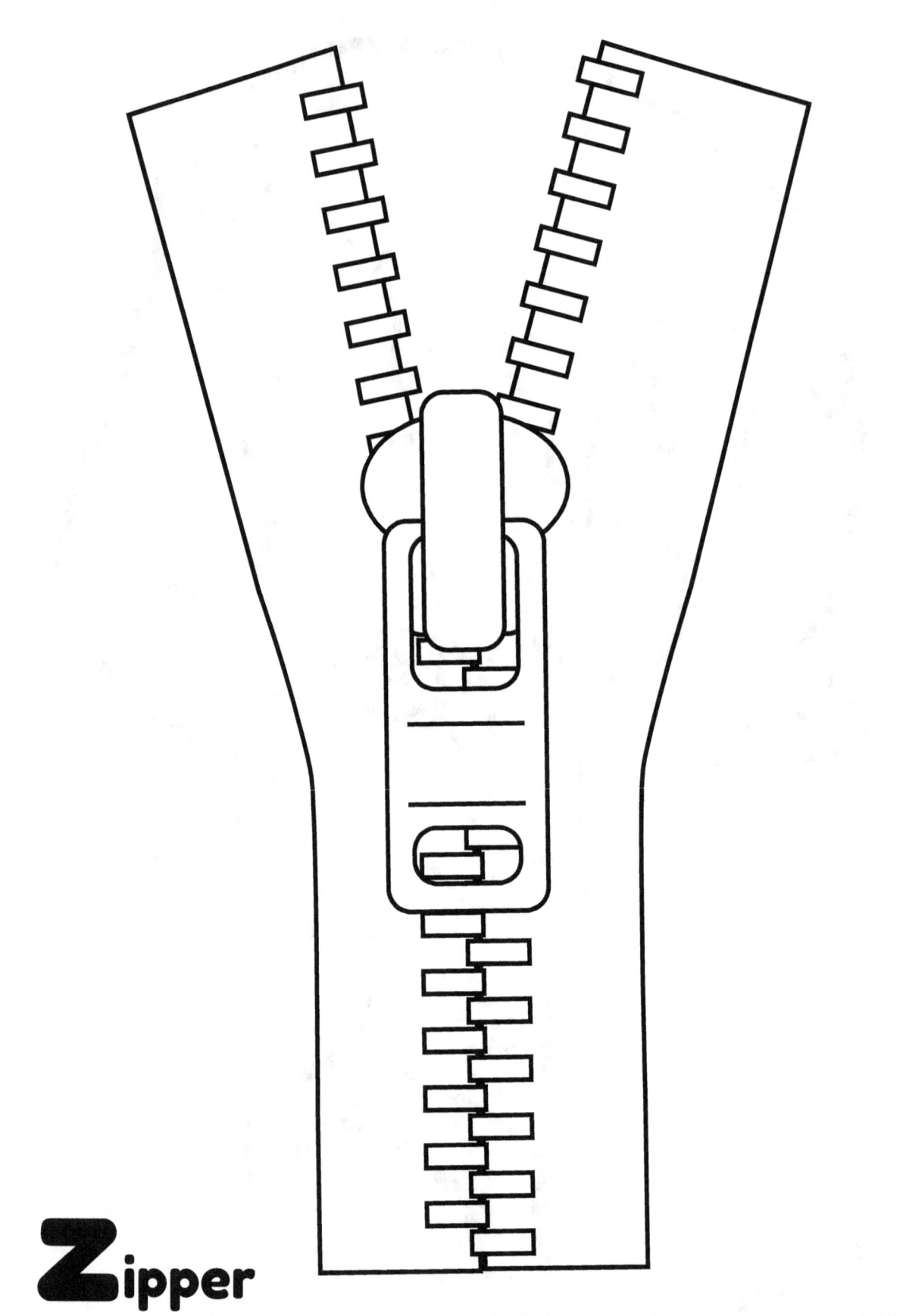

Zipper

Name:

www.ingramcontent.com/pod-product-compliance
Lightning Source LLC
Chambersburg PA
CBHW080544220526
45466CB00010B/3033